Hidden Mickeys

A Field Guide to Walt Disney World's Best Kept Secrets
7th Edition

Also by Steven M. Barrett

Disneyland's Hidden Mickeys:
A Field Guide to Disneyland® Resort's Best Kept Secrets

Hidden Mickeys Go To Sea:
A Field Guide to the Disney Cruise Line®'s Best Kept Secrets

HIDDEN MICKEYS

A Field Guide to

Walt Disney World®'s

Best Kept Secrets

7th edition

Steven M. Barrett

HIDDEN MICKEYS

A Field Guide to Walt Disney World®'s
Best Kept Secrets
7th edition

Published by
The Intrepid Traveler
P.O. Box 531
Branford, CT 06405
http://intrepidtraveler.com

Copyright ©2015 by Steven M. Barrett
Seventh Edition
Printed in the United States of America
Cover design by Foster & Foster
Interior Design by Starving Artist Design Studio
Maps designed by Evora Taylor
Library of Congress Control Number: 2014946170
ISBN-13: 978-1-937011-46-8

10 9 8 7 6 5 4 3

Trademarks, Etc. ● ● ● ● ● ● ● ● ● ● ● ● ●

Photo by Vickie Barrett

About the Author • • • • • • • • • • • •

Author Steven M. Barrett paid his first visit to Disney World in the late 1980s, after attending a conference in Orlando. He immediately fell under its spell, visiting it twice yearly with family and friends for the next several years, offering touring advice to the less initiated, and reading almost everything written about the WDW theme parks. When a job in his field opened up not far from WDW in 1998, Barrett relocated to the Orlando area from Houston, Texas. He began visiting the WDW parks every chance he got to enjoy the attractions, sample the restaurants, escort visiting friends and relatives, and find Hidden Mickeys! His interest in Hidden Mickeys led him to take pen in hand. The result is this book of Hidden Mickey scavenger hunts arranged to help you spend the least possible time waiting in line as you hunt for the elusive Mouse.

Dedication •

I dedicate this book to my wife Vickie and our son Steven, who willingly accompanied me on countless research visits to Disney World and added invaluable insight to this book. Furthermore, updating this book would not be possible without the many wonderful Hidden Mickey fans I've met through my website and in the Disney parks. Thanks to you all.

Thank You, My Fellow
Hidden Mickey Hunters

No Hidden Mickey hunter works alone. Scores of dedicated Mickey sleuths have helped me find the elusive Mouse in WDW. Thanks to each and every one of you. You'll find your names in the Acknowledgements, beginning on page 295.

★ ★ ★

Finding Mickey
Without Scavenger Hunting

Want to look for Hidden Mickeys in an attraction, restaurant, shop, or resort without scavenger hunting? Turn to the Index on page 307. If Mickey is hiding there, the Index will direct you to the page(s) with the appropriate Clues. If the venue isn't listed, Mickey isn't hiding there. Or if he is, I haven't yet found him.

★ ★ ★

Hidden Mickeys Are Elusive

New Hidden Mickeys appear from time to time and old ones may disappear (see page 17, paragraph above "My Selection Process"). When that happens— and it will—I will let you know on my website:

www.HiddenMickeyGuy.com

So if you can't find a Mickey—or if you're looking for just a few more—be sure to check it out.

– *Steve Barrett*

Table of Contents . . . .

Maps

Tip: To find a specific attraction, restaurant, shop, or resort, turn to the Index, page 307.

Read This First! . . . .

My guess is that you have visited Disney World before, perhaps many times. But if I've guessed wrong, and this is your first visit, then this note is for you.

Searching for Hidden Mickeys is lots of fun. But it's not a substitute for letting the magic of Disney sweep over you as you experience Walt Disney World (WDW) for the first time. For one thing, the scavenger hunts I present in this book do not include all the attractions in WDW. That's because some of them don't have Hidden Mickeys! For another, this book doesn't cover many things the first-time visitor should know and do to make that first trip to Disney World as magical as possible.

That doesn't mean you can't search for Hidden Mickeys, too. Just follow the suggestions in Chapter One of this book for "Finding Hidden Mickeys Without Scavenger Hunting."

CHAPTER 1

Hidden Mickey Mania

••••••••••••••••••••••••••••••••

Have you ever marveled at a "Hidden Mickey"? People in the know often shout with glee when they recognize one. Some folks are so involved with discovering them that Hidden Mickeys can be visualized where none actually exist. These outbreaks of Hidden Mickey mania are confusing to the unenlightened. So let's get enlightened!

Here's the definition of an official Hidden Mickey: a partial or complete image of Mickey Mouse that has been hidden by Disney's Imagineers and artists in the designs of Disney attractions, hotels, restaurants, and other areas. These images are designed to blend into their surroundings. Sharp-eyed visitors have the fun of finding them.

The practice probably started as an inside joke among the Imagineers (the designers and builders of Disney attractions). According to Disney guru Jim Hill (JimHillMedia.com), Hidden Mickeys originated in the late 1970s or early 1980s, when Disney management wanted to restrict Disney characters like Mickey and Minnie to the Magic Kingdom. The Imagineers designing Epcot couldn't resist slipping Mickey into the new park, and thus "Hidden Mickeys" were born. Guests and "Cast Members" (Disney employees) started spotting them and the concept took on a life of its own. Today, Hidden Mickeys are anticipated in any new construction at Walt Disney World, and Hidden Mickey fans can't wait to find them.

Hidden Mickeys come in all sizes and many forms. The most common is an outline of Mickey's head formed by three intersecting circles, one for Mickey's round head and two for his round ears. Among Hidden Mickey fans, this image is known as the "classic" Hidden Mickey, a term I will adopt in this book. Other Hidden Mickeys include a side or oblique (usually three-quarter) profile of Mickey's face and head, a side profile of his entire body, a full-length silhouette of his body seen from the front, a detailed picture of his face or body, or a three-dimensional Mickey Mouse. Sometimes just his gloves, handprints, shoes, or ears appear. Even his name or initials in unusual places may qualify as a Hidden Mickey.

And it's not just Mickeys that are hidden. The term "Hidden Mickey" also applies to hidden images of other popular characters. There are Hidden Minnies, Hidden Donald Ducks, Hidden Goofys, and other Hidden Characters in Disney World, and I include many of them in this book.

The sport of finding Hidden Mickeys has caught on and adds even more interest to an already fun-filled Walt Disney World vacation. This book is your "field guide" to more than 1,250 Hidden Mickeys in WDW. To add to the fun, instead of just describing them, I've organized them into six scavenger hunts, one for each of the major theme parks, one for the Walt Disney World Resort hotels, and one for all the rest of WDW: the water parks, Disney Springs, and beyond. The hunts are designed for maximum efficiency so that you can spend your time looking for Mickeys rather than cooling your heels in lines. Follow the Clues and you will find the best Hidden Mickeys WDW has to offer. If you have trouble spotting a particular Hidden Mickey (some are extraordinarily well camouflaged!) you can turn to the Hints at the end of each scavenger hunt for a fuller description.

Scavenger Hunting for Hidden Mickeys

To have the most fun and find the most Mickeys, follow these tips:

★ **Reserve FastPass+ attractions before your visit** to Walt Disney World to speed your hunts in the parks. Keep in mind, however, that many great Hidden Mickeys can only be seen from the Standby (regular) queue. You'll miss them if you take the FastPass+ route. Therefore, I recommend reserving FastPass+ for the following:

• At Magic Kingdom: *Peter Pan's Flight, Buzz Lightyear's Space Ranger Spin,* and the *Tomorrowland Speedway.*

• At Epcot: *Mission: SPACE* (choose orange level for more intense, or green level for less intense), *Spaceship Earth,* and *Living with the Land.*

• At Disney's Hollywood Studios: *The Twilight Zone Tower of Terror, Voyage of The Little Mermaid,* and *Fantasmic!.*

• At Disney's Animal Kingdom: *Kilimanjaro Safaris, Festival of the Lion King,* and *Finding Nemo—The Musical.*

★ **Arrive early** for the theme park hunts, say 30 minutes before the official opening time. Pick up a Guidemap and a Times Guide and plot your course. Then look for Hidden Mickeys in the waiting area while you wait for the rope to drop. You'll find the Clues for those areas by checking the *Index to Mickey's Hiding Places* in the back of this book. Look under "Entrance areas." If you arrive later in the day, skip down a few Clues to stay ahead of the crowds.

★ **"Clues" and "Hints"**
Clues under each attraction will guide you to the Hidden Mickey(s). If you have trouble spotting them, you can turn to the Hints at the end of the hunt for a fuller description. The Clues and Hints are numbered consecutively, that is, Hint 1 goes with Clue 1, so it's easy to find the right Hint if you need it. In some cases (*The Great Movie Ride* in Disney's Hollywood Studios is a good example), you may have to ride the attraction more than once to find all the Hidden Mickeys.

★ **Scoring**
All Hidden Mickeys are fun to find, but all Hidden Mickeys aren't the same. Some are easier to spot than others. I assign point values to Hidden Mickeys, identifying them as easy to find (a value of 1 point) to difficult to find the first time (5 points). I also consider the complexity and uniqueness of the image: the more complex or unique the Hidden Mickey, the higher the point value. For example, the brilliantly camouflaged Mickey hiding in The Garden Grill Restaurant mural in Epcot is a five-pointer.

★ **Playing the game**
You can hunt solo or with others; competitively or just for fun. There's room to tally

your score in the guide. Families with young children may want to focus on one- and two-point Mickeys that the little ones will have no trouble spotting. (Of course, little ones tend to be sharp-eyed, so they may spot familiar shapes before you do in some of the more complex patterns.) Or you may want to split your party into teams and see who can rack up the most points (in which case, you'll probably want to have a guide for each team).

Of course, you don't have to play the game at all. You can simply look for Hidden Mickeys in attractions as you come to them (see "Finding Hidden Mickeys Without Scavenger Hunting," below).

★ Following the Clues
The hunts often call for crisscrossing the parks. This may seem illogical at first, but trust me, it will keep you ahead of the crowds. Besides, it adds to the fun of the hunt and, if you're playing competitively, keeps everyone on their toes. Warning: Many Hidden Mickeys are waiting to be found in the Disney Parks, and depending on the crowds and the park hours when you visit, you may not be able to complete the Scavenger Hunt in one day!

★ Waiting in line
Don't waste time in lines. If the wait is longer than 15 minutes, get a FastPass+ (if available and you're eligible) and move on to the next attraction. The lines at popular attractions should not be too long if you start your scavenger hunt when the park opens and follow the hunt Clues as given. If you do encounter long lines, come back later during a parade or in the hour before the park closes. Alternatively, if you need to board an attraction with a long wait without a FastPass+, use the Single Rider queue if available (check your Guidemap for a big "S" symbol next to the attraction).

★ Playing fair
Be considerate of other guests. Many Hidden Mickeys are in restaurants and shops. Ask a Cast Member's permission before searching inside sit-down restaurants, and avoid the busy mealtime hours unless you are one of the

diners. Tell the Cast Members and other guests who see you looking around what you're up to, so they can share in the fun. (Note: Some restaurants, such as the Coral Reef, do not welcome drop-in Hidden Mickey Hunters. I don't include these restaurants in the Hunts, but I do post their Hidden Mickeys on my website, www.HiddenMickeyGuy.com, so you can search inside if you have dining reservations.)

Finding Hidden Mickeys Without Scavenger Hunting

If scavenger hunts don't appeal to you, you don't have to use them. You can find Hidden Mickeys in the specific rides and other attractions you visit by using the *Index to Mickey's Hiding Places* in the back of this book. For easy lookup, in addition to being listed alphabetically, attractions in Magic Kingdom, Epcot, and Disney's Animal Kingdom are listed under their appropriate "lands" or "areas" (for example, Fantasyland in Magic Kingdom, Future World East in Epcot, and Asia in Animal Kingdom). In Epcot, attractions are also listed by pavilion. To find Hidden Mickeys in the attraction, restaurant, hotel or shop you are visiting, simply turn to the *Index*, locate the appropriate page, and follow the Clue(s) to find the Hidden Mickey(s).

Caution: You won't find every WDW attraction, restaurant, hotel or shop in the Index. Only those with confirmed Hidden Mickeys are included in this guide.

Hidden Mickeys, "Gray Zone" Mickeys, Wishful Thinking

The classic (three-circle) Mickeys are the most controversial, for good reason. Much debate surrounds the gathering of circular forms throughout Walt Disney World. The sideways classic Mickey made of blue bubbles on the *Living with the Land* entrance-queue wall mural (Clue 88 in the Epcot Scavenger Hunt) is surely the work of a clever artist. However, three-circle configurations occur spontaneously in art and nature, as in collections of grapes, tomatoes, pumpkins, bubbles, oranges, cannonballs, and the like. Unlike the bubbles Hidden

Mickey in Epcot, it may be difficult to attribute a random "classic Mickey" configuration of circles to a deliberate Imagineer design.

So which groupings of three circles qualify as Hidden Mickeys as opposed to wishful thinking? Unfortunately, no master list of actual or "Imagineer-approved" Hidden Mickeys exists. Purists demand that a true classic Hidden Mickey should have proper proportions and positioning. The round head must be larger than the ear circles (so that three equal circles in the proper alignment would not qualify as a Hidden Mickey). The head and ears must be touching and in perfect position for Mickey's head and ears.

On the other hand, Disney's recent mantra is: "If the guest thinks it's a Hidden Mickey, then by golly it is one!" Of course, I appreciate Disney's respect for their guests' opinions. However, when the subject is Hidden Mickeys, let's apply some guidelines. My own criteria are looser than the purists' but stricter than the "anything goes" Disney approach. I prefer to use a few sensible guidelines.

To be classified as a real classic Hidden Mickey, the three circles should satisfy the following criteria:

1. Purposeful (sometimes you can sense that the circles were placed on purpose).

2. Proportionate sizes (head larger than the ears and somewhat proportionate to the ears).

3. Round or at least "roundish."

4. The ears don't touch each other, and the ears are above the head (not beside the head).

5. The head and ears touch or are close to touching.

6. The grouping of circles is exceptional or unique in appearance.

7. The circles are hidden or somewhat hidden and not obviously intended to be part of the décor.

Having spelled out some ground rules, allow me to now bend the rules in one instance. Some Hidden Mickeys are sentimental favorites with Disney fans, even though they may actually represent "wishful thinking." (My neighbor, Lew Brooks, calls them "two-beer Mickeys.") Who am I to defy tradition? For example, the nuts in the jar along the queue at *Jungle Cruise* in the Magic Kingdom are all about the same size. Nevertheless, although the image doesn't meet our classic Mickey criteria, many guests and even Cast Members call the jar nuts a Hidden Mickey. So I include the jar-nuts Mickey in the Magic Kingdom Scavenger Hunt in Chapter 2 (Clue 161).

Hidden Mickeys vs. Decorative Mickeys

Some Mickeys are truly hidden, not visible to the tourist. They may be located behind the scenes, accessible only to Cast Members. You won't find them in this field guide, as I only include Hidden Mickeys that are accessible to the guest. Other Mickeys are decorative; they were placed in plain sight to enhance the décor. For example, in a restaurant, I consider a pat of butter shaped like Mickey Mouse to be a decorative (aka décor) Mickey. Disney World is loaded with decorative Mickeys. You'll find obvious images of Mickey Mouse on items such as manhole covers, displays in shop windows, and restaurant menus. I do not include these ubiquitous and sometimes changing images in this book unless they are unique or hard to spot.

Hidden Mickeys can change or be accidentally removed over time, by the process of nature or by the continual cleaning and refurbishing that goes on at Disney World. For example, the "Steamboat Willie" Hidden Mickey in the star map in Mickey's Star Traders shop in Tomorrowland disappeared when the shop was remodeled. Moreover, Cast Members themselves sometimes create or remove Hidden Mickeys.

My Selection Process

I trust you've concluded by now that Hidden Mickey Science is an evolving specialty. Which raises the question, how did I choose the Hidden Mickeys in the scavenger hunts in this guide?

I compiled my list of Hidden Mickeys from all resources to which I had access: my own sightings, friends, family, Cast Members, websites, and books. (Cast Members in each specific area usually—but not always!—know where some Hidden Mickeys are located.) Then I embarked on my own hunts, and I took along friends or family to verify my sightings. I have included only those Hidden Mickeys I could verify.

Furthermore, some Hidden Mickeys are visible only intermittently or only from certain vantage points in ride vehicles. I don't generally include these Mickeys, unless I feel that adequate descriptions will allow anyone to find them. So the scavenger hunts include only those images I believe to be recognizable as Hidden Mickeys and visible to the general touring guest. It is likely, though, that one or more of the Hidden Mickeys described in this book will disappear over time.

I'll try to let you know when I discover that a Hidden Mickey has disappeared for good by posting the information on my website:

www.HiddenMickeyGuy.com

If you find one missing before I do, please email me care of my website to let me know.

I have enjoyed finding each and every Hidden Mickey in this book. I'm certain I'll find more as time goes by, and I hope you can spot new Hidden Mickeys during your visit.

So put on some comfortable walking shoes and experience Walt Disney World like you never have before!

Happy Hunting!

— *Steve Barrett*

CHAPTER 2

Magic Kingdom Scavenger Hunt

••••••••••••••••••••••••••••••

Before You Start

• *Many great Hidden Mickeys are in Standby queues. You'll miss them if you take the FastPass queue, so I recommend reserving FastPass+ for the following rides:* Peter Pan's Flight, Buzz Lightyear's Space Ranger Spin, *and* Tomorrowland Speedway.

Be sure to keep track of your three FastPass+ windows and return to those attractions at the appropriate times. In the Scavenger Hunt below, if you come to your FastPass+ attraction and it's not time for it yet, you can skip to the next stop in the Hunt and return to the FastPass+ attraction during your time window.

• *Some of the Hidden Mickeys in this park are in restaurants and shops. Be considerate of fellow guests and Cast Members as you search. Tell them what you're looking for, so they can share in the fun.*

Clue 1: As you approach the security area, look down for Mickey under your feet.
3 points

★ Check your Times Guide for any morning, afternoon, and evening parades, shows, and fireworks. There are generally both decorative and Hidden Mickeys in the shows and on the floats, vehicles, and banners.

Tip: For Hidden Mickeys in the current parades and shows, check out the "General Magic Kingdom" section on the Catalog page of www.HiddenMickeyGuy.com

Clue 2: Once you are in the park, examine the scrollwork of the roof of the Main Street Train Station.
2 points

main street, u.s.a

1. WDW Railroad
2. Mickey's Meet 'N Greet in Town Square Theater

adventureland

3. Swiss Family Treehouse
4. Walt Disney's Enchanted Tiki Room
5. The Magic Carpets of Aladdin
6. Jungle Cruise
7. Pirates of the Caribbean

frontierland

8. Frontierland Shootin' Arcade
9. Country Bear Jamboree
10. Splash Mountain
11. WDW Railroad
12. Big Thunder Mountain Railroad
13. Raft to Tom Sawyer Island

liberty square

14. The Hall of Presidents
15. Liberty Square Riverboat
16. Haunted Mansion

fantasyland

17. "it's a small world"
18. Peter Pan's Flight
19. Mickey's PhilharMagic
20. Prince Charming Regal Carrousel
21. Enchanted Tales with Belle
22. Princess Fairytale Hall
23. Fairytale Garden
24. The Many Adventures of Winnie the Pooh
25. Seven Dwarfs Mine Train
26. Under the Sea ~ Journey of The Little Mermaid
27. Ariel's Grotto
28. Pete's Silly Sideshow
29. Casey Jr. Splash 'N' Soak Station
30. WDW Railroad
31. The Barnstormer
32. Dumbo the Flying Elephant
33. Mad Tea Party
34. Castle Forecourt Stage

tomorrowland

35. Tomorrowland Speedway
36. Stitch's Great Escape!
37. Monsters, Inc. Laugh Floor
38. Buzz Lightyear's Space Ranger Spin
39. Walt Disney's Carousel of Progress
40. Tomorrowland Transit Authority PeopleMover
41. Astro Orbiter
42. Space Mountain

21

★ If the park is not open yet, you may want to hunt for Hidden Mickeys on **Main Street, U.S.A.** (See Clues 185 to 202.)

★ Head for Fantasyland and **Seven Dwarfs Mine Train**.

Clue 3: Study the gems along the Standby entrance queue.
4 points for one or more images

Clue 4: On the ride, check out a Hidden Mickey next to Dopey.
5 points

Clue 5: Watch for Grumpy on your right side. Do you see a Hidden Mickey near him?
5 points

Clue 6: Don't miss Oswald the Lucky Rabbit on your left side. He's etched in wood on a beam.
5 points

★ Walk to Tomorrowland and line up for **Space Mountain**. (You can enjoy the ride after walking through the entrance queue, or exit the attraction just before boarding.)

Clue 7: In the interactive games on the left wall of the entrance queue, pay attention to the space construction objects that guests can move around and interconnect.
5 points

Clue 8: Watch the instructional video near the loading dock for two Hidden Mickeys.
4 points for both

★ Head back to Fantasyland and line up for **The Many Adventures of Winnie the Pooh**. Study Mr. Sanders' big tree.

Clue 9: Search for a Mickey made of rocks embedded inside the tree.
3 points

Clue 10: Look for a submarine image in the wood of the tree. (Tip: This is a Hidden Tribute rather than a Hidden Mickey.)
4 points

Clue 11: Find a side profile of Mickey in the bark outside.
4 points

Clue 12: Locate Mickey on a wooden post by a window outside.
5 points

Clue 13: Next check out two Hidden Mickeys inside the entryway play area.
4 points for both

★ Now hop in your honey pot and find five Hidden Characters.

Clue 14: Examine the flower-pot marker in Rabbit's Garden.
4 points

Clue 15: In Owl's house, find the picture of Mr. Toad and Owl.
3 points

Clue 16: Near the end of Owl's house, locate a picture of Mole with Winnie the Pooh.
3 points

★ Walk to **Under the Sea ~ Journey of The Little Mermaid**. Spend some time in the Standby entrance queue to find all the great Hidden Mickeys here (let people walk by you in line if you need to).

Note: Many collections of circular rock impressions in both the entrance and exit areas and inside this attraction suggest classic Hidden Mickeys. I include below my favorite images, which seem intentional.

Clue 17: Spot a Hidden Mickey on a rock just outside the Standby entrance queue.
4 points

Clue 18: In the outside Standby queue, be alert for another Hidden Mickey on a rock in the lagoon near a waterfall.
5 points

Clue 19: Gaze way above and to the right of the rock in the lagoon to find another classic Hidden Mickey on the rock wall.
5 points

Clue 20: Look down over the right side of a bridge railing for a classic Hidden Mickey.
5 points

Clue 21: Now stare way above this railing for a small classic Hidden Mickey in the rock.
5 points

Clue 22: Also in the outside Standby queue, study the rock walls for a submarine image. (Not a Hidden Mickey, but an awesome Hidden Image!)
5 points

Clue 23: In the inside Standby entrance queue, at a large opening in the rock ceiling on your right and just past a carved wooden figure, stay alert for a classic Mickey in light on the lower wall to your left. This Hidden Mickey is designed to appear only on November 18 (Mickey's birthday) around noon, but it just might appear other times of the year!
10 bonus points

Clue 24: Along the inside Standby entrance queue, find a Hidden Mickey in the rock wall above some bottles on your left.
5 points

Clue 25: Search for Mickey on the ceiling just as you enter the room with Scuttle, the talking seagull.
5 points

Clue 26: On the ride, look for a purple-coral classic Mickey on your right.
5 points

Clue 27: Keep your eyes peeled and gaze to the left side to spot a green fish with a Hidden Mickey.
4 points

Clue 28: Don't miss the frogs with Hidden Mickeys!
4 points for one or more

Clue 29: Along the inside exit walkway, study the wall near the floor to your left for Mickey.
4 points for one or more

Clue 30: Look through the large opening in the exit walkway's left wall for another classic Hidden Mickey.
4 points

Clue 31: Outside the cave exit, look around for Steam-boat Willie!
5 points

★ At or shortly after 10:30 a.m., amble over to the entrance area for **Be Our Guest Restaurant** and line up for lunch.

Clue 32: As you enter Be Our Guest Restaurant, study the walls behind the suits of armor for some Hidden Mickeys.
3 points for one or more

Clue 33: Search the room to the right for a Hidden Mickey on a suit of armor.
5 points

Clue 34: In the food order room, spot two Hidden Mickeys on books.
4 points for both

Clue 35: Look for Mickey bubbles on a wall in the Rose Gallery seating area to the right (as you enter the restaurant) of the restaurant's Ballroom.
5 points

Clue 36: Find Mickey in fabric hanging in the West Wing seating area, located to the left of the Ballroom.
5 points

Clue 37: Pay attention as you exit the restaurant and walk along the bridge toward the rest of Fantasyland. Glance to your right before you reach the end of the bridge.
4 points

Clue 38: At the entrance walkway to Be Our Guest Restaurant, examine a short rock wall for a classic Mickey at the side of the check-in station
5 points

★ Go to **Peter Pan's Flight** at your FastPass+ time.

Clue 39: Study the overhead attraction sign at the entrance for two decent Mickey images.
5 points for spotting both

Clue 40: On the ride, keep looking down for a brown classic Mickey on the ground.
5 points

★ If you're lucky, you may spot Mickey on the rotating moon and earn yourself some bonus points.
5 bonus points

Clue 41: Search for a classic Mickey near mermaids.
3 points

Clue 42: Squint your eyes for two shadow Hidden Mickeys near two different sets of cannonballs.
5 points for each one

★ Cross over to Frontierland and ride **Splash Mountain**.

★ Hop in line and keep your eyes peeled for two Hidden Mickeys in the queue, six on the ride, and at least four more after you exit.

Clue 43: Along the queue, look to your left for a red Mickey hanging on the wall.
4 points

Clue 44: Look up for Mickey in the last stretch of the entrance queue.
3 points

Clue 45: Soon after you start the ride, search for barrels that form a classic.
3 points Mickey

Clue 46: Just as your boat goes outside, spot a tiny classic Mickey on a "moonshine" barrel!
5 points

Clue 47: Look for a rabbit with a broom and then try to catch a moving Hidden Mickey silhouette on a wall nearby.
5 points

Clue 48: Just past Brer Frog, find the fishing bobbers that form a Hidden Mickey.
4 points

Clue 49: In the room with jumping water, spot the hanging rope classic Mickey.
4 points

Clue 50: As your boat ascends toward the big drop, look toward the opening for a side profile of Mickey's face.
3 points

Clue 51: Along the exit walkway, look for the birdhouse with at least two acorn classic Mickeys.
3 points for two or more

Clue 52: Do you see a Hidden Mickey in the children's play area along the exit?
3 points

Clue 53: After the ride, take another look at the mountain from the outside viewing area to spot that Clue 50 side profile (again).
3 points

★ Now get in line to ride **Big Thunder Mountain Railroad**.

Clue 54: During the first climb, search the cavern floor to the right of the coaster.
4 points

Clue 55: Study the reddish rock along the exit walkway for a Hidden Tinker Bell.
4 points

★ Head for **Haunted Mansion** in Liberty Square. Find six classic Mickeys, two Donald Ducks, and a Mr. Toad!

Clue 56: Along the interactive "Scenic" left-side entrance queue, search for a Mickey made of barnacles.
4 points

Clue 57: In the first room inside the entrance, look for some classic Mickeys in the border design around a portrait.
3 points

Clue 58: During the ride, be alert for Donald Duck on two different chairs.
4 points each

Clue 59: Find the Mickey on the ghostly banquet table.
2 points

Clue 60: Spot plates on the floor in the attic.
4 points

Clue 61: Look closely to your far right at the "Grim Reaper" by the opera-singing lady.
5 points

Clue 62: Outside, as you exit, look for a classic Mickey next to a gate.
3 points

Clue 63: Find Mr. Toad along the exit walkway.
3 points

★ Enter **Columbia Harbour House** restaurant and look for a classic Hidden Mickey. (Be considerate of the diners.)

Clue 64: Check the art on the downstairs walls.
2 points

28

★ Walk into Adventureland for **Pirates of the Caribbean** and find four Hidden

Mickeys along the left entrance queue. Then find six classic Hidden Mickeys on the ride and four more after the ride.

Clue 65: Spot some cannonballs along the left queue.
3 points

Clue 66: Look near a faux fireplace along the queue for a Hidden Mickey.
5 points

Clue 67: Now search for two classic Mickey locks in the left queue.
4 points for spotting both

Clue 68: If Davy Jones appears in the mist on the ride, look up for a classic Mickey. (Note: it's usually Blackbeard you'll see.)
5 bonus points

Clue 69: Try to spot the classic Mickey shadow above the drunken pirate's cat.
4 points

Clue 70: Near the end of the ride, look left at the recessed doors in the wall.
4 points

Clue 71: Don't miss the treasure room's open door.
4 points

Clue 72: Now glance at the wall behind Jack Sparrow.
4 points

Clue 73: As you exit the ride, search for some coins and jewels.
5 points for both

Clue 74: In the gift shop, spot a classic Mickey in a painting.
3 points

Clue 75: Outside the attraction entrance, look around for a Hidden Mickey on a cart.
3 points

★ Stop by the **Frontierland Shootin' Arcade**.

Clue 76: Find a classic Mickey in front of the target area.
1 point

★ Then turn right to **Liberty Square** and cross the street.

Clue 77: Find the classic Mickey near the *Liberty Square Riverboat* entrance.
1 point

★ At your FastPass+ Time, cross the bridge to Tomorrowland and go to the **Tomorrowland Speedway**. (Exit before boarding the ride after you find the FastPass+ Hidden Mickeys.)

Clue 78: Spot two classic Hidden Mickeys on a wall in the FastPass+ queue.
5 points for both

Clue 79: Look for a shadow on the pavement near the *Tomorrowland Speedway* that's shaped like a classic Mickey.
3 points

★ Go to **Walt Disney's Carousel of Progress**. Check the first scene for Clue 80, the third scene for Clue 81, the last scene for Clues 82 to 87, and the exit for Clue 88.

Clue 80: Admire a classic Mickey on a mirror.
3 points

Clue 81: Search for Mickey's blue hat.
4 points

Clue 82: Observe a painting on the rear wall.
4 points

Clue 83: Find a Mickey nutcracker.
2 points

30

Clue 84: Spot a Mickey Mouse doll.
2 points

Clue 85: Search around for green Mickey ears.
3 points

Clue 86: Look fast for a classic Mickey on a space-ship.
5 points

Clue 87: View objects with Mickey ears in the kitchen.
3 points

Clue 88: Don't miss Hidden Mickeys along the exit walkway.
2 points

★ Go to **Buzz Lightyear's Space Ranger Spin** at your allotted FastPass+ time and be on the lookout for ten Hidden Mickeys along with another Hidden character.

Note: Some of the planets with Hidden Mickeys appear in several places along the entrance queue and on the ride.

Clue 89: Inside the building on the right wall, find the planet with a continent shaped like the side profile of Mickey Mouse.
3 points

Clue 90: On this same poster, spot classic Mickey craters.
3 points

Clue 91: Look for the side-profile Mickey continent further along the entrance queue to the left.
2 points

Clue 92: Search for a Hidden Mickey in Sector 2 nearby.
3 points

Clue 93: Pay attention to the right wall in the very first interactive room on the ride for a tiny classic Mickey in the stars. (This one is tough to spot.)
5 points

Clue 94: During the first part of the ride, spot another side profile of Mickey. Look to the left of your vehicle in the room with batteries.
3 points

Clue 95: Also in the battery room, to the right of your vehicle, stare at the star field to the right of the cone over Zurg to find a blue classic Mickey star.
5 points

Clue 96: Catch another view of the planet with a side-profile Mickey in the space video room.
3 points

Clue 97: Just past the space video room, look straight ahead to spot that side-profile Mickey planet one more time.
2 points

Clue 98: Along the exit, look for an alien pointing to a classic Mickey.
2 points

Clue 99: Spot Stitch's spaceship nearby.
3 points

★ Walk to the far side of **Astro Orbiter** and search carefully for a small classic Mickey traced in the cement nearby.

Clue 100: Check the side facing *Space Mountain*.
5 points

★ Go to the outside of the **Monsters, Inc. Laugh Floor**.

Clue 101: Find the moon with classic Mickey craters.
1 point

Clue 102: Spot the asteroid shaped like a classic Mickey.
1 point

★ Get in line for *Monsters, Inc. Laugh Floor*. (After finding the Hidden Mickey, you can exit before the show or stick around and enjoy the jokes.)

Clue 103: As you enter the waiting area, search for a classic Mickey in a window display.
4 points

★ Walk over to **The Hall of Presidents** in Liberty Square. (Again, after spotting the Hidden Mickey, you can exit before the show.)

Clue 104: In the waiting room for the show, study the paintings for a tiny classic Mickey.
4 points

★ From near *Big Thunder Mountain Railroad*, float on the **raft** over **to Tom Sawyer Island**. (It sometimes closes at 5:00 p.m. or at dusk.)

Clue 105: Look across the river for a classic Mickey rock formation at the right end of the bridge in Frontierland. (Note: This Hidden Mickey is also visible from the *Liberty Square Riverboat*.)
4 points

Clue 106: Search one of the caves for Goofy.
3 points

Clue 107: In Fort Langhorn, look around in the rear right Rifle Roost for a Mickey in wood.
4 points

★ Float back to Frontierland and then walk to Fantasyland to see **Mickey's PhilharMagic**.

Clue 108: In the first waiting area inside, squint at the wall mural.
4 points for two or more

Clue 109: Inside the main theater, examine the border of the video screen.
2 points

Clue 110: In the show, look for a shadow Mickey on a table.
4 points

Clue 111: Stare at Ariel's jewels for a classic Mickey in a ring.
5 points

Clue 112: Keep alert for a classic Mickey during the magic carpet ride.
5 points

Clue 113: Stop in the gift shop at the exit and find a classic Mickey.
2 points

★ Go to **"it's a small world"** and try to spot two classic Hidden Mickeys.

Clue 114: In the Africa room, look up at the vine with purple leaves.
3 points

Clue 115: In the South Pacific Room, search for an animal classic Mickey.
3 points

★ Walk over to the **"Tangled" Tower restroom area**.

Clue 116: Spot a Hidden Mickey on a wall poster.
3 points

★ Head **toward Peter Pan's Flight**.

Clue 117: Find grapes arranged like a classic Mickey.
2 points

★ Enter **Pinocchio Village Haus** restaurant.

Clue 118: Look for a tiny, dark classic Mickey on the wall near the exit to the restrooms.
4 points

Clue 119: Locate a minuscule, white classic Mickey near the word "All."
4 points

Clue 120: Keep searching this wall for another tiny, white classic Mickey at the other side of the same mural.
5 points

★ Stroll over to **Fairytale Garden**.

Clue 121: Find a classic Mickey on a light pole.
3 points

Clue 122: Search for a Hidden Character on a wall.
4 points

★ Walk over to **Sir Mickey's Store**.

Clue 123: Observe a classic Mickey outside the store.
1 point

Clue 124: Gaze inside a display window of the store
to find more classic Mickeys.
4 points for two or more

★ Enter the **Castle Couture** shop.

Clue 125: Search high on a wall for a bronze frieze
with a tiny classic Mickey on a bush.
5 points

★ Now walk to the **exit area** of the **Fantasyland
Train Station** in Storybook Circus.

Clue 126: Check the pavement near the exit from the
station for at least two Hidden Mickeys.
5 points for two or more

★ Stand outside **Casey Jr. Splash 'N' Soak
Station**.

Clue 127: Look over the boxcars in *Casey Jr. Splash
'N' Soak* for a classic Mickey.
5 points

★ Cruise over to **The Barnstormer**.

Clue 128: Find a classic Mickey near a picture of
Goofy outside *The Barnstormer*.
3 points

Clue 129: Study a large billboard outside
The Barnstormer for a Hidden Mickey.
5 points

★ Walk back to **Pete's Silly Sideshow**.

Clue 130: Search for a classic Mickey on a poster outside *Pete's Silly Sideshow*.
5 points

★ Check out the large tent next to *Pete's Silly Sideshow*.

Clue 131: Locate tiny Mickey balloons.
5 points for finding eight balloons

★ Explore inside the **Big Top Souvenirs** store.

Clue 132: Spot Mickey on an animal on the wall.
5 points

★ Return to the **area near Dumbo the Flying Elephant**.

Clue 133: Look for a classic Mickey near the entrance to the *Dumbo* FastPass+ queue.
3 points

★ Amble over toward **Ariel's Grotto**.

Clue 134: Find a Hidden Mickey at the Disney Vacation Club kiosk.
2 points

Clue 135: Search for a Hidden Mickey in the walkway near the Disney Vacation Club kiosk.
5 points

★ Locate **Gaston's Statue**.

Clue 136: Study the statue for a Hidden Mickey.
5 points

★ Gaze around inside the **Bonjour Village Gifts** shop.

Clue 137: Find a Hidden Mickey on a wall.
2 points

36

Clue 138: Donald Duck is in the shop, too!
3 points

★ Walk toward **Enchanted Tales with Belle**.

Clue 139: Before you reach the entrance walkway to Be Our Guest Restaurant, keep your eyes down for a horseshoe Hidden Mickey.
4 points

Clue 140: In the main walkway, not far from the entrance sign for *Enchanted Tales with Belle*, search for a pebble image of Oswald the Lucky Rabbit. (Psst: it's not in the side walkway to *Enchanted Tales with Belle*!)
5 points

★ Stroll over to Town Square Theater on Main Street, U.S.A. and visit **Mickey's Meet 'N' Greet**.

Clue 141: In the queue, look for some special mail.
2 points

Clue 142: In Mickey's Room, find a Hidden Mickey made of rings.
2 points

Clue 143: Spot another classic Mickey in Mickey's magic chest. (It's sometimes covered by a scarf.)
2 points

Clue 144: Don't miss Oswald the Lucky Rabbit!
4 points

Clue 145: Look around for Sorcerer Mickey.
4 points

Clue 146: In the gift shop at the exit, find Mickey hanging on a table.
2 points

Clue 147: In the gift shop, search for Mickey on a house.
3 points

★ From Main Street, ride the **WDW Railroad** to search for another Hidden Mickey. Exit the train at the Frontierland station.

Clue 148: Sit toward the left side of the train and watch the ground as you leave Main Street station.
4 points

★ Walk over and look inside **Ye Olde Christmas Shoppe** in Liberty Square.

Clue 149: Spot a stack of logs with a Hidden Mickey.
2 points

★ Walk into the **Liberty Tree Tavern**.

Clue 150: Search for a classic Mickey in the waiting area.
3 points

Clue 151: Now look for a classic Mickey in a painting in one of the seating areas to the left of the waiting area. (Psst! You'll have to climb some stairs to find this Hidden Mickey.)
4 points

★ Enter the **Frontier Trading Post** in Frontierland.

Clue 152: Look for two rope classic Mickeys.
3 points for spotting both

Clue 153: Spot a cowboy with a Hidden Mickey.
3 points

★ Check out the inside of **Pecos Bill Tall Tale Inn and Cafe**.

Clue 154: Squint for a classic Mickey on a plate that's sitting on a ledge.
4 points

★ Head for Adventureland and stop inside **Tortuga Tavern**.

Clue 155: Search for a candle image.
3 points

38

★ Enjoy **Walt Disney's Enchanted Tiki Room**.

Clue 156: Find classic Mickeys at the bottom of two bird perches. One is in the left corner as you enter; you'll find the other in the right corner as you exit.
3 points each

Clue 157: Near the entrance to *Walt Disney's Enchanted Tiki Room*, look around for a Hidden Mickey on a statue.
3 points

Clue 158: Study the cement for a tiny classic Mickey between the Agrabah Bazaar shop and *The Magic Carpets of Aladdin* ride.
4 points

★ Eat dinner either before or after riding *Jungle Cruise*. One choice: The Columbia Harbour House.

★ Ride **Jungle Cruise** and search for six Hidden Mickeys and two Hidden Donalds.

Clue 159: Study the sign outside for a Hidden Mickey.
2 points

Clue 160: Along the Standby entrance queue, look for a map with a Hidden Mickey.
4 points

Clue 161: Along the entrance queue, spot some nuts that resemble Mickey.
2 points

Clue 162: Study a tree across the river from the loading dock for a small white classic Mickey.
4 points

Clue 163: Watch for Donald Duck's face on a canoe.
4 points

Clue 164: Stay alert for a Hidden Mickey on an airplane.
4 points

Clue 165: Search the riverbanks for Donald Duck's face on a native.
4 points

Clue 166: Coming out of the temple, look hard at the first undecorated column on the left for a chipped area of brick that forms part of a profile of Mickey's head and face. (This is a tough one!)
5 points

★ Walk through the **Swiss Family Treehouse**.

Clue 167: Keep alert for Mickey on the tree trunk.
5 points

Clue 168: Look around outside the attraction in a seating area for Mickey on a rock.
4 points

★ Check the shields on the **Adventureland bridge to the Hub** in front of Cinderella Castle.

Clue 169: Find two Hidden Mickeys.
3 points for both

★ Head for Fantasyland and join the Standby queue for **Enchanted Tales with Belle**.

Clue 170: In Maurice's cottage, study the window glass to the left. Can you see a Disney Character?
5 points

Clue 171: Look near the fireplace in the first room for two Hidden Mickeys.
5 points for both

Clue 172: Search below your feet in the Wardrobe Room for a Hidden Mickey.
3 points for one or more

Clue 173: Spot Hidden Mickeys on a book near the back wall of the Library.
5 points for both

★ Now cross the park to Tomorrowland and go to **Tomorrowland Transit Authority People-Mover**. Find a Hidden Mickey as you ride.

Clue 174: In the last part of the ride, ob-

serve the accessories of the woman getting her hair done.
3 points

★ Walk to the **Merchant of Venus** shop.

Clue 175: Find a classic Mickey on a wall mural.
2 points

Clue 176: Can you spot a Mickey hat?
2 points

★ Now scan the wall mural inside **Mickey's Star Traders** shop.

Clue 177: Look for the train on the mural.
2 points

Clue 178: Find the Hidden Stitch.
3 points

Clue 179: Spot Mickey hats on a building.
2 points

Clue 180: Look up higher at the satellite dishes.
2 points

Clue 181: Scan the road layout.
3 points

Clue 182: Find three clear domes.
2 points

Clue 183: Follow the mural around to another classic Mickey on a building.
1 point

★ Stroll toward *Space Mountain* and into the **To-morrowland "Cool Scanner" Station**.

Clue 184: Look up for tiny Hidden Mickeys.
3 points for one or more

★ Cross the nearest bridge to **Main Street, U.S.A.** and search for 18 or more classic Mickeys as you stroll toward the park entrance.

Clue 185: Look around the outside of The Crystal Palace restaurant.
3 points

Clue 186: As you enter the short side street off of Main Street, study the area near the bricks outside the entrance to the Crystal Arts store for a tiny classic Mickey.
5 points

Clue 187: Near the Emporium store outside, search for Hidden Mickeys on a sign.
3 points for all

Clue 188: Find Mickey in stained-glass windows high on the Emporium exterior.
3 points

Clue 189: Study the outside display windows of the Emporium store for a Hidden Mickey in a logo.
4 points

Clue 190: Inside the Emporium store, study the merchandise stands.
2 points

Clue 191: Look for a tiny Mickey on a building in an outside display window of the Emporium store.
5 points

Clue 192: Find a Hidden Mickey made of gears or circles in a display window of the Main Street Confectionery store near Town Square.
2 points

Clue 193: Spot another classic Hidden Mickey made of something sweet in a display window of the Main Street Confectionery store.
3 points

Clue 194: Observe the overhead moving candy bins in the Main Street Confectionery store.
3 points

★ Closely examine the **Caffe Italiano coffee cart** (present seasonally) near Tony's Town Square Restaurant to earn some bonus points.
2 bonus points

Clue 195: Inside **Tony's Town Square Restaurant**, spot Mickey on a bookshelf.
3 points

Clue 196: As you enter Tony's dining area, study the floor near the left wall for a classic Mickey.
5 points

Clue 197: Now look around inside the restaurant for a classic Mickey under a painting.
3 points

Clue 198: Look up for a classic Mickey as you exit the restaurant.
3 points

Clue 199: Find Hidden Mickeys on Main Street's horse-drawn trolley.
2 points for one or more

Clue 200: Stand in Town Square plaza and look for a classic Mickey on a ceiling.
2 points

Clue 201: Look around the Main Street Train Station for a Hidden Mickey on a ticket.
4 points

Clue 202: Find a Hidden Mickey on the wall inside the Main Street Train Station. (Psst! It's near the ticket Hidden Mickey.)
3 points

★ Enjoy the **evening parade**. You'll likely find a few Hidden Mickeys (and several decorative Mickey images) on the floats.

Clue 203: If it's the Main Street Electrical Parade, search for a classic Mickey on the front of a vehicle.
2 points

★ You can often spot a classic Mickey in the sky during the evening **Wishes fireworks** show. If you see one, give yourself bonus points!
5 bonus points for spotting one or more

★ Keep your eyes peeled for another Hidden Mickey or two as you end your day in the park.

Clue 204: As you leave Main Street under the train station, search for Mickey on a gate.
2 points

★ Ride the **ferryboat** from the Magic Kingdom to the Transportation and Ticket Center (TTC).

Clue 205: As you walk onto the ferry and as you exit the ferry at the TTC, look around for a classic Mickey.
4 points for one or more

★ If you go through the **Transportation and Ticket Center**, check out a cool Hidden Mickey and earn some bonus points.

Clue 206: Study the TTC ceiling skylights.
5 bonus points

Now tally your score.

Total Points for Magic Kingdom =

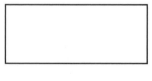

How'd you do?

Up to 294 points – Bronze
295 to 586 points – Silver
587 points and over – Gold
734 points – Perfect Score

If you earned bonus points in *Under the Sea ~ Journey of the Little Mermaid, Peter Pan's Flight, Pirates of the Caribbean,* on Main Street, U.S.A., at the fireworks, or in the TTC, you may have done even better.

**Caution:
Don't peek at this
section unless you
really want help!**

Magic Kingdom Entrance

Hint 1: Classic Mickeys are formed in the bell clapper designs of some of the commemorative bricks in the walkways in front of the Magic Kingdom.

Main Street, U.S.A. – Train Station

Hint 2: The periphery of the Main Street Train Station roof, second level, has scrollwork that repeats a classic Mickey motif.

Fantasyland

– Seven Dwarfs Mine Train

Hint 3: Bright colored gems are in the interactive games along the Standby entrance queue. At times in these games, three gems come together to form a classic Hidden Mickey. One good image, made of a green gem for the "head" and two clear gems for the "ears,"

45

is at the top of the first barrel in the "Spin the Barrels" game.

Hint 4: On the right side of your train and to the right of Dopey's ears, a classic Hidden Mickey is formed by jewels. Find the larger red jewel for Mickey's head—the left ear is a smaller red jewel and the right ear, an amber diamond.

Hint 5: Along the ride on your right side, three gems (a purple "head" and one green and one light purple "ear') are stuck in the wall behind Grumpy's head.

Hint 6: After passing Doc going up the second lift, Oswald the Lucky Rabbit can be seen as a 3-D image on the left hand side of the ride on a horizontal log. You can see his tiny legs, his belly pooching out, his round tan face with eyes and nose, and his right hand to the upper left of his face. His dark ears flop back from the top of his head and are less distinct. (This image is difficult to spot; you'll only get a fleeting glimpse.)

Tomorrowland

– Space Mountain

Hint 7: In one or more of the interactive games on the left wall of the entrance queue, guests can at times connect space construction objects together to form classic Mickeys.

Hint 8: In the instructional video near the loading area, a man with a full-face image of Mickey Mouse on the front of his T-shirt sits down in the front seat of a ride vehicle. At another time in the video, a woman removes her Mickey ears before riding.

Fantasyland

– The Many Adventures of Winnie the Pooh

Hint 9: Inside the big tree, a classic Mickey is formed by embedded rocks above the frame of the smaller children's entrance.

Hint 10: Above the frame of the larger entrance inside the big tree is a depression in the wood shaped like a submarine: a tribute to *20,000 Leagues Under the Sea* the previous attraction near this location; thus, a Hidden Tribute rather than a Hidden Mickey.

Hint 11: On the outside of the big tree, in back, a side profile of Mickey is carved into the bark. It's at the upper left corner above the lower window.

Hint 12: Outside on the far side of the big tree, behind the fence, a classic Mickey is etched into the wood in the middle of a vertical brown post on the left side of a window.

Hint 13: Two Hidden Mickeys are in Rabbit's Garden along the entry area (accessed through the Standby queue):
   - A head of lettuce and two tomatoes form a classic Mickey.
   - Three watermelon drums are positioned to create a classic Mickey.

Hint 14: At the beginning of the ride, in Rabbit's Garden, the small marker with radishes (in the middle pot to the left of the "Letus" sign) has one radish shaped like a classic Hidden Mickey.

Hint 15: At the beginning of the left wall of Owl's house (the second room on the ride) is a picture of Mr. Toad handing the deed to the house over to Owl (a tribute to the previous attraction in this building, *Mr. Toad's Wild Ride*).

Hint 16: Near the end of this room, on the right side of the floor, is a picture of Mole standing with Winnie the Pooh.

– Under the Sea ~ Journey of The Little Mermaid

Hint 17: A classic Hidden Mickey made of three circular impressions in the rock is to the upper right of the sign at the Standby entrance to the attraction.

Hint 18: On the right side along the outside Standby entrance queue, a classic Mickey made of impressions is at the top right side of a rock that sits in the middle of the small lagoon in front of the waterfall.

Hint 19: Above the lagoon rock with the Hidden Mickey is another small classic Mickey made of impressions in the rock wall. Look for it on a flat sloping wall face just below the very top of the rock wall. The Hidden Mickey is above the right edge of the large opening in the wall; the waterfall spills over the left side of this opening.

Hint 20: Directly below the right side of a bridge with a rope-covered side rail is a classic Hidden Mickey made of impressions in the rock. You're facing a rock arch with a waterfall, and the Hidden Mickey is at the right side of the base of the stream below you. Water streaming over the Mickey blurs the image.

Hint 21: Now stare up at the higher part of the rock arch. To the right of the small waterfall, a tiny classic Mickey impression is in the rock in the upper middle of the arch.

Hint 22: At the left side of the outside Standby entrance queue, a Nautilus submarine impression is in a rock wall behind a small pond. When you reach a fence on your left strewn with ropes and nets, look back to your left and study the rear rock wall near the waterline. First spot the round porthole that resembles an eye; the nose of the submarine points to the left.

Note: "Nautilus" is the submarine, commanded by Captain Nemo, in Jules Verne's novel *Twenty Thousand Leagues Under the Sea*. It was the ride vehicle in the WDW ride of the same name, which closed in 1994.

Hint 23: Each year on Mickey Mouse's birthday (November 18) the noontime sun shines through holes carved in the rockwork above you at just the right angle to form a classic Mickey on the wall of the inside entrance queue. The Mickey-shaped light lasts for several minutes. The top of Mickey's head is formed by the carving in the highest rock, and the lower part of his head is formed by the carving in the rock closer to you. Stay alert, because the sunlight just might shine through both rock openings at other times of the year to form Mickey!

Hint 24: Along the left side of the inside Standby entrance queue, a classic Mickey tilted to the left is formed by holes in the rock above some bottles on a table.

Hint 25: A side profile of Mickey Mouse, looking left, is etched in the ceiling. He's at the beginning of the room with the talking Scuttle, high to your left as you enter and near a cubed light cover.

Hint 26: In the first part of the room where the song "Under the Sea" is playing, three oval purple corals clinging to a rock to the right of your ride vehicle form a classic Mickey. They're just past and behind the singing chorus line of fish that are standing on their tails.

Hint 27: Just past Ariel in the "Under the Sea" room, a green fish with a purple seashell hat has a classic Hidden Mickey at the top of her earring. For the best vantage point, look back to the earring after you pass by the fish.

Hint 28: Toward the end of the ride, check the pond (to your right) for frogs with dark green spots on their backs that form sideways classic Mickeys. The frogs are perched on lily pads to the left of a boat with Ariel and Eric.

Hint 29: Along the left side of the exit walkway inside the cave, spot a classic Hidden Mickey made of a large depression for the "head" and two smaller depressions for the "ears." This upright Hidden Mickey is just inches up from the floor and below a large opening in the left wall that looks into the exit path from *Ariel's Grotto*.

Hint 30: Through the large opening mentioned above, you can see another Hidden Mickey: a classic Mickey formed of three impressions in the rock wall along the left side of the exit from *Ariel's Grotto*. This image is tilted to the left and it's about halfway up the wall and below a ceiling light. (Note: You'll probably find other rock impressions along the exit that resemble classic Mickeys.)

Hint 31: At the end of the exit walkway from *Under the Sea*, turn to your right to spot an amazing Hidden "Steamboat Willie" Mickey Mouse. The Imagineers sculpted this image on a series of rocks. His left leg and shoe are closest to you, then his right leg and shoe are on the next rock. Two holes in the rocks represent the buttons on his shorts. His whitish face is on a flat rock, and he's looking left. His tall hat is the last rock above his head. There's even a ship's wheel in the rock to the left of his face!

– Be Our Guest Restaurant

Hint 32: Just inside the entrance to Be Our Guest Restaurant, in the room with the suits of armor, classic Hidden Mickeys are formed at times in the corners and intersections of the border design on the wall behind the suits of armor.

Hint 33: In the room with suits of armor, the ax blade at the end of the room on the right has a classic Hidden Mickey hole cut out of it.

Hint 34: At the right rear terminal as you enter the food order room, take a look at the stack of books. Two images form Hidden Mickeys; one is at each corner of the top book cover, and another is on the spine of the second book from the bottom.

Hint 35: On the left side of the rear wall of the Rose Gallery seating area (to the right of the restaurant's Ballroom dining room), look for a small painting of Mrs. Potts and Chip. Chip is playing in a dish filled with bubbles. Three of those bubbles form a classic Mickey.

Hint 36: Inside the Be Our Guest Restaurant, walk to the West Wing room and stand in front of the rose at the rear of the room. Now turn and look up to your right to spot a small Hidden Mickey hole in tattered fabric hanging from the ceiling.

Hint 37: Outside along the bridge, on your right as you exit toward the rest of Fantasyland, a classic Hidden Mickey is etched in stone. The Hidden Mickey, tilted left, is on the back of the partial wall behind the check-in station.

Hint 38: A faint classic Mickey in swirls is on top of a short rock wall to the left of the check-in station (as you face the station) at the beginning of the entrance walkway to Be Our Guest Restaurant. It's on top of the last flat rectangular stone before the wall ends.

– Peter Pan's Flight

Hint 39: At the lower right of the entrance-sign cloud formation is an incomplete classic cloud Mickey. It's just to the right of the "t" in "Flight." Peter Pan is standing between the ears of another Hidden Mickey in the sign; you can see just the top of Mickey's head and his ears.

Hint 40: Three brown rocks in the yard in front of the doghouse form a classic Mickey. The rocks are in the brown dirt section of the yard. Mickey's smiling face may be on the "head" rock, but it's hard to spot!

Bonus Points Hint: When the rotating moon is in just the right position, you can see a faint dark classic Mickey on the moon, above the silhouettes of the flying Peter Pan and his entourage. Unfortunately, since the moon rotates, you can't spot this Hidden Mickey on every ride through the attraction.

Hint 41: On the rocky edge of the mermaid lagoon, three flowers on the grass form a classic Mickey; the "head" is yellow and the "ears" are light orange.

Hint 42: As you fly over one side of the ship with the pirates and then back over the other, look down for two sets of cannonballs, one on each side of the ship. Shadows directly below the first pile of cannonballs form a classic Hidden Mickey. A more pronounced "shadow" classic Mickey is next to and apart from the second pile of cannonballs; this Hidden Mickey appears to be painted on the deck of the ship.

Frontierland

– Splash Mountain

Hint 43: A red classic Hidden Mickey is painted on a yoke that hangs on a left wall of the entrance queue. It's in the first tunnel. Start looking for it when you reach the part of the tunnel with lights on the wall. You can spot it from both the Standby and FastPass+ queues. (It's growing fainter with time.)

Hint 44: Along the entrance queue, just after you pass by the *WDW Railroad* tracks (you can see the tracks just behind this part of the entrance queue), a Mickey Mouse sticker is glued on the first hexagonal light cover you pass under.

Hint 45: As you ride halfway up the second crankhill, on the right side, three barrels in the lower right corner of a stack of barrels form a classic Mickey.

Hint 46: During the first part of the ride, when your boat is outside, look to your right for a barrel with "Muskrat Moonshine" painted on the side. A classic Mickey is formed by holes in the paint, above the "s" in "Muskrat."

Hint 47: On the right side of your boat and to the left of the rabbit sweeping a porch, small animal silhouettes run right to left along the top of a hill on the rear wall. Just before the last animal disappears, its head becomes a classic Mickey silhouette. These moving animal silhouettes repeat at regular intervals.

Hint 48: Look for a picnic basket up on a small ledge. You'll spot it just past Brer Frog, who is sitting on an alligator and fishing with his toe. Near the basket are three red-and-white-striped fishing bobbers in the shape of a classic Hidden Mickey.

Hint 49: On the right side of your boat, in the room with jumping water, a classic rope Mickey is hanging halfway down from the ceiling. It's in the shadows behind a lantern and just past a turtle lying on a geyser.

Hint 50: The hole in the mountain at the top of the big drop is sculpted to form a side profile of Mickey's face. As you approach the big drop in your boat, Mickey's nose juts out from the left side of the hole. (You can also see this one from the outside viewing area; see Hint 53.)

Hint 51: As you pass the photo viewing area on your way out, look over to the entrance queue to spot two classic Mickeys formed by acorns on a birdhouse with a rope ladder. One classic Mickey formation is above a door and below blue roof slats. The other is near the peanut-shell chimney, above the curve of the red rail.

Hint 52: Along the exit walkway, at the Laughin' Place children's play area, a classic Mickey is formed by the ends of three logs stuck to the wall to the right of the "Laughin' Place" sign.

Hint 53: Walk in front of *Splash Mountain* after your ride. The hole in the mountain for the big drop forms a side profile of Mickey's face. From the outside, Mickey's nose juts out from the right side of the hole.

– Big Thunder Mountain Railroad

Hint 54: Three stalagmites in the cavern to your right at the beginning of the ride form a classic Mickey. Look down at the left side of the floor of the cavern to spot it.

Hint 55: On the left side as you exit the ride (in the exit closest to the Standby line entrance), a cutout in the reddish rock resembles a side profile of Tinker Bell. She's behind the fence, behind a cactus and between two metal carts.

Liberty Square

– Haunted Mansion

Hint 56: Along the interactive "Scenic Route," a classic Mickey made of barnacles is on a huge bathtub with the words "Here Floats Captain Culpepper Clyne." The classic Mickey is tilted right and is below and between the letters "R" and "C" in the name.

Hint 57: Just inside the entrance to the first room, you'll find some small classic Mickeys in the oval border design around the portrait of the dressed-up aging man above the fireplace.

Hint 58: As you pass by the library room (at the beginning of the ride) and then the "endless hallway" on your right, check out the backs of two purple chairs for an abstract Donald Duck. Near the top of the chairs, you can see his cap, which sits above his distorted eyes, face, and bill. (Note that the chairs may change locations at times.)

Hint 59: A plate and two saucers on the ghostly banquet table are arranged to form a classic Mickey. They're usually at the bottom left corner of the table.

Hint 60: In the first part of the attic area, on the floor to your left under a small table with shelves, plates form a classic Mickey.

Hint 61: To the right of the opera-singing lady (her left) is a ghost resembling the Grim Reaper. He is holding up his left arm. Hanging from his left hand is a cloth with dark markings at the top that form a classic Hidden Mickey.

Hint 62: Outside, at the left end of the covered walkway, a classic Mickey metal latch holds a wrought-iron gate open.

Hint 63: In the pet cemetery on the left side of the outside exit walkway, a Mr. Toad tombstone stands at the rear left corner.

– Columbia Harbour House restaurant

Hint 64: In the downstairs table area, a wall across from the food-order counters is decorated with three small circular maps covered by a single piece of glass. (The central map is labeled "Charles V.") The three circles form a classic Mickey.

Adventureland

– Pirates of the Caribbean

Hint 65: About halfway along the left queue, a pile of cannonballs appears on the floor to your left. A classic Mickey made of cannonballs is at the lower left of the pile.

Hint 66: Along the left entrance queue is a room with a faux fireplace on the right side. A classic Mickey is in the plaster on the sloping area to the right and above the fireplace mantle. It's about seven feet up from the floor. (This image is fading with time.)

Hint 67: Tall gun cabinets stand on both sides of the left entrance queue. On two of the cabinets are classic Mickey-shaped locks (one on each side).

Hint 68: At the beginning of the ride, Davy Jones's image is sometimes projected on a wall of mist in front of the boat. Look up at the left side of his hat (his right side, viewers' left). Below and to the left of the bottom of the "V" at the front of his hat, three tiny gold balls form a classic Mickey.

Hint 69: About halfway through the ride and past the red-haired lady, a cat behind an intoxicated pirate casts a classic Hidden Mickey moving shadow on the corner of the wall above and behind it.

Hint 70: As your boat approaches the last scene (the treasure room), a classic Mickey lock hangs on large wooden recessed doors to the left.

HINTS HINTS HINTS HINTS HINTS HINTS HINTS HINTS HINTS HINTS HINTS HINTS HINTS

Hint 71: As the treasure room comes into view, a classic Mickey lock hangs at the middle of the wooden door that's swung open on the left. A long key with a cord hanging from it juts out of the keyhole of the lock.

Hint 72: Classic Mickey locks hang on the cabinets behind Captain Jack Sparrow in the treasure room.

Hint 73: Just as you enter the gift shop after exiting your boat, several classic Mickeys are formed by coins and jewels in two hanging plates near the right wall. Look along the edges of the plates for some of the best images.

Hint 74: Inside the gift shop, turn left and find a painting at the lower right of a wall map on the shop's rear wall. In the painting, a lady in a multicolored gown has a classic Mickey on her left shoulder.

Hint 75: Along a side pathway outside the entrance to the *Pirates of the Caribbean* attraction, the wheel of a cart forms a classic Mickey with two barrels above it. To spot it, walk to the side of the cart away from the main Adventureland path.

Frontierland

– Frontierland Shootin' Arcade

Hint 76: In the front center of the target area is a group of cactus plants. One near the middle, just below the gray tombstone, has three lobes forming a classic Hidden Mickey.

Liberty Square

– Stocks near the Liberty Square Riverboat entrance

Hint 77: Padlocks on the stocks near the entrance are shaped to resemble classic Hidden Mickeys (even though the "ears" are a bit small).

Tomorrowland

– Tomorrowland Speedway

Hint 78: Find a *Tomorrowland Speedway* map to your left on the purple wall at the end of the FastPass+ queue. Look for two small classic Hidden Mickeys formed of blue "heads" with two faint white "ears." One is at the right middle of the map (a red object points to this Hidden Mickey). The second Hidden Mickey is in the right lower corner of the map, next to an angle in the blue field.

Hint 79: A tall lamppost casts a classic Mickey shadow on the pavement outside *Tomorrowland Speedway*. It's best seen on a sunny day in the late morning or early afternoon.

– Walt Disney's Carousel of Progress

Hint 80: In the first scene, on the right side of the stage, where the daughter is getting ready for the evening (on Valentine's Day), a classic Mickey made of cloth decorates the top of her mirror.

Hint 81: In the third scene, Mickey's Sorcerer's Hat sits at the right side of the room, next to the girl in the shaker machine.

Hint 82: In the last scene, an abstract Mickey Mouse as the Sorcerer's apprentice from the film *Fantasia* is in a painting on the dining room wall. To spot it, look immediately to the left rear of the scene as it rotates into view. The painting is on the dining room's right rear wall.

Hint 83: On the left side of the room, a nutcracker shaped like Mickey Mouse stands on the left side of the mantelpiece.

Hint 84: Under the Christmas tree, a plush Mickey Mouse is behind the wrapped boxes.

Hint 85: On the last stage, one of the Christmas presents under the tree (near the grandfather's chair) is decorated with a large classic Mickey head cut out of green paper and glued to the side of the gift, which is sometimes partially hidden by another present, so you may only see the ears and part of the top of Mickey's head. The green Mickey ears are to the right of Grandpa's lower leg.

Hint 86: A classic Mickey appears (just for a few seconds) on the top of a spaceship in the middle of the television screen. Look for it just as the game starts on the TV, before Grandma starts playing.

Hint 87: Salt and pepper shakers on the kitchen counter have Mickey ears.

Hint 88: Along the exit ramps, classic Mickeys are on the backs of the round signs for the attraction.

– Buzz Lightyear's Space Ranger Spin

Hint 89: Just inside the building, in the entrance queue, the second poster on the right wall is called "Planets of the Galactic Alliance." In Sector 1, the central continent on the planet "Pollost Prime" is shaped like a side profile of Mickey Mouse's head.

Hint 90: At the right lower corner of this poster, a purple planet ("Planet Z") has three craters that form a sideways classic Mickey with "ears" to the left. (Planet Z with its Mickey craters appears in several posters along the queue.)

Hint 91: The side-profile Mickey continent appears in the top left of a recessed wall farther along the entrance queue, just before the last right turn in the queue.

Hint 92: Sector 2 in this same mural contains a planet made of many spheres, some of which form classic Mickeys. One of them is at the outer edge of the planet at about the "ten o'clock" location.

Hint 93: On the ride, in the very first interactive room with targets, a tiny classic Mickey with a green head and blue ears is on the first part of the lower right wall. You have to rotate back and to the right in your vehicle to see it. The Hidden Mickey is below and between two five-point green stars.

Hint 94: You go through three different rooms during the first part of this ride. When you enter the room with lots of batteries, look to the left of the ride vehicle. You'll see a side profile of Mickey's head in the rear left under the words, "Initiate Battery Unload."

Hint 95: Also in the battery room, look to the right of your vehicle and high over Zurg's left (your right) shoulder to spot a tiny blue classic Mickey star, tilted to the left. It's in the star field to the right of the large blue and yellow cone suspended over Zurg.

Hint 96: As the ride vehicle moves through the space video room, planet "Pollost Prime," with continent Mickey, flies by on the right wall.

Hint 97: Just past the space video room, in the final battle scene on the ride, "Pollost Prime" shows up yet again on a wall straight ahead and to the upper left.

Hint 98: A yellow classic Mickey is on the wall across from the video monitors that show ride photos. An alien is pointing up to it.

Hint 99: Stitch's spaceship is flying through space in a corner of the first mural on the right wall as you exit the ride.

– Astro Orbiter

Hint 100: A small classic Mickey is traced in the cement close to a *Tomorrowland Transit Authority PeopleMover* support beam near *Astro Orbiter* on the side toward *Space Mountain*, between Cool Ship and The Lunching Pad.

– Monsters, Inc. Laugh Floor

Hint 101: On the outside wall, a picture advertising a Recreational Rocket has a moon with craters shaped like an upside-down classic Mickey.

Hint 102: Also on the outside wall, a sign advertising a Space Collectibles Convention includes an asteroid shaped like a classic Mickey.

Hint 103: As you enter the attraction, look for a window display of a city on the rear of the right-hand wall just past the entrance doors to the second room. A classic Mickey is under the apex of the triangular roof segment on the building in the front center of the window display.

Liberty Square

– The Hall of Presidents

Hint 104: On a wall painting in the waiting room for the show, a tiny classic Mickey is at the end of the object George Washington holds in his left hand.

Frontierland

– Tom Sawyer Island

Hint 105: Across the river from the island docks, look at the right end of the bridge in Frontierland for three rocks that form a classic Mickey. They're located between the last two vertical posts that support the handrail, about one foot down from the top of the rocks. The Hidden Mickey is in the second row of rocks from the top. (Note: This Hidden Mickey is also visible from the *Liberty Square Riverboat.*)

Hint 106: Halfway through Old Scratch's Mystery Mine, bright shining gems embedded in the wall form a side profile of Goofy. He's looking to your right.

Hint 107: In Fort Langhorn, enter the Rifle Roost at the far right corner. (To get there, climb up the stairs to your immediate right after you enter the fort and walk across the right upper walkway to the far right Rifle Roost.) On top of the right handrail, about halfway up the steps to the top of the Rifle Roost, there is a Hidden Mickey created by: a wood knot, an additional mark, and an indentation in the wood.

Fantasyland

– Mickey's PhilharMagic

Hint 108: In the first waiting area inside, the wall mural with musical instruments has several small white classic Mickeys.

Hint 109: On the right vertical border of the video screen in the main theater, a classic Mickey hides inside a French horn.

Hint 110: In the "Be Our Guest" portion of the movie, there is a point where you are watching Lumiere dancing on the table with other characters. The view goes to an overhead shot and there are shadows cast on the table from the candle hands of Lumiere. These shadows come together at times to form what appear to be Hidden Mickeys.

Hint 111: In "The Little Mermaid" segment, Ariel throws jewels out into the water in front of her. Stay focused on the right side of the screen (your right), to spot a ring as it rotates slowly from a side position to an open circle. A dark classic Mickey image is visible just as you first spot the open center of the ring. The image disappears as the ring finishes its rotation.

Hint 112: Watch closely as Aladdin and Jasmine ride their magic carpet in the sky. Stare at the bottom left of the screen for a quick glimpse of three round buildings on the ground. They're clustered to form a classic Mickey.

Hint 113: Music stands shaped like classic Mickeys are on shelves high up above the merchandise in Fantasy Faire at the exit of *Mickey's PhilharMagic*.

– "it's a small world"

Hint 114: Toward the end of the Africa room, vines on the right above the giraffes and to the left of your boat have purple leaves shaped like classic Mickey heads.

Hint 115: Near the end of the South Pacific room, several koala bears hang on a tree. As you approach the bears on your left, the back of the blue bear's head forms a classic Mickey.

– "Tangled" Restroom area

Hint 116: On a wall poster outside the Ladies' Restroom near the "Tangled" Tower, a classic Hidden Mickey is on a Mime's lips. Smaller round, solid black circles form the "ears" just above the upper lip.

– Near Peter Pan's Flight

Hint 117: Between the entrance to *Peter Pan's Flight* and Columbia Harbour House, you'll find paintings of grape clusters on the walls. The lower three grapes in the second cluster from the right at the bottom form a classic Mickey.

– Pinocchio Village Haus restaurant

Hint 118: As you head from the dining area to the restrooms, a tiny dark classic Mickey appears above the word "dreams" on the "When You Wish Upon A Star" mural. You'll find it on the left wall near the exit to the restrooms.

Hint 119: A tiny white classic Mickey is in this same area of the mural, below and left of the word "All."

Hint 120: On the left side of the same mural, a tiny white classic Mickey hides near a sparkling star. It's to the left of the Fairy, at mid-thigh level, and her right thumb points to it.

– Fairytale Garden

Hint 121: At the base of the first light pole on the right as you enter, a classic Mickey that looks like a piece of different-colored stucco is in the cement on the side next to the fence.

Hint 122: A side profile of Pluto's head is on the wall, upper left of the stage. It's left of the brick circle and above the stairs.

– Sir Mickey's Store

Hint 123: You'll find a classic Mickey toward the top of the store's sign-shield. The shield is hanging under a vine, across from Castle Couture shop.

Hint 124: In a display window to the right of the main entrance to the store, classic Mickeys are on the border of the archer's collar in a painting on the rear wall of the display. You can also usually find classic Mickeys made by arrangements of buttons on the floor of the display.

– Castle Couture shop

Hint 125: To find a tiny classic Mickey on the wall, walk through the entrance doors to the right of the Cinderella fountain. Then turn right and look up at the bronze horizontal frieze near the ceiling. You'll spot a series of arches over bushes with flowers. Walk forward to the far end of the frieze and count back six arches to a bush with three flowers at its upper left that form a classic Mickey. If you have trouble spotting it, ask a Cast Member to point it out for you.

– Storybook Circus area

Hint 126: Between the exit of the Fantasyland Train Station and the nearby restrooms is a trail of large and small (mother and baby) elephant tracks. These prints in the pavement come together at times to form classic Mickeys.

Hint 127: On the "Giraffes" boxcar in *Casey Jr. Splash 'N' Soak Station*, a classic Mickey is hidden in the clouds behind a giraffe in a painting on the side of the boxcar facing the restrooms. This cloud Hidden Mickey is behind the lower neck of the tall giraffe and it's tilted to the right.

Hint 128: Under the entrance sign to *The Barnstormer*, two classic Mickeys are in the scrollwork below Goofy's picture. The images are at the top corners on each side of the faux ticket booth window.

Hint 129: On the huge billboard on the right side of *The Barnstormer* (the billboard the ride train hurtles through), a tiny gray classic Mickey hides in the middle of the propeller of the lower plane on the far right side of the billboard.

Hint 130: A poster of Daisy Duck ("Madame Daisy Fortuna") is outside to the left of the entrance to *Pete's Silly Sideshow*. A faint classic Mickey is traced on the upper part of her light green blouse, just to the right of her right index finger.

Hint 131: Eight tiny Mickey balloons are scattered around the large "Storybook Circus" painting at the rear of a tent next to *Pete's Silly Sideshow*.

Hint 132: A classic Hidden Mickey is on a sleeping cheetah inside Big Top Souvenirs. The cheetah is on a wall painting behind a register counter and its leg hangs down from a tree branch. The reddish-brown Mickey spot is on the hanging left lower leg, just above the ankle area.

Hint 133: A classic Mickey is formed by a manhole cover (the "head") and two elephant tracks (the "ears") near the entrance to the FastPass+ queue for *Dumbo the Flying Elephant*.

– Enchanted Forest area

Hint 134: A classic three-circle Mickey metal design sits atop the Disney Vacation Club sign.

Hint 135: Embedded in the cement walkway in front of the Disney Vacation Club kiosk and across from *Ariel's Grotto* is a classic Hidden Mickey formed of a survey marker and two adjacent pebbles. It's near a cart track indented in the cement.

– Gaston's Tavern area

Hint 136: A tiny classic Mickey made of dark impressions hides on the rock that forms the base of Gaston's Statue, which stands in front of Gaston's Tavern. The Hidden Mickey is near the waterline below the back of Gaston's left leg.

Hint 137: Groups of circles in several antique maps on the wall inside the Bonjour Village Gifts shop resemble classic Mickeys. The most convincing image is on the "Terrestrial Globe" map on the left wall, on which a globe forms the head of an upside-down classic Mickey.

Hint 138: A Hidden Donald Duck is at the upper left corner of a portrait in the Bonjour Village Gifts shop. The portrait is centered on the wall at the rear of the store and hangs near the ceiling.

Hint 139: A classic Hidden Mickey is formed by horseshoe prints in the sidewalk. Find it as you walk from Gaston's Tavern toward Be Our Guest Restaurant; it's near the end of the short rock wall on your right and close to a pole with lanterns. Two horseshoe prints form the "head" and two other prints form the "ears."

– Near Enchanted Tales with Belle

Hint 140: An image that resembles Oswald the Lucky Rabbit is formed by three embedded pebbles in the middle of a walkway. To find the image, stop across from the *Enchanted Tales with Belle* entrance (and waiting time) sign and look down in the middle of the main walkway to Be Our Guest Restaurant.

Main Street, U.S.A.

– Town Square Theater

Hint 141: In the last room in the queue just before you enter Mickey's Dressing Room for *Mickey's Meet 'n' Greet*, there are mail slots for the theater cast. Mickey has his own personal mail slot.

Hint 142: A classic Mickey made of metal rings lies in the right upper compartment of Mickey's open magic chest in the Greeting Room.

Hint 143: Inside Mickey's magic chest, on the right, there's a classic Mickey lock on a chain. (It's sometimes covered by a scarf.)

Additional Mickey-shaped locks can often be spotted in various locations in the Greeting Room.

Hint 144: Oswald the Lucky Rabbit is drawn on a piece of paper at the upper right of a bulletin board at the back of the room. He's to the right of a drawing of Mickey Mouse.

Hint 145: To the right of the exit door from the Greeting Room, three large Mickey Mouse playing cards are held upright by a long clip on the floor. In the middle of the clip, a classic Mickey wearing a triangular "hat" resembles a Sorcerer Mickey.

Hint 146: Classic Mickey locks hang from the side of a metal display table in the gift shop.

Hint 147: A birdhouse from the now-closed Mickey's Toontown Fair sits on a tall merchandise cabinet at the left side of the shop (as you enter from Mickey's greeting area). The front door of the birdhouse is shaped like a classic Mickey.

– From the WDW Railroad

Hint 148: As you ride the train away from the Main Street Station and toward Adventureland, watch for three wheels on the ground that form a classic Hidden Mickey. (The "ears" aren't the same size but the image seems purposeful.) Spot the wheels after the first road crossing on the left side of the tracks; they're between a side road and a barrel.

Liberty Square

– Ye Olde Christmas Shoppe

Hint 149: In the framed log collage under a register in the middle of the store, a classic Hidden Mickey formed by three logs hides in the upper left corner of a stack of logs.

– Liberty Tree Tavern

Hint 150: Look for a spice rack to the right of the fireplace on the rear wall of the waiting area. Three grapes in a small still-life painting on the spice rack form a classic Mickey.

Hint 151: Turn left from the waiting area and go up the stairs. Then turn right and enter a brown room with a fireplace on the inside. Go up to the fireplace (you'll have to climb a few more steps) and look for a classic Mickey in the clouds. You'll find it on the left side of the upper part of the painting that's hanging to the left of George Washington's portrait.

Frontierland

– Frontier Trading Post store

Hint 152: A "How to Pin Trade" sign, behind a register inside the store to the right, sports a rope classic Mickey. Another rope classic Mickey is attached to a pole. It stands above the merchandise and near the middle entrance to the store.

Hint 153: In the "How to Pin Trade" posters, a cowboy's lanyard has a black classic Mickey.

– Pecos Bill Tall Tale Inn and Cafe

Hint 154: Inside the cafe, find the plates sitting upright along a ledge near the ceiling behind the middle of the serving counter. On the third plate from the left, at the upper left and near the inside circle of the plate, three red spots behind the white bird form a classic Mickey.

Adventureland

– Tortuga Tavern

Hint 155: In a window display about pirates inside the Tortuga Tavern restaurant, three candles stuck in a bowl form a classic Hidden Mickey.

– Walt Disney's Enchanted Tiki Room

Hint 156: Upside-down classic Mickeys are camouflaged in the designs at the bottom of two bird perches. One perch is in the left corner as you enter the theater. The other is to the right of the exit door.

Hint 157: To the right of the entrance to *Walt Disney's Enchanted Tiki Room*, a statue with several faces has classic Mickeys formed by beads in the middle of the forehead, above the nose.

– Near The Magic Carpets of Aladdin

Hint 158: A charm embedded in the cement between *The Magic Carpets of Aladdin* exit and the Agrabah Bazaar shop contains a tiny classic Mickey. It's near a shop pole that has blue paint above its base.

– Jungle Cruise

Hint 159: Check the big sign outside. On the side of the sign that faces the attraction, three barnacles under the "J" in "Jungle Cruise" form a classic Mickey.

Hint 160: About halfway along the Standby entrance queue, a classic Hidden Mickey made of dark round circles and tilted to the right is at the lower left of a map of Africa in a display cabinet on a wall. The display cabinet is to the right of several masks on the wall.

Hint 161: Along the entrance queue, on a shelf facing the cruise boats, three walnuts in a jar resemble a classic Mickey.

Hint 162: Across the river from the loading dock, look for a hut with a tall tree behind it that leans to the right. There's a white classic Mickey marking on the tree bark above the hut. To spot it, follow the right-leaning tree trunk high up to the Mickey marking. It's about two-thirds of the distance up the trunk, where the trunk angles slightly more to the right.

Hint 163: Along the right side of the boat, watch for the Pygmy War Canoes sitting

on a beach. The bow of the middle canoe resembles Donald Duck.

Hint 164: After the waterfall, a wrecked silver plane sits to the right of the boat. Look back to spot three circles etched in the metal at the lower right of the visible section of fuselage. The circles are all the same size, but many folks and Cast Members consider them a Hidden Mickey.

Hint 165: Along the left side of the boat, be alert for menacing natives with spears. The last isolated native of the group wears a Donald mask.

Hint 166: The first undecorated column on the left wall (the third column from the end as you come out of the temple) has a chipped area of brick on the third block from the top. The chipped area forms part of a profile view of Mickey's head and face. Don't get discouraged if you have trouble spotting it; this one is tough to find—especially the first time.

– Swiss Family Treehouse

Hint 167: A side profile of Mickey, facing to the right, is on a section of the tree trunk that touches a wall of the treehouse. Mickey is in a clearing inside a large patch of green algae. You'll find it on the right as you descend the steps from the boys' bedroom and on the left as you walk down from the very top of the trail.

Hint 168: At the rear of the outdoor stone seating area next to the entrance to the *Swiss Family Treehouse*, a classic Mickey is etched in a rock. The rock rests on the seating area against a wooden pole. Mickey's head is made of circles and his ears are depressions in the rock.

– Adventureland bridge to the Hub

Hint 169: Shields are propped at the sides of the bridge connecting Adventureland with the Hub in front of Cinderella Castle. Two classic Mickeys with smiley faces for "ears" appear on separate shields. One with white ears is at the bottom of one shield, while the other, an upside-down classic Mickey with blue ears, is at the top of a second shield.

Fantasyland

– Enchanted Tales with Belle

Hint 170: Along the Standby entrance queue, in the window to your left as you enter the first room of Maurice's cottage, look at the lower left pane. An image of Donald Duck is in the glass swirls at the middle right side of the pane.

Hint 171: Inside the first room of Maurice's cottage, a stack of firewood stands to the left of the fireplace. An upright classic Mickey made of three logs is at the lower middle of the stack, and a sideways classic Mickey is at the upper middle left of the stack. Other combinations of logs also resemble classic Mickeys.

Hint 172: The red carpet in the Wardrobe Room has a number of small Hidden Mickeys. A pseudo-triangle looks like a hat on each Mickey head.

Hint 173: In the Library where you meet Belle, a book with Mickey-shaped bookmarks on its spine is at the right rear corner of the room. It's the fifth book from the right, above a blue and gold horizontal frieze midway up the wall.

Tomorrowland

– Tomorrowland Transit Authority PeopleMover

Hint 174: The woman getting her hair done sports a belt buckle with a classic Hidden Mickey.

– Merchant of Venus shop

Hint 175: Face the cash registers and look at the mural on the wall behind the register on the left. In the foreground is one of Stitch's cousins holding a Mickey balloon. (Mickey's face is on the balloon.)

Hint 176: In the same mural, another cousin of Stitch is wearing Mickey ears.

– Mickey's Star Traders shop

Hint 177: On the mural, the headlights of a train form a classic Mickey.

Hint 178: Stitch races beside a train in the mural.

Hint 179: Mickey hats sit atop windows halfway up the sides of a building.

Hint 180: Satellite dishes form a classic Mickey on top of this building.

Hint 181: Across the room on another mural, the middle circle of freeway loops forms a classic Mickey.

Hint 182: Over one of the entrance doors, clear domes form a classic Mickey.

Hint 183: The blue glass dome covering one building is a classic Mickey with ears.

– Tomorrowland "Cool Scanner" Station

Hint 184: Several tiny, dark classic Mickeys are formed by holes underneath the overhead dome of the station.

Main Street, U.S.A.

Hint 185: On the roof of The Crystal Palace restaurant, the circles in the middle row of the tower above the main entrance resemble Mickey ears.

Hint 186: A tiny classic Mickey is impressed in the cement outside the Crystal Arts store entrance. It's on a gray flagstone between the red cement and the bricks of the side street off of Main Street. Find a long crack (between red cement sections) that's parallel to Main Street and starts in front of the entrance pillars at the store entrance. The gray flagstone is at the end of this crack, and the Hidden Mickey is at the lower right corner of the flagstone as you face the store.

Hint 187: Outside along Main Street, just to the right of the Emporium shop and near the Athletic Club, a sign on a door has two classic Mickeys, at the top and bottom along the border.

Hint 188: The cupola above the Emporium, in the middle recessed area of the store, has stained-glass windows just below the highest eaves. The central flower circle in each window is joined with two frosted "ear" panels to form classic Mickeys.

Hint 189: In an outside display window in the middle recessed area of the Emporium store, a classic Mickey image hides on a piano above the words "Steinmouse & Sons." The display window is under a sign that says "Collectibles."

Hint 190: In the Emporium store, metal poles that hold up merchandise shelves sport classic Mickey holes. (You can also spot Mickey holes on merchandise poles in other Disney stores.)

Hint 191: In the outside Aladdin display window of the Emporium store, you'll find a small classic Mickey window in a building wall.

Hint 192: At the Main Street Confectionery store, classic Hidden Mickeys made of circular objects, such as gears, are often present in an outside display window facing Main Street.

Hint 193: An upside-down classic Hidden Mickey made of three colorful lollipops hides in a framed poster in a Confectionery shop window display facing Main Street. You can find the same image inside the store. It is just to the right of the entrance door as you enter from Town Square through the door at the corner of the store. Is the image an upside-down Minnie Mouse because of the bow?

Hint 194: Candy bins in the Main Street Confectionery move along a track suspended from the ceiling. On the lower

front and back sides of the bins, holes form classic Mickeys.

Bonus Points Hint: The sign on the Caffe Italiano cart, which appears seasonally in front of Tony's Town Square Restaurant, includes a classic Mickey in its design.

Hint 195: Inside Tony's Town Square Restaurant, as you enter the main dining area from the entrance waiting area, three white flowers form a classic Mickey on a bookshelf to the upper left.

Hint 196: When you enter Tony's inside dining area, look left to the corner and find the second floor tile to the right of the corner. There's a classic Mickey impression at the center right side of this black tile. If you view the Hidden Mickey from the seating area, it will appear upside-down.

Hint 197: A classic Mickey made of bread rolls is to the right as you enter the dining area inside Tony's Town Square Restaurant. It's sitting on an armoire under a painting from *Lady and the Tramp*.

Hint 198: A small classic Hidden Mickey is on the middle back of the overhanging entrance sign to Tony's Town Square Restaurant. Look up as you exit the restaurant.

Hint 199: Several classic Mickeys adorn the gear on the horse pulling the Main Street Trolley.

Hint 200: In Town Square plaza, walk about seven or eight steps away from the island curb toward the train station. As you approach the station, a classic Mickey is formed by circles on the train station ceiling. You might call this a "positional" classic Mickey because you have to be in just the right position to see it.

Hint 201: At the Main Street Train Station's faux ticket office upstairs, an image that looks like Mickey is on a baggage ticket next to the letter "K" inside the front window to the right. (Walk up the outside stairs to the office window, which faces Main Street.)

Hint 202: A classic Mickey-shaped lock can also be found inside the faux ticket office. Look for the lock hanging on the right wall behind the windows.

– Evening Parade

Hint 203: In the *Main Street Electrical Parade*, a classic Mickey is formed by circles on the front of the train Goofy is driving.

– Train Station Exit from Main Street

Hint 204: Classic Mickeys are repeated atop a tall gate, which is usually folded inside a recess beside the entrance and exit tunnel walkway under the Main Street Train Station.

Ferryboat Landing at Magic Kingdom

Hint 205: Ropes coiled into classic Mickeys can often be spotted at the ferry loading docks at the Magic Kingdom and at the Transportation and Ticket Center. Look next to a large post on either side as you walk onto or leave the boat at either loading dock. Cast Members usually maintain these rope images.

Transportation and Ticket Center

Hint 206: An imprint of Mickey's face, full frontal image, has remained over the years. It looks as though it was made by a balloon that melted against the glass. This Hidden Mickey is in the second overhead glass bubble from the tram, in the first row of bubble skylights to the right as you walk from the trams toward the monorail entrance ramps. The image is fading with time, so try different viewing angles to spot it. However, bright sunlight may block it from view.

Epcot Scavenger Hunt

· ·

Before You Start

• *Many great Hidden Mickeys are in Standby queues. You'll miss them if you take the FastPass queue, so I recommend reserving FastPass+ for the following rides:* Mission: SPACE *(choose either Orange level—more intense, or Green level—less intense),* Spaceship Earth, *and* Living with the Land. *Be sure to keep track of your three FastPass+ windows and return to those attractions at the appropriate times.*

In the Scavenger Hunt below, if you come to your FastPass+ attraction and it's not time for it yet, you can skip to the next stop in the Hunt and return to the FastPass+ attraction during your time window.

• *Some of the Hidden Mickeys in this park are in restaurants and shops. Be considerate of fellow guests and Cast Members as you search. Tell them what you're looking for, so they can share in the fun. Avoid searching restaurants at busy meal times unless you are one of the diners.*

★ Walk to **Test Track**. Let folks pass by you in line while you search for three Hidden Mickeys in the Standby queue.

Clue 1: In the Standby entrance queue, look for a classic Mickey traced on the wall.
5 points

Clue 2: Now spot a white classic Mickey on the wall.
4 points

Clue 3: Watch for an interactive touch screen on the right wall of the Standby entrance queue. Make your own classic Mickey on top of the car!
5 points

75

Epcot®

international gateway

Lagoon

world showcase

future world

odyssey center

front entry/exit

monorail station

to bus facility

76

FUTURE WORLD

1 Spaceship Earth Pavilion

2 Universe of Energy Pavilion
Ellen's Energy Adventure

3 Mission: SPACE Pavilion

4 Test Track Pavilion

Imagination! Pavilion

5 Captain EO

6 Journey Into Imagination
With Figment

7 ImageWorks

The Land Pavilion

8 Living with the Land

9 The Circle of Life

10 Soarin'

11 The Seas with Nemo &
Friends Pavilion
Turtle Talk with Crush

12 Innoventions East

13 Innoventions West

14 Innoventions Plaza

15 Epcot Character Spot

WORLD SHOWCASE

16 Mexico:
Gran Fiesta Tour

17 Norway:
Frozen-themed attraction
(opening 2016)

18 China:
Reflections of China

19 Germany

20 Italy

21 The American Adventure:
The American Adventure show

22 Japan

23 Morocco

24 France:
Impressions de France

25 United Kingdom

26 Canada:
O Canada!

Clue 4: On the ride, watch for a road sign on your right to spot a Hidden Mickey.
5 points

Clue 5: Look for a small, red Hidden Mickey to your left before the fast drive outside.
5 points

Clue 6: Keep your eyes left for a small, purple Hidden Mickey on the wall.
5 points

★ Cross Future World to The Land pavilion and get in line for **Soarin'**. (Ask a Cast Member at the entrance if the interactive games are playing along the Standby entrance queue. If they aren't, the Cast Member can call to activate the games.)

Clue 7: Along the entrance queue, five screens show changing artistic landscapes. (Note: These landscapes are not the interactive games; the games appear every few minutes on these same screens.) Search for Mickey in the landscape with the purple mountain ridge in the lower background.
4 points

Clue 8: Interactive games appear at times on these screens on the right wall of the entrance queue. Watch for the snowman!
4 points

Clue 9: In the "Bird Race" interactive game, stay alert for a Mickey image in a rock archway over a river.
5 points

Clue 10: Just before boarding, be ready for the words "Palm Springs" on the video monitor and look for Mickey!
5 points

Clue 11: In the pre-show video, spot the Mickey ears.
2 points

Clue 12: In the pre-show video, stay alert for Hidden Character clothing logos.
4 points for spotting two

Clue 13: While soaring, look left for a Mickey balloon.
4 points

Clue 14: Then look right for a Mickey shadow.
4 points

Clue 15: Don't blink at the golf ball!
5 points

Clue 16: A huge classic Mickey in the sky greets you at the end of your *Soarin'* ride.
3 points

★ Return to **Mission: SPACE** at your FastPass+ time. Three Hidden Mickeys wait to be found along the entrance queue.

Clue 17: Search for a Hidden Mickey on a planet.
4 points

Clue 18: Spot a Hidden Mickey in "status lights" on a monitor.
4 points

Clue 19: Look for waveform images on a monitor that form a Hidden Mickey.
4 points

Clue 20: Just before launch, keep your eyes open for two identical Hidden Mickeys.
4 points

Clue 21: As you land on Mars, glance around for a Hidden Mickey on a building.
4 points

Clue 22: After the ride, look for a Hidden Mickey on a video console in the exhibit area.
2 points

Clue 23: Spot a Hidden Mickey on the ceiling of the gift shop at the attraction exit.
4 points

Clue 24: Search for Donald and Pluto on the ceiling.
4 points for spotting both

Clue 25: Study the spaceship in a mural in the gift shop.
3 points

Clue 26: Now squint for a small black Hidden Mickey in the same mural.
3 points

Clue 27: While you're at it, examine the mural for an upside-down classic Mickey.
3 points

Clue 28: Now glance low for classic Mickeys near the floor.
2 points

Clue 29: Find two classic Mickeys and a side-profile Mickey on the wall of the gift shop.
2 points for spotting all three

Clue 30: Outside in the front plaza, search for a classic Mickey on the moon.
3 points

Clue 31: Look down for a classic Mickey in the blue tile area out front.
5 points

Clue 32: In a blue tile stripe out front, spot a white classic Mickey near a gray disk.
4 points

Clue 33: Find two more classic tile Mickeys near a drain cover.
4 points for spotting both

★ Walk across Future World to The Seas with Nemo & Friends pavilion. Check out **Turtle Talk With Crush**. In the waiting area, search for two Hidden Mickeys.

Clue 34: Spot a tiny Mickey in the coral on the wall.
5 points

Clue 35: Admire a Hidden Mickey on a starfish.
4 points

Clue 36: During the show, study the undersea images on the show screen for a classic Mickey.
3 points

★ Line up for the **Epcot Character Spot**.

Clue 37: When you go inside to meet the characters, spot Mickey listening to music.
1 point

Clue 38: Outside the *Character Spot*, look around for a Mickey hat.
3 points

★ After World Showcase opens at 11:00 a.m., head toward the Mexico Pavilion. Take the path behind MouseGear shop for a hard-to-find Hidden Mickey. (This path is between MouseGear and Test Track, and it connects to the main walkway to World Showcase.)

Clue 39: As you walk, stare at the cement until you discover a Hidden Mickey.
5 points

★ Eat an early lunch to avoid the crowds. The San Angel Inn Restaurante in the Mexico pavilion is an ideal choice if you have 11:30 a.m. or so reservations. If not, try fast food at Mexico's La Cantina de San Angel or the Kringla Bakeri Og Kafe in Norway. Ride *Gran Fiesta Tour Starring the Three Caballeros* before or after lunch.

★ If you eat in the San Angel Inn, look for classic Mickeys in the smoke rising from the volcano (see Clue 46).

★ Go to **Gran Fiesta Tour Starring the Three Caballeros** in Mexico and keep your eyes peeled for classic Mickeys.

Clue 40: At the beginning of the ride, take a close look at the smoke rising from the volcano.
4 points

Clue 41: In the first tunnel, search for Mickey on a necklace.
5 points

Clue 42: Find Mickey on a video screen on the wall.
5 points

Clue 43: Spot classic Mickeys in a small blue pond to the left of the boat.
4 points

Clue 44: Don't miss Mickey in a barge!
3 points

Clue 45: In the final scene, turn on a light (your camera, phone, etc.) and highlight a Hidden Mickey under the platform to the left of your boat. (Psst! There are three of them. You might get lucky and see all three!)
5 points for one or more

★ After exiting the ride, walk to the outside of the San Angel Inn Restaurante (if you haven't already been there) and look for classic Mickeys that appear and disappear.

Clue 46: Observe the smoke rising from the volcano.
4 points

★ Stroll over to **China**.

Clue 47: Search for Hidden Mickeys on posts in the courtyard.
4 points

★ Now study the water for possible bonus points.
2 bonus points for one or more Hidden Mickeys

★ Cross over the bridge to the **Outpost**.

Clue 48: Check out the wooden poles.
3 points

Clue 49: Locate Mickey's name (twice) hidden high inside the **Village Traders Shop**.
5 points for both

★ Walk left to **Germany** to find five classic Hidden Mickeys.

Clue 50: As you walk into the plaza, look for the classic Mickey on a suit of armor on the building to your right.
3 points

Clue 51: Spot Mickey behind a large bell.
3 points

Clue 52: Search for Mickey near a lion.
3 points

Clue 53: Admire the outside display windows of the Karamell-Küche shop to find a small Hidden Mickey.
5 points

Clue 54: Study the woodwork inside Karamell-Küche for a Hidden Mickey.
5 points

★ Check out the landscaping around the train attraction to earn yourself some possible bonus points. (Note: These Hidden Mickeys come and go.)
1 bonus point for each one you spot.

★ Stop at **Italy** to inspect the shops, statues, and restaurants.

Clue 55: A classic Mickey is near the wine!
2 points

Clue 56: Look for Mickey behind a statue.
3 points

★ Go to **The American Adventure** pavilion.

Clue 57: Admire the banner over the entrance to the rotunda to locate a Hidden Mickey.
5 points

Clue 58: Search the walls inside for a classic Mickey in roses.
4 points

★ Now inspect the rear wall of the rotunda, upstairs and down, for classic Hidden Mickeys.

Clue 59: Study a picture in the rotunda for Hidden Mickeys on two metal beams.
3 points for spotting both

Clue 60: Take a good look at the bronze eagle reliefs in the rotunda.
2 points for each floor; 4 points total

★ Watch **The American Adventure show** and keep an eye out for three hard-to-spot classic Hidden Mickeys. (Tip: Try to sit on the right side of the theater for the best view of the Hidden Mickeys.)

Clue 61: At the beginning of the film, look at the rocks behind a kneeling female pilgrim.
4 points

Clue 62: Stay alert for a Mickey image on a stockade.
3 points

Clue 63: Study some fruit at the gas station.
3 points

Clue 64: At the end, watch the fireworks' explosions behind the Statue of Liberty Torch.
4 points

★ Stroll over to **Japan**.

Clue 65: Search for a classic Mickey in the koi fish pond.
2 points

Clue 66: Check out the grates at the bases of the trees in the courtyard.
2 points

Clue 67: Study the pond by Katsura Grill.
4 bonus points

Clue 68: Look around for Mickey in the bushes by the lagoon.
3 points

Clue 69: On your way to Morocco, don't miss the rock Mickey near the Mitsukoshi store!
5 points

★ Meander to **Morocco**.

Clue 70: Gaze at the front of the shop on the promenade for Hidden Mickeys.
2 points for one or more

Clue 71: Find a Mickey made of basket lids on the wall of a shop.
4 points

Clue 72: Study a mural at the rear of the pavilion for three Hidden Mickeys.
5 points for spotting all three

★ Go to **France**.

Clue 73: Examine the grates at the bases of the trees in the courtyard.
2 points

Clue 74: Find the classic Mickey bush on the right side of the ornamental garden.
3 points

Clue 75: Look high for classic Mickeys on the outside of a shop.
2 points

Clue 76: Search for Remy the rat inside a shop in the pavilion.
4 points

Clue 77: In the movie *Impressions de France*, spot Mickey's head and ears in the background of the wedding scene.
4 points

★ Enter the **United Kingdom**.

Clue 78: Check out a classic sports Mickey from the street.
2 points

★ Now walk over to **Canada** to find more classic Mickeys.

Clue 79: Look around outside for a fence with a small Hidden Mickey made of holes.
3 points

Clue 80: Examine the totem pole on the left near the steps into the pavilion.
3 points

Clue 81: Inside a store, search for a classic Mickey on an animal.
4 points

Clue 82: Study the front of the stone steps near the theater for a classic Mickey.
4 points

Clue 83: Step inside Le Cellier Steakhouse to find a Mickey made of wine.
3 points

★ Return to Future World and walk to **Club Cool** at the end of Innoventions West. Enjoy free exotic and refreshing soft drinks from foreign countries.

Clue 84: At the front entrance, look near the outside sign for Mickey.
3 points

Clue 85: Search inside Club Cool for a classic Mickey in the interior design.
3 points

Clue 86: Find a Hidden Mickey on the rear doors.
3 points

Clue 87: Spot Mickey outside above the rear entrance.
3 points

★ Go to the **Living with the Land** ride in The Land pavilion at your FastPass+ time. Study the wall murals to find three classic Hidden Mickeys.

Clue 88: Take a good look at the bubbles in the mural at the rear of the entrance queue.
3 points

Clue 89: Examine the mural behind the loading area near the farmer's hat.
3 points

Clue 90: Now check the lower part of the mural behind the loading area.
3 points

Clue 91: On the ride, keep alert for a Cast Member with a Hidden Mickey on a video screen.
4 points

Clue 92: Search for a garden hose classic Mickey.
4 points

Clue 93: Spot Mickey in a horizontal water tube. (Minnie may be in there, too!)
4 points for Mickey and 4 bonus points for Minnie

Clue 94: Along the ride, stay alert for one or more plastic gourds shaped like Mickey.
3 points

Clue 95: Look for plants arranged to form a Hidden Mickey.
4 points

Clue 96: Toward the end of the ride, find the green Hidden Mickey in the round test tube holder in a lab room.
3 points

Clue 97: Spot Mickey's name in this same lab room.
2 points

★ Go to the outside railing of **The Garden Grill** restaurant upstairs and take a good look at the back wall.

87

Clue 98: Find and then marvel at the green face of Mickey Mouse on the left side of the large mural of vegetation. He's in three-quarter profile on the right side of a single fern and he's well camouflaged by the fern's leaves. (He's easier to spot from inside the restaurant.)
5 points

★ Go to the **interior railing** to the left of the pavilion's main entrance.

Clue 99: Focus on the side of one of the globes hanging over the lobby to spot another Mickey.
3 points

★ Now walk **outside** under the overhang **and face the entrance doors**.

Clue 100: Study the mosaic mural on the wall to your right for a classic Mickey in jewels.
4 points

Clue 101: Search the same mosaic mural for a classic Mickey in grapes.
4 points

★ Walk down the sloping walkway (from the pavilion) until you come to **"The Land" sign** out front.

Clue 102: Search for a classic Mickey in the stones embedded in a support for "The Land" sign. (Tip: The support is covered with tiles and stone designs.)
4 points

★ Head over to **The Seas with Nemo & Friends** to find twelve or more Hidden Mickeys.

Clue 103: Look up along the entrance queue for the ride for a Hidden Mickey.
3 bonus points (This image is not always present.)

Clue 104: On the ride, keep alert for a Mickey in the rock. Look below the fifth video screen to spot it.
5 points

Clue 105: Walk upstairs and search for one or more Hidden Mickeys on the aquarium floor.
5 points for one or more

Clue 106: Stroll to the upper level of the manatee viewing area and look for Hidden Mickeys on the wall. (These Hidden Mickeys come and go.)
3 bonus points

Clue 107: Cross to the upper display room above *Turtle Talk with Crush* to find two Hidden Mickeys on the wall in a lower panel.
5 points for both

Clue 108: Study an upper panel in this same display window for another Hidden Mickey.
5 points

Clue 109: Downstairs, find two Hidden Mickeys in bubbles on the wall near the manatees.
5 points for spotting both

Clue 110: In Bruce's room downstairs, look around for classic Mickeys in two different windows.
4 points for spotting both

Clue 111: Now search for Mickey near the exit gift shop.
3 points

★ Go to the Imagination! pavilion and ride **Journey Into Imagination with Figment**.

Clue 112: Locate a small Buzz Lightyear figure along the entrance queue.
5 points

Clue 113: On the ride, find a Hidden Mickey on a greaseboard. (Note: It's not always there.)
5 bonus points

Clue 114: Squint for a black pair of Mickey ears in the Sight Room.
4 points

Clue 115: Look up at Figment's bathtub for a classic Mickey.
3 points

Clue 116: Now look up again in Figment's bathroom for another classic Mickey near the bathtub.
3 points

Clue 117: Find a classic Mickey on a cloud in the rainbow room.
3 points

Clue 118: Search for a Mickey in snow.
5 points

Clue 119: Look for a classic Mickey on the wall along the exit hallway.
3 points

★ When you reach **ImageWorks** . . .

Clue 120: Look down inside for a classic Mickey.
4 points

★ Walk over to the **Captain EO** show.

Clue 121: Check out Captain EO's ship for a Hidden Mickey.
3 points

★ Stroll inside Innoventions West to the **"Where's the Fire?"** attraction.

Clue 122: Look for Mickey in the logo.
3 points

Clue 123: Stare at a computer monitor screen.
3 points

Clue 124: Search for a classic Mickey near books.
2 points

Clue 125: Don't forget Goofy! (Tip: He's upside down.)
4 points

Clue 126: Walk by **"The Great Piggy Bank Adventure"** attraction and spot a Hidden Mickey on the wall.
3 points

Clue 127: Now find classic Mickeys near the floor.
2 points

★ Walk to **Innoventions East** and enjoy *Habit Heroes*, then look around outside for a nearby restaurant.

Clue 128: During the interactive game, pay attention for a Hidden Mickey on the wall.
3 points

Clue 129: Look outside for Mickey on a restaurant sign.
3 points

★ Check out the Universe of Energy. Find a Hidden Mickey as you take in the show and ride.

Clue 130: After the dinosaur section of the ride, watch the movie and look for the shadow of Disney's Hollywood Studios' "Earful" Tower (the tower with Mickey ears) in the door of a church in the background.
5 points

★ Head for **Spaceship Earth** at your FastPass+ time. Line up for the ride.

Clue 131: During the ride, keep alert for classic Mickey light patterns on the floor to your right.
5 points

Clue 132: Now look quickly to your left for a Hidden Mickey in scrolls.
5 points

Clue 133: During the ride, notice the Hidden Mickey on the document in front of the sleeping monk.
4 points

Clue 134: In the Renaissance section, look quickly to your left to spot the classic Mickey formed by paint circles on a tabletop near a painter.
4 points

Clue 135: Look for a chalkboard with the name of a famous Mickey Mouse cartoon.
4 points

Clue 136: Just after the garage scene and as the ceiling darkens over you, shine your camera red light or your phone flashlight app toward the ceiling. Spot Mickey up there!
5 points

Clue 137: After you exit the ride vehicle, look up for Mickey in the "Project Tomorrow" area.
3 points

★ Go to the **MouseGear** shop, where you'll find a number of Hidden Mickeys and décor Mickeys.

Clue 138: Before you enter MouseGear, find the classic Mickey in the sign above the shop entrance.
1 point

★ Now step inside, and keep your eyes peeled.

Clue 139: Examine the nuts on the display racks' bolts.
1 point

Clue 140: Observe the gauges on the wall.
1 point

Clue 141: Search for Donald's shadow.
3 points

Clue 142: Spot a set of Hidden Mickey gears.
2 points

Clue 143: Can you find an image of Donald Duck with a classic Mickey on him?
2 points

Clue 144: Finally, look at the tops of the garment display mannequins.
1 point

★ Keep your reservations for dinner. If you don't have reservations, eat at the Food Court in The Land.

Time now to tally your score.

Total Points for Epcot =

How'd you do?
Up to 200 points – Bronze
201 to 400 points – Silver
401 points and over – Gold
501 points – Perfect Score

If you earned bonus points in China, Germany, Japan, *Living with the Land,* and/or *The Seas with Nemo & Friends,* you may have done even better!

Notes

**Caution:
Don't peek at this
section unless you
really want help!**

Test Track

Hint 1: On the wall, along the right side of the Standby entrance queue is a photo collage of artists and designers. A classic Mickey is traced on a transparent drawing board, just above the right hand of a man wearing glasses and drawing with a Magic Marker.

Hint 2: In the middle of the photo collage of artists and designers, a tiny white classic Mickey lies above a white vertical dashed line. This Hidden Mickey is above the left forearm of a girl who is drawing on white paper.

Hint 3: A bit further along on the right wall of the Standby queue, look for an interactive screen with design criteria (efficiency, etc.) listed above a car. Touch the area along the top of the car and circles will appear. You can arrange these circles with your finger to form a classic Mickey.

Hint 4: On the ride, about halfway along the inside track, a classic Mickey hides on the first road sign on your right.

Hint 5: Before the long fast drive outside, look for the words "Scan Complete" on the wall to the left of the vehicle. A small, red classic Mickey is on the wall under the "C" in "Complete."

Hint 6: Keep your eyes left just before you burst onto the outside track. A small, purple classic Mickey is on the wall, above eye level.

The Land

– Soarin'

Hint 7: Along the right side of the entrance queue, five screens show changing artistic landscapes. In the landscape with the purple mountain ridge in the lower background, a large green tree halfway up the right side of the screen holds a classic Mickey group of flowers. (In the different scenes, round trees—and also groups of flowers or leaves on the various trees— come together at times to form classic Mickeys.)

Hint 8: Watch for the interactive games on the screens along the right wall of the Standby entrance queue. In the game with the snowy scene, a snowman appears at the left side of the screen. His head is a side profile of Mickey Mouse.

Hint 9: In the "Bird Race" interactive game, watch as the bird follows a river. More than halfway through the game, a side-profile Mickey looking to the left appears as a cutout in the rock archway over the river.

Hint 10: At the final queue-up for boarding, look for the words "Palm Springs" to appear in the clouds on the video monitor before the preshow. A classic Hidden Mickey tilted to the right is in the clouds below and to the left of "Palm Springs."

Hint 11: In the pre-show video, a man who is wearing Mickey Mouse ears is asked to take them off.

Hint 12: In the pre-show video, a boy sitting in his ride seat is wearing a red shirt with a Grumpy logo and shorts sporting Mickey Mouse.

Hint 13: On the ride, when you soar over the hills and spot a golf course, look immediately to your lower left and find a golf cart. The man standing on the other side of the cart is holding a blue Mickey balloon (and he quickly pulls it down out of sight!).

Hint 14: Now look to the right side of the golf course. About halfway along the fairway a slightly distorted classic Mickey shadow is cast on the green grass by a cluster of three trees. The "ears" of the shadow Mickey touch the right side of the white cart path.

Hint 15: Look straight ahead and then down to the golf course. Spot the man who is about to swing a golf club. When he strikes the golf ball, it will head directly toward you. Watch the ball's rotation to see the dark classic Mickey on the surface of the ball.

Hint 16: As you complete your *Soarin'* ride over Disneyland, the second burst of fireworks forms a huge classic Mickey in the sky.

Mission: SPACE

Hint 17: On the far right and left (outer) video monitors in the Mission Control room, classic Mickey circles appear on the lower part of the surface of Mars.

Hint 18: Continue to watch the video loops as three "status lights" form a classic Mickey at the lower right side of the rightmost monitor screen.

Hint 19: During the video loop on either of the middle monitors, three small waveform images merge into a classic Mickey on the lower left of the screen.

Hint 20: You'll see identical faint classic Hidden Mickeys above a horizontal bar on both sides of the launch door before it opens and before you see the sky.

Hint 21: As your spacecraft is landing on Mars, look sharp for a classic Mickey made of satellite dishes on top of the second building from the end, on the right side of the landing strip.

Hint 22: In the Expedition Mars section of the exit exhibit area, you'll find small classic Mickeys in the design of the video-game joystick consoles at the upper left and upper right corners.

Hint 23: In the center of the gift shop near the exit doors, a large side profile of Mickey Mouse is painted on the ceiling in the middle square.

Hint 24: On either side of Mickey's side profile on the ceiling are side profiles of Donald Duck and Pluto (or is it Goofy?).

Hint 25: On the right side of the mural behind the gift shop's cash register, the three round thrusters behind the blue X-2 spaceship form an upside-down classic Mickey.

Hint 26: Look for Minnie Mouse in the same mural. There's a small black classic Mickey in the dirt under her left foot.

Hint 27: On the left side of the mural behind the gift shop's cash register, you'll find an upside-down classic Mickey on the lower part of the moon.

Hint 28: The bases of some of the merchandise stands near the gift shop exit contain "support arches" in the shape of Mickey.

Hint 29: You can spot Hidden Mickeys in the electrical tubing on the wall on both sides of the exit door from the gift shop. There's a classic Mickey on one side and both a classic Mickey and a side-profile Mickey on the other.

– In the entrance plaza

Hint 30: Spot three craters that approximate a classic Mickey at the upper left of the Luna 8 landing site on the back side of the moon.

Hint 31: In the middle of a blue tile area, very near and to the left of a gold strip (as you face the attraction), you'll find a tiny tile classic Mickey (black head and blue ears).

Hint 32: A small classic Mickey formed of white tiles is toward the bottom of a blue tile stripe. Look for a gray disc in the cement, near the lowest part of the stripe. Mickey is hiding about four feet from the disc as you go toward the Mars planet.

Hint 33: Two more tile or stone classic Mickeys (black head and white ears) lie next to a drain cover. Look for the cover in a circle of tiles to the left of the *Mission: SPACE* sign.

The Seas with Nemo & Friends

– Turtle Talk With Crush

Hint 34: In the waiting room, a tiny classic Mickey hides in the pink and brown coral in the first window painting to the right as you enter the room. At the lower part of the painting, the Mickey is left of the third tallest (leftmost) blue tube, about one quarter of the distance up the side of the tube.

Hint 35: Also in the *Turtle Talk With Crush* waiting room, look at the upper left of the second window to the right (as you enter the room) to spot "Peach" the starfish. An upside-down classic Mickey lies above the left side of Peach's "eyebrow."

Hint 36: During the show, look closely at the middle left side of the rear screen, near the edge, to spot a classic Mickey made of coral circles on the rock. Mickey's ears are angled to the left.

Epcot Character Spot

Hint 37: At the left side of the first greeting bay, a metal 3-D Mickey head wears earphones.

Hint 38: On an outside wall of Innoventions West, a Mickey Mouse hat appears in a mural of silhouettes. The wall faces The Land pavilion and borders the walkway from Innoventions Plaza to Future World West.

Behind MouseGear store

Hint 39: Outside and behind MouseGear is a classic Mickey in the walkway cement. Exit the shop at the rear heading toward Test Track; then take the first right onto a walkway (heading toward World Show-case). Just before the path changes to an octagonal shape, look down near the left railing to find a small classic Mickey indented in the concrete.

Mexico

– Gran Fiesta Tour
Starring the Three Caballeros

Hint 40: At the beginning of the boat ride, smoke rises from the volcano. Every half minute or so, holes in the smoke form classic Mickeys that quickly disappear.

Hint 41: Along the left wall inside the first tunnel, look at the fifth man from the end. He is wearing green shorts and has a partially covered blue classic Mickey on the front of his necklace.

Hint 42: Watch for a video screen to the right of your boat that shows a broad expanse of water in the fore-ground and, in the background, a shoreline edged with modern buildings set against the backdrop of a mountain. Donald Duck is parasailing over the water, but you want to focus on the buildings on the shore-line. One building on the right side of the scene has a dark classic Mickey tree in front of it.

Hint 43: About halfway through the ride, in the small blue pond to the left of the boat,

classic Mickeys appear in the bubbles after Donald is taken away. Look above and also to the lower left of the octopus.

Hint 44: Toward the end of the ride, as you enter the fireworks room, three drums form a classic Hidden Mickey at the lower right of the "Viva Donald" barge to the left of your boat.

Hint 45: These Hidden Mickeys can only be seen with a light from your camera, cell phone, etc. As your boat floats by the last scene of the ride with the map of Mexico on the wall, look down at tiles that line the base of the platform to your left. The tiles are just above the side of your boat. You can spot three Mickey stickers on the tiles! They're located about one-third of the distance along the row of tiles as you float along. The first one is a full-body Mickey on tile #17 (counting from the start). Several tiles further along, on tile #20, are Mickey's face and ears. Finally, another full-body Mickey sticker is on tile #25, which is halfway along the 50 tiles on the platform.

– San Angel Inn Restaurante

Hint 46: Smoke rising from the volcano by the river forms classic Mickeys that quickly disappear.

China

Hint 47: Classic Mickey-shaped flowers are sculpted on the bases of several decorative light posts on the outside front of the pavilion.

Bonus Points Hint: In the ponds, the floating lily pads sometimes come together to form recognizable classic Mickeys.

Outpost
between China and Germany

Hint 48: At the Outpost, three of the short wooden posts at the corner closest to the bridge form a classic Mickey when looked at from above.

Hint 49: At the Outpost, a piece of brown luggage is perched high on a rear wall in the left room inside the Village Traders shop. The luggage tag is signed "M. Mouse," and a red sticker on the bottom of the luggage says "Mickey Mouse" and "Disney Magic."

Germany

Hint 50: On the second floor of the building to your right, to the right of the glockenspiel clock, are three suits of armor. The one closest to the glockenspiel has a classic Mickey on its crown.

Hint 51: In the rear of the courtyard, a three-circle classic Mickey formation is in the ironwork support behind the bell on the front of the clock tower. It's formed by the circular metal support (not by holes in the metal) and is tilted to the left.

Hint 52: At the left of the entrance to the Biergarten Restaurant, you can see a wrought-iron lion behind a lamp on the outside wall. The lion's front and rear paws are resting on an upside-down classic Mickey.

Hint 53: At the Karamell-Küche shop, in an outside display window that faces the inner courtyard and is close to the main promenade, a caramel apple at the lower right corner of a page in an open cookbook has a small light reflection that forms a white classic Mickey.

Hint 54: Inside the Karamell-Küche shop, a small orange classic Hidden Mickey is painted on the merchandise shelf siding. The image is about halfway up on a vine on the right shelf siding closest to the door to the main World Showcase promenade.

**– Landscaping around
the miniature train exhibit**

Bonus Points Hint: Check the dirt, grass, bushes, and decorations for Hidden Mickey images that come and go during the year.

Italy

Hint 55: In the wine shop, Enoteca Castello, a classic Mickey appears in the woodwork along the relief design of the upper front counter.

Hint 56: Behind the statue on the right side of the walkway in front of the restaurants, a classic Mickey impression hides on the left side of the rock wall.

The American Adventure

Hint 57: A red, white, and blue banner is on the railing over the entrance to the rotunda of The American Adventure, and a small, faint classic Mickey hides on the banner. It's in the middle of the white star next to the "A" in "Adventure."

Hint 58: A classic Mickey made of roses decorates a lady's hat in a painting on the first floor on the far left wall (as you enter). Look for the painting in which a man is speaking to a crowd in front of a hardware store. The lady with the rose-trimmed hat is at the lower middle of the painting and the Hidden Mickey is on the right side of her hat.

Hint 59: A picture on a first-floor wall at the right rear of the rotunda (indoors) shows workers building a skyscraper. The tops of two vertical beams behind the workers sport classic Mickeys.

Hint 60: On the rear wall of the rotunda, first and second floors, large bronze eagle reliefs have classic Mickeys in the corners.

– The American Adventure show

Hint 61: At the beginning of the film, a classic Mickey appears on the rock behind (and to your right of) a kneeling female pilgrim.

Hint 62: Early in the show, a classic Mickey lock hangs on the right side of a stockade in a scene of the American Revolution time period.

Hint 63: In the scene with the old gas station, a classic Mickey is formed by three red apples in a crate at the lower right of the scene.

Hint 64: At the end of the show, fireworks light up the sky behind the Statue of Liberty Torch as it rises from the floor. One of the last fireworks at the upper right fizzles into a classic Mickey head (best seen from the right side of the theater).

Japan

Hint 65: In the koi fish pond across from the Mitsukoshi store, a drain cover in the water near the bamboo fence sports a classic Mickey.

Hint 66: The trees in the courtyard are encircled by metal grates with classic Mickey designs.

Hint 67: Visit the pond next to Katsura Grill for a possible bonus Hidden Mickey. Cast Members sometimes arrange rocks in the pond to form a classic Mickey.

Hint 68: Out on the promenade, next to the lagoon, three round bushes to the left of the Torii Gate form a classic Mickey.

Hint 69: A classic Mickey formed by three rocks is deep inside a hole in a large bush. It's on the right side of the pavilion, next to the far right sidewalk to the Mitsukoshi store, and near a juniper tree.

Morocco

Hint 70: Three brass plates are arranged to form a classic Mickey on the left green door at the entrance to the Souk-al-Magreb "Gifts of Morocco" shop on the promenade. (Sometimes, the plates are on the nearby red door, and you might find more than one plate classic Mickey on the doors!)

Hint 71: Basket lids usually form a sideways classic Mickey on the wall inside the Brass Bazaar shop (located at the right side of the Morocco pavilion behind the Tangierine Café). As you face the rear of the pavilion from inside the shop, look above the right side of the archway.

Hint 72: Across from Restaurant Marrakesh, three small classic Mickeys hide on a mural on the rear wall of a small room. One is at the top of a tower on the right side of the mural's street. Another is on the left side of the street, next to a double archway. The third is a tiny black Mickey in an upper doorway on the left middle part of the mural.

France

Hint 73: The trees in the courtyard are encircled by metal grates with classic Mickey patterns.

Hint 74: In the patterned hedge (parterre) garden, a bush in the middle right area (on the side nearest the canal) is trimmed to the shape of a classic Mickey.

Hint 75: Classic Mickey images are high on the outside molding of Les Vins de France shop, near the entrance to *Impressions de France*.

Hint 76: Inside Les Vins de France, a small plush figure of Remy (the rat from the movie *Ratatouille*) sits in a basket on a shelf near the ceiling, behind the service counter.

– Impressions de France

Hint 77: In the movie's outdoor wedding scene, you can see a Mickey head and ears in a second floor window of the house in the background. It's in the center screen.

United Kingdom

Hint 78: Outside the Sportsman's Shoppe, a sign has a classic Mickey with a tennis racket head, a soccer ball for one ear, and a rugby ball for the other.

Canada

Hint 79: Holes in a wooden fence railing form a classic Hidden Mickey outside in the Canada pavilion. Find it on the upper railing in the second fence section from the left end of the fence (as you face the fence with your back to the drink cart).

Hint 80: Past the steps into the pavilion, the left totem pole has black classic Mickeys on both sides near the top by the raven's wings.

Hint 81: A small black classic Mickey is on the side of a fish, which is hanging on the outside of a box at the left rear of the first room as you enter the Northwest Mercantile shop.

Hint 82: A classic Hidden Mickey is etched on the front facing of a stone step inside Canada, close to the theater. Start at the theater and walk up the steps. You will come to a landing with a light and a trail that branches off to the left. Continue walking up the steps. The Mickey image appears before you reach the next landing.

Hint 83: Behind the check-in desk at Le Cellier Steakhouse, three horizontal bottles at the center top of a wine display form a classic Mickey.

Future World West

– Club Cool near Innoventions West

Hint 84: Holes in the metal bracket supports behind the outdoor sign form classic Mickeys.

Hint 85: Above you, on a colorful decorative border in the middle of the club, green circles form an upside-down classic Mickey.

Hint 86: A classic Mickey is formed when the rear doors open. Stand inside and watch the door on your left. When it's fully open, circles on the door and the glass wall come together to form a Hidden Mickey in the center of the door.

Hint 87: Classic Mickeys are near the bottom of the blue banners that are located outside and above the rear entrance to Club Cool.

The Land

– Living with the Land

Hint 88: In the middle section of the giant wall mural at the rear of the queue, bubbles align to form a classic Mickey, ears angled to the left.

Hint 89: A classic Mickey is formed by shrubs (the "head" has yellow dots on it) to the right of the brim of the farmer's hat near the top of the loading dock mural.

Hint 90: In the lower right area of the mural behind the boat loading area, three circles form a small classic Mickey (a purple circle forms the head and blue circles form the ears). The head is tilted slightly to the right.

Hint 91: In the first part of the ride, a female Cast Member on the last video screen on your left has a Mickey Mouse face hiding on the upper part of her name tag.

Hint 92: A garden hose is coiled into a classic Mickey to the right of the boat about halfway through the fish farming section. (Cast Members usually arrange this Mickey image every morning.)

Hint 93: A classic Mickey made of wire mesh can be found in the aquaculture section. Cast Members generally place it in one of the horizontal display tubes that are part of the landscape on either side of your boat. (A wire mesh Hidden Minnie, with her hair bow, may also appear in the aquatubes, not far from Mickey.)

Hint 94: Along the ride, you can often spot hanging plastic gourds shaped like classic Mickeys. They're used to grow fruit or vegetables into Mickey shapes.

107

Hint 95: Plants of different colors are usually arranged in groups to form a classic Mickey in the greenhouses. Often the plants are lettuces.

Hint 96: Toward the end of the ride, a large circular test-tube holder on the right side of a "Biotechnology Lab" room has a green classic Mickey in the center. Mickey is formed by the test tubes' green stoppers.

Hint 97: On one of the tables in this biotech lab, a sign advertises the plant product, "Mickey's Mini Gardens."

– The Garden Grill

Hint 98: On the left side of the large wall-mural of vegetation inside the restaurant, a Mickey is hiding behind the most prominent fern that extends all the way to the top of the mural. Counting up horizontally from the bottom of the fern, his face is mostly behind the fifth through eighth leaves on the fern's right side. He's looking slightly downward and to the right in a three-quarter profile. Two black circles that form his eyes are visible above the sixth fern leaf on the right, more than halfway to the end of the leaf. Mickey's ears jut above the seventh leaf, and his mouth and nose are below the sixth leaf. His face and ears are green, and his mouth is slightly open. This Hidden Mickey is a real classic!

– Around The Land's main entrance

Hint 99: From the upper level railing, just to the left as you walk in the main entrance, a classic Mickey is on the Earth above the lobby. It's in water swirls, to the left of the tip of South America.

Hint 100: A classic Mickey hides in the mosaic mural on the pavilion's right outside wall (as you enter). Find the word "LAND" on the mural and look slightly above and to the right about six feet or so to a reddish plateau. Just above the left side of the flat upper part of the plateau are three jewels, a green "head" and two reddish "ears."

Hint 101: In the same mosaic mural, look for a cluster of grapes to the upper left of

the word "LAND." A classic Mickey, tilted to the right and almost upside down, is formed by three grapes. The grape Mickey is almost completely beneath the translucent signboard.

Hint 102: The Land sign outside the pavilion's entrance rests on two large stone- and tile-covered supports. On the end of the right-hand support, embedded stones decorate the upper portion of the green-tiled area. A small classic Mickey, formed of three stones, lies near the center of the stone decoration.

The Seas with Nemo & Friends

Hint 103: As you reach the wooden rails of the walkway along the inside entrance queue for the ride, a classic Mickey made of blue moving water circles lies above you on the right side. (Note: This image isn't always present.)

Hint 104: On the ride, a classic Mickey impression in rock lies below the fifth video screen from the start. It's slightly above and between two pink clusters of standing corals, to the right of center in the rock ledge.

Hint 105: Spot one or more classic Mickeys formed of rocks at the bottom of the aquarium. They're best seen from the upstairs viewing corridor and circular viewing area. Recently, one of the images had starfish-shaped rocks for its "ears." Note: These rock Mickeys may change locations on the aquarium floor, and some may disappear at times. You may need to look through several windows in the observation area to find them.

Hint 106: You can often see classic Mickeys on the chalkboard at the upper level of the Manatee viewing area. The board lists the names and other information about the manatees in the pool. Hidden Mickeys on this chalkboard come and go.

Hint 107: Search the room upstairs directly above *Turtle Talk with Crush*. In the far left display window (as you enter the room), look for two classic Hidden Mickeys in bubbles in the lower row of panels. You'll find them in the upper right corner of the second panel from the right side of the large window.

Hint 108: In this same display window, look high in the upper left panel under the words "Finding Solutions" for another bubble classic Hidden Mickey.

Hint 109: In the manatee viewing room, lower level, bubbles in wall displays form two classic Mickeys. One is on the left wall (as you exit), in the left middle square containing the words "Manatee Zone ... Slow Speed." Another is on the right wall (as you exit) in the lower left square with the polar bear.

Hint 110: As you enter Bruce's room on the lower level, check out the second windows on both the right (labeled "Did You Know?") and left (labeled "Bruce's Scrapbook"). In both windows, an oyster contains three pearls arranged as a classic Mickey.

Hint 111: Bubbles come together to form several classic Mickeys on the garbage cans you see in the pavilion.

Imagination!

– Journey Into Imagination with Figment

Hint 112: On the right side along the entrance queue, a small Buzz Lightyear is hiding in a display across from Professor Phillip Brainard's office door.

Hint 113: As you enter the Sight Room, a tiny dark classic Mickey is hidden at the lower right of a greaseboard on a wall to your right. The greaseboard is below the words "Focus Group." (Note: This Hidden Mickey may change locations on the board or even disappear at times.)

Hint 114: In the center of the Sight Room, headphones on the left of two tables have Mickey ears on an earpiece!

Hint 115: Three bubbles make a classic Mickey near Figment's hand on the edge of his bathtub.

Hint 116: In Figment's Upside-Down House, his toilet forms a classic Mickey with two red circles on the floor.

Hint 117: When you feel a blast of air and the walls open, you'll see a rainbow and balloons. Look down and to the right to see classic Mickey circles appear on a cloud at the bottom right of the stage.

Hint 118: In this same scene at the end of the ride, find the letters that spell "Action" that stand in the middle of the scene. Snow covers the top of the letter "A," and a classic Mickey sits in the snow at the bottom left of the snow cap. The Hidden Mickey image tilts to the left.

Hint 119: On the left wall of the exit hallway, a sideways classic Mickey is behind and between the "I" and "m" of the ImageWorks sign.

– ImageWorks

Hint 120: Behind a pillar in the middle of Image-Works, a classic Hidden Mickey is on the floor made of tan-colored tile.

– Captain EO

Hint 121: In the movie, the three lower thrusters on the back of Captain EO's spaceship form a classic Hidden Mickey.

Innoventions West

– "Where's the Fire?"

Hint 122: A partial classic Mickey is at the lower left of the "Where's the Fire?" logo, which appears between shows on all the monitors in this attraction.

Hint 123: In one of the rooms, look for a computer monitor screen on a desk. You can make out classic Mickeys in the changing graphics on the screen.

Hint 124: A classic Mickey bookend is visible on the desk in the Kids' Bedroom.

Hint 125: Goofy is on an upside-down magazine draped over a lamp in the Kids' Bedroom.

– "The Great Piggy Bank Adventure"

Hint 126: On the yellow wall inside the attraction, circles below the sign "Start saving early" form a classic Mickey tilted to the left. You can see the image from the outer walkway. Other circles on the walls inside may resemble classic Mickeys.

Hint 127: Also from the outer walkway, check out the classic Mickey-shaped holes in the sides of the children's wooden stools on the floor inside. You'll find the stools in the last room before the exit.

Innoventions East

– Habit Heroes

Hint 128: In this interactive game, you run around in the third room and tap your card to protect cities around the world from being attacked. The city on the far right as you enter the room, has an Italian flag, and a dark classic Hidden Mickey hides on the city's Roman Coliseum.

– Electric Umbrella

Hint 129: A tiny white classic Hidden Mickey is at the apex atop an outdoor sign on the roof for the Electric Umbrella restaurant.

Universe of Energy

Hint 130: After the dinosaur section of the ride, the movie shows a man driving a car out of a barn and toward a church building in the background (the fourth building from the left). A shadow of the Disney's Hollywood Studios' "Earful" Tower appears in the door of the church.

Spaceship Earth

Hint 131: After the fall of Rome, you see three Islamic scholars seated around a table on the floor. They are illuminated by lights that form patterns on the floor. The outer circles of light patterns form classic Mickeys.

Hint 132: Across from the Islamic scholars, on a wall to your left, are shelves with cubbyholes full of scrolls and books. In one of the last cubbyholes you pass before you leave the scene, the round ends of three stacked scrolls lying horizontally form a classic Mickey. It's on the second shelf up from the bottom, in the right lower corner of the second cubbyhole from the right wall.

Hint 133: During the ride, in a scene to the left, monks are writing at desks. In front of the sleeping monk is a document with a small ink blot at the upper right corner. The blot is shaped like a classic Mickey and becomes visible as your vehicle passes by.

Hint 134: Just after the Gutenberg printing press scene, in the first part of the Renaissance section, look for the first painter to the left of your ride vehicle. Three white paint circles form a classic Mickey on the top left of the table near the painter. You have to look fast for this one.

Hint 135: On the right side, as you're passing the section showing black and white movies, a chalkboard marquee on the ground lists upcoming features. One is "The Band Concert," a famous Mickey Mouse cartoon.

Hint 136: A Mickey Mouse sticker is stuck above you on an unlighted part of the ceiling, just past the garage scene. It is visible after you pass beyond the section of overhead lighting and before you emerge out into the vastness of stars and space. But you can't see the sticker unless you shine your camera's red light or your phone flashlight up toward the ceiling. It appears about six feet or so after the lighted ceiling section ends.

Hint 137: At the exit of *Spaceship Earth,* several classic Mickeys float along on overhead blue screens in the Project Tomorrow interactive area.

Future World East

– *MouseGear*

Hint 138: The signs above the shop entrances have classic Mickeys with two round ears above the letter "G" as the head.

Hint 139: The large wing nuts on the bolts of the display racks form Mickey ears.

Hint 140: Some of the gauges on the wall are arranged as classic Mickeys.

Hint 141: The shadows of Donald Duck and his relatives are on the upper part of a wall in the center of the store.

Hint 142: Classic Mickey gears hang above a display on a wall opposite the cash registers.

Hint 143: Look for a large Donald Duck on a wall in the part of the store near the main walkway to the east side of Future World to find a classic Mickey made of gears.

Hint 144: Some of the garment-display mannequins have classic Mickeys at the top.

Disney's Hollywood Studios Scavenger Hunt

• •

Before You Start

• Many great Hidden Mickeys are in Standby queues. You'll miss them if you take the FastPass queue, so I recommend reserving FastPass+ for the following rides: The Twilight Zone Tower of Terror, Voyage of The Little Mermaid, and Fantasmic! Be sure to keep track of your three FastPass+ windows and return to these attractions at the appropriate times.

In the Scavenger Hunt below, if you come to your FastPass+ attraction and it's not time for it yet, skip to the next stop in the Hunt and return to the Fast-Pass+ attraction during your time window.

• Line up for shows 20-30 minutes ahead of start time.

• Many of the Hidden Mickeys in this park are in restaurants and shops. Be considerate of fellow guests and Cast Members as you search. Tell them what you are looking for, so they can share in the fun. Avoid searching restaurants at busy meal times unless you are one of the diners.

★ Your scavenger hunt in Disney's Hollywood Studios (aka "the Studios") starts even **before you enter the park**.

Clue 1: Look closely at the brackets on the signs above the ticket windows.
2 points

Clue 2: Examine the fence at the entrance turnstiles.
1 point

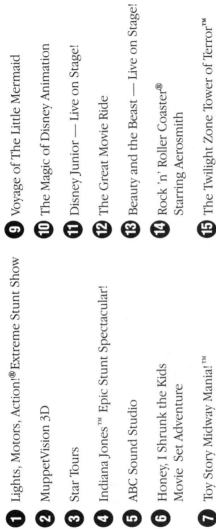

1. Lights, Motors, Action!® Extreme Stunt Show
2. MuppetVision 3D
3. Star Tours
4. Indiana Jones™ Epic Stunt Spectacular!
5. ABC Sound Studio
6. Honey, I Shrunk the Kids Movie Set Adventure
7. Toy Story Midway Mania!™
8. Walt Disney: One Man's Dream
9. Voyage of The Little Mermaid
10. The Magic of Disney Animation
11. Disney Junior — Live on Stage!
12. The Great Movie Ride
13. Beauty and the Beast — Live on Stage!
14. Rock 'n' Roller Coaster® Starring Aerosmith
15. The Twilight Zone Tower of Terror™
16. Fantasmic!

★ Walk first to **Toy Story Midway Mania!**

Clue 3: Search carefully for a blue classic Mickey along the Standby (i.e., regular) entrance queue.
5 points

Clue 4: As your ride starts, glance back at a big book for Donald and Mickey. (Sometimes, the book is positioned so that these images cannot be seen from the vehicle.)
5 bonus points for both

Clue 5: On the interactive screens, look behind the target balloons in front of the volcano to spot a classic Mickey.
5 points

Clue 6: On another screen, watch the white plates for a classic Mickey image.
3 points

Clue 7: Stay alert for a classic Mickey below an exclamation point on the wall.
5 points

Clue 8: Along the exit walkway, spot another classic Mickey on a wall.
2 points

Clue 9: Study a book along the exit for a tiny classic Mickey.
5 points

Clue 10: Outside of the attraction, look around for popcorn Mickey.
3 points

Clue 11: Then search outside for Mickey on a plate.
2 points

★ Now go to **Rock 'n' Roller Coaster Starring Aerosmith**. (You can find the Hidden Mickeys here without riding the coaster, the first ten by exiting before the ride, six in—and on the way to—

the gift shop by walking in through the exit from outside, and four outside in the courtyard.)

Clue 12: Study the tile floor along the entrance queue for two classic Mickeys.
5 points for both

Clue 13: Look down at the carpet along the entrance queue for Hidden Mickeys.
4 points

Clue 14: Don't miss the tiny Mickey on a wall poster just before the pre-show room.
4 points

Clue 15: Search around the pre-show room for a classic Mickey.
4 points

Clue 16: After the pre-show, look for three Mickeys on a poster.
5 points for spotting all three

Clue 17: Look across the track for Mickey on the wall.
5 points

Clue 18: At the loading gate, look at the rear license plates of the limo ride vehicles. (Then exit if you wish.)
4 points

Clue 19: As you step out of your ride vehicle at the end, glance to your far left to spot Mickey on a wall. (If you haven't taken the ride, walk in through the gift shop to find this and the following five Mickeys.)
3 points

Clue 20: At the exit, find a box with a classic Mickey in the word "box."
4 points

Clue 21: Search for another box with a classic Mickey in a word.
4 points

Clue 22: In the gift shop, spot a Hidden Mickey on a guitar.
4 points

119

Clue 23: In the gift shop, look around for a Hidden Oswald the Lucky Rabbit (with long ears).
3 points

Clue 24: Also in the shop, find Mickey and Minnie made of guitar picks!
4 points for both

Clue 25: Outside in the courtyard, locate a Hidden Mickey on a food kiosk sign.
3 points

Clue 26: Also in the courtyard, search for three Hidden Mickeys on the wall of the attraction.
5 points for spotting all three

★ Walk to **The Twilight Zone Tower of Terror** at your FastPass+ time and explore the entry queue area and pre-show for three Hidden Mickeys.

Clue 27: During the pre-show film in the library, find the plush Mickey Mouse doll held by a little girl.
3 points

Clue 28: Linger in the left library to spot the words "Mickey Mouse" on sheet music on a desktop.
4 points

Clue 29: Notice a classic Mickey stain on the wall in the boiler room.
4 points

(Tip: For the best vantage point for the ride Hidden Mickeys (Clues 30 to 32), take the right queue when the line for the ride splits. Then tell the Cast Member you're hunting for Hidden Mickeys and ask to be seated in the rightmost ride vehicle.)

Clue 30: At the first stop on the ride, search for a Hidden Mickey above you.
4 points

Clue 31: Also look for a Mickey Mouse doll here.
4 points

Clue 32: Stare at the star field (the doors to the elevator shaft just before they open!) to spot a classic Hidden Mickey in the stars.
5 points

Clue 33: As you exit, spot Mickey on the floor!
4 points

Clue 34: Outside the gift shop at the exit, check out the rock wall at the smoking area for a classic Mickey.
4 points

★ Your next stop is **Star Tours—The Adventures Continue**.

Clue 35: Don't miss a classic Mickey on a tree along the outside queue.
5 points

Clue 36: Along the inside entrance queue, look for a Hidden Mickey near C-3PO.
3 points

Clue 37: Now wait for a shadow Hidden Mickey in a video on a wall display along the entrance queue. (Note: You may have to cool your heels awhile to spot this one!)
4 points

Clue 38: Next, study the entrance queue luggage scanner for Mickey and other Disney characters and images.
5 points total for finding Mickey and two or more other Disney images

Clue 39: Just after you're seated for the ride, watch C-3PO to your right for a tiny Hidden Mickey.
5 points

Clue 40: At the end of the ride, if you land on the Coruscant planet (as opposed to other random end destinations for the ride), look for classic Mickeys on a rear wall.
5 bonus points

Clue 41: Spot a blue-light classic Mickey on a counter in the gift shop at the exit.
4 points

Clue 42: Find classic Mickey on the front of another counter in the gift shop.
3 points

Clue 43: Just before you exit the gift shop, look on your left for a Hidden Mickey on the wall.
4 points

★ Stroll over to **The Great Movie Ride**. First find two classic Mickeys among the celebrity impressions in the cement in front of the Chinese Theater and then take the ride.

Clue 44: Check Harry Anderson's square.
3 points

Clue 45: Now see if you can spot a Mickey in Carol Burnett's square.
3 points

Clue 46: In the middle of the loading dock mural, search for the Hidden Minnie above a tree stump. (Psst! It's visible at loading and unloading.)
5 points

Clue 47: On the right side of this mural, squint for a tiny black Hidden Mickey.
5 points

Clue 48: As you start down Gangster Alley, look for Mickey's brown shoes under a James Cagney poster.
4 points

Clue 49: At the end of Gangster Alley, find Mickey's shadow in a window near the top of the "Chemical Company" building.
5 points

Clue 50: In the "Western" section, spot two references to Pocahontas.

5 points for both

Tip: To spot all of the Hidden Images in the "Raiders of the Lost Ark" room (Clues 51 to 54, below) look quickly first to your left, then to your right, then left again, and finally right again as your vehicle moves through the room.

Clue 51: Look left for R2-D2 and C-3PO on the wall!
5 points

Clue 52: Stare to the right of your vehicle for a small white classic Mickey on a tablet below the ark container.
5 points

Clue 53: Find Mickey and Donald on the left wall, at the end of the "Raiders of the Lost Ark" room.
(Psst! Mickey is facing Donald.)
5 points

Clue 54: Now glance quickly to your right for a hieroglyphic Mickey.
5 points

Clue 55: In the "Tarzan" room, stare at the trees high above and to your right for a classic Mickey.
3 points

Clue 56: In the "Wizard of Oz" room, search for Mickey in the flowers.
3 points

Clue 57: Look up to spot Mickey in the trees in the "Wizard of Oz" room.
5 points

Clue 58: After you exit, study the design above the outside entrance door for a classic Mickey image.
3 points

★ Walk over to **Voyage of The Little Mermaid** at your FastPass+ time.

Clue 59: Look for a classic Mickey in the inside waiting room.
3 points

(You can stay for the show in the theater or exit out the doors you just entered to continue your Hidden Mickey search.)

★ Take a lunch break. Keep your reservations if you have them. If not, try the Backlot Express for burgers and sandwiches, the Pizza Planet Arcade for pizza, or the ABC Commissary for salads and sandwiches.

★ Check your Times Guide for convenient show times later for *Beauty and the Beast—Live on Stage*. While you're eating **scan your Studios Guidemap** for a Hidden Mickey.

Clue 60: Turn the Disney's Hollywood Studios map about 45 degrees counterclockwise (so that the right corner is at the top) and search for Mickey.
4 points

Clue 61: Now study the map for tiny classic Hidden Mickeys.
3 points

★ Catch the next performance of **Lights, Motors, Action! Extreme Stunt Show**.

Clue 62: Don't miss classic Mickeys along the entrance walkway.
4 points for one or more

Clue 63: Search for a small full-body Mickey Mouse at the rear of the set.
5 points

Clue 64: Find a classic Mickey in a set window.
5 points

Clue 65: Stay alert for fiery Mickey ears.
5 points

Clue 66: Exit to the left for Mickey beyond the fence.
4 points

★ Go to **MuppetVision 3D** and find seven Hidden Mickeys and a Hidden Surprise.

Clue 67: Look for a Mickey Mouse in the fountain outside MuppetVision.
2 points

Clue 68: On the wall near the far turn of the long outside waiting queue, check out the poster about 3D glasses to find a classic Mickey.
3 points

Clue 69: In the waiting room for the pre-show, find bicycles that form a Hidden Mickey.
2 points

Clue 70: During the first part of the pre-show on the video monitors, observe the test pattern.
4 points

Clue 71: In the first part of the movie, keep your eyes open for shelves on a wall with trophies. Look for Mickey there!
5 points

Clue 72: Try to spot the Mickey balloons while Kermit rides in on a fire truck.
3 points

Clue 73: Study the license plate on the fire truck for a Hidden Surprise.
4 points

Clue 74: Find a Mickey image just outside the theater exit doors.
3 points

★ Walk up the Streets of America. Turn right and pass by the *Honey, I Shrunk the Kids Movie Set Adventure* to **Studio Catering Co**.

Clue 75: Search for a Hidden Mickey on a wall. (Psst! It's at one side of the restaurant.)
3 points

★ Walk down Mickey Avenue to **Walt Disney: One Man's Dream**.

Clue 76: During your walk through the attraction, locate a Hidden Mickey in a painting that Walt is holding.
3 points

Clue 77: Farther along, look around for a Hidden Donald near Walt, who is holding a pointer.
3 points

Clue 78: Now find Mickey on the wall near Walt.
3 points

Clue 79: Study the Tokyo display for a Hidden Mickey.
3 points

★ Check out the show **Disney Junior—Live on Stage!** in Animation Courtyard.

Clue 80: Watch for Mickey in the lighting and stage effects.
3 points for two or more

★ Exit Animation Courtyard through the arch and veer left to **The Hollywood Brown Derby** restaurant. Admire the mural on the wall outside, above the restaurant.

Clue 81: Look for two classic Mickeys in the mural.
4 points for spotting both

★ Now look at the pictures in the waiting area inside the restaurant.

Clue 82: Spot the man with Mickey Mouse ears.
3 points

★ Turn left as you leave and **head down Sunset Boulevard**.

Clue 83: Search for a classic Mickey in scrollwork on a blue building.

4 points

★ Walk to **Rosie's All-American Café**.

Clue 84: Look around the food order area for Mickey.
4 points

★ Catch a performance of **Beauty and the Beast —Live on Stage**.

Clue 85: Watch for Mickey on the back of one of the characters.
3 points

★ Turn left onto Hollywood Boulevard, then right to **Hollywood & Vine restaurant**.

Clue 86: Seek a Hidden Character above the restaurant's entrance.
3 points

★ Enter the restaurant and examine the left wall.

Clue 87: Find a stick-figure Mickey.
2 points

Clue 88: Search the wall for some classic Mickeys.
3 points

★ Step inside the waiting area for the **50's Prime Time Café** and look closely at the tables.

Clue 89: Check out what's holding them together.
1 point

★ Check your Times Guide for a convenient performance of **Mulch, Sweat & Shears**.

Clue 90: Look for a Hidden Mickey in the props.
4 points

★ Enter the **Backlot Express** restaurant.

Clue 91: Look for standing Mickeys.
4 points for finding four or more

★ Ask a restaurant Cast Member to let you check out the **Sci-Fi Dine-In Theater Restaurant** inside.

Clue 92: Look for a classic Mickey in the waiting area of the Sci-Fi Dine-In Theater Restaurant.
3 points

Clue 93: Find a full-body Mickey in the waiting area.
3 points

Clue 94: Search for Mickey in the left hallway to the dining area.
4 points

Clue 95: Study the right rear mural. Look for two Hidden Mickeys along the treetops.
5 points for both

Clue 96: Stare at a small mosaic mural at the rear of the restaurant for a side profile of Mickey Mouse.
5 points

Clue 97: Watch the movie reel for three Hidden Characters.
8 points for spotting all three

Clue 98: Stay alert for a classic Hidden Mickey on a spacesuit.
4 points

Clue 99: When popcorn appears on the screen, search for a Hidden Mickey.
5 points

Clue 100: Find a Hidden Mickey on a dining car.
3 points

★ Get yourself some coffee or other refreshment at **The Writer's Stop**. Look up while you enjoy it.

Clue 101: See anything familiar on the overhead theater lights?
2 points

Clue 102: Check out the outside display windows for a Hidden Mickey.
1 point

★ Mosey over to the ***Pizza Planet Arcade*** and find three Hidden Mickeys.

Clue 103: Search for a small classic Mickey in the stars above the counter registers. Focus on the left side of the pizzeria's rear wall.
4 points

Clue 104: Swing your eyes over to the right side of the rear wall to find a bright classic-Mickey star cluster.
3 points

Clue 105: Now find a three-quarter Mickey profile above the arcade games on the wall mural. (Psst! He's looking left.)
5 points

★ Wander into the ***Stage 1 Company Store*** and find four Hidden Mickeys.

Clue 106: Locate a classic Mickey near a bird.
2 points

Clue 107: Take a good look at the old bureau that's loaded with hats and paint cans.
3 points

Clue 108: Spot a classic Mickey on the wall.
3 points

Clue 109: Search for some famous shorts.
3 points

Clue 110: Now find several Hidden Mickeys outside the store.
5 points for four or more

★ In the waiting area for ***Mama Melrose's Ristorante Italiano***, search for four classic Mickeys.

Clue 111: Check out the Dalmatian.
3 points

Clue 112: Examine the plaster on the right wall.
3 points

Clue 113: Find a classic Mickey leaf near the check-in podium. (Note: This Hidden Mickey moves around or disappears at times!)
4 bonus points

Clue 114: Locate a small Hidden Mickey marking on the wall behind the check-in podium.
5 points

Clue 115: Now look at the plaster on the wall to the left of the check-in podium.
3 points

★ Stroll to **Radiator Springs**, where the *Cars* characters sign autographs.

Clue 116: Study Mater for a Hidden Mickey.
3 points

★ Walk down the **Streets of America**.

Clue 117: Search for a San Francisco newspaper with a Hidden Mickey.
4 points

Clue 118: Keep looking around for a reference to a Disney movie.
3 points

Clue 119: Glance at a nearby wall poster for three or more Hidden Mickeys.
4 points for three or more

Clue 120: Study the sidewalk not far from the Funeral Director's office for a Hidden Mickey.
5 points

Clue 121: Along the street, locate a dog with a Hidden Mickey.
3 points

Clue 122: Find a Mickey Mouse watch in a window.
4 points

Clue 123: Don't miss the photo of Walt with Mickey!
4 points

Clue 124: Search for four classic characters in a window near a cruise ship.
5 points for spotting all four

Clue 125: Spot a classic Mickey in the sand in a New York window.
3 points

★ Walk past *The Great Movie Ride* to the **entrance arch to Animation Courtyard**.

Clue 126: Search this area for Hidden Characters.
4 points for finding two characters

Clue 127: Find a Hidden Mickey outside above the entrance to *Voyage of The Little Mermaid*.
3 points

★ Enjoy **The Magic of Disney Animation**.

Clue 128: Look around the stage during the theater presentation for Hidden Mickeys.
5 points for two or more

Clue 129: In the theater video, watch for the cloud of smoke around Mushu the dragon.
5 points

Clue 130: Then keep watching the video for Hidden Mickeys on a mug.
4 points

Clue 131: Look around the courtyard outside the theater for Mickey.
3 points

Clue 132: Study the carpets inside as you walk toward the Character Greeting areas.
2 points

Clue 133: Search the Character Greeting areas for Hidden Mickeys and a Hidden Pluto.
5 points for Pluto and two or more Hidden Mickeys

★ Stroll **toward Hollywood Boulevard**.

Clue 134: On the way, look for Mickey on the large plaza between *The Great Movie Ride* and Hollywood Boulevard. (Note: he's not always present.)
3 points

Clue 135: While in the plaza, look toward Min and Bill's Dockside Diner for a Hidden Mickey.
3 points

Clue 136: At the intersection of Hollywood and Sunset Boulevards, discover Mickey Mouse's previous moniker. (Psst! Read the impressions in the sidewalks, near the curb.)
5 points

Clue 137: Walk behind Keystone Clothiers and search for a classic Mickey.
2 points

★ Enter **Mickey's of Hollywood** to look for four Hidden Mickeys.

Clue 138: Check the posts holding up merchandise racks.
2 points

Clue 139: Admire the merchandise bins!
3 points for two Hidden Mickeys

Clue 140: Next find "MICKEYS" spelled out on vertical dividers.
1 point

★ Go to the **Cover Story** store and take a good look at the outside.

Clue 141: See any classic Mickeys in the design?
2 points

★ Stroll to the area just inside the **park entrance**.

Clue 142: Locate a Hidden Mickey on an animal.
4 points

★ Walk outside the park to the **charter bus area**.

Clue 143: Search the cement next to a bench.
5 points

★ In the evening, arrive 30 to 40 minutes before show time (even though you have FastPass+) and stay alert during the **Fantasmic!** show for a Hidden Mickey.

Clue 144: Look for large bubbles floating up the water screen that form a classic Mickey.
5 points

**Total Points for
Disney's Hollywood Studios =**

How'd you do?

Up to 210 points – Bronze
211 to 418 points – Silver
419 points and over – Gold
524 points – Perfect Score

You may have done even better if you earned bonus points in *Toy Story Midway Mania!*, *Star Tours,* and/ or the check-in podium of Mama Melrose's Ristorante Italiano.

Notes

**Caution:
Don't peek at this
section unless you
really want help!**

– Park entrance area

Hint 1: Metal brackets at the bottoms of signs above the ticket purchase windows are shaped like classic Mickeys.

Hint 2: You'll see classic Mickeys on top of the fence at the turnstiles.

– Toy Story Midway Mania!

Hint 3: An upside-down blue paint classic Mickey is on the wall past the large map of the U.S.A. It is below a green dinosaur and an orange fish (Nemo), near the floor and behind the handrails on the left side of the queue.

Hint 4: Just as your vehicle leaves the loading area, glance back at the large "Tin Toy" book. On the back of the book, near the spine, spot full-body images of Donald Duck at the upper right corner and Mickey Mouse two figures below Donald. (Sometimes, the back of the book is positioned so that these images cannot be seen from your ride vehicle.)

Hint 5: Watch for the screen with target balloons in front of the volcano spewing lava. If you pop the middle 100-point balloon on the second tier, a light classic Mickey appears on the rear surface in the lava behind the balloons.

Hint 6: Be alert for the screen with moving white plates. At one point, a large plate aligns with smaller plates behind it to form a classic Mickey.

Hint 7: Look for the words "Circus Fun!" on the wall to your right as you rotate into position for the last screen stop. The dot below the exclamation point is a classic Mickey.

Hint 8: On the wall to the left of the ride vehicles, a classic Mickey is formed by three ovals that outline Mr. Potato Head, Slinky Dog, and Bullseye the horse. You can see this image at loading and unloading, and you can study it as you take the exit walkway.

Hint 9: On the upper spine of the large "Tin Toy" book along the exit, a tiny white classic Mickey is in a chicken's eye. It's the fourth image from the top of the spine.

Hint 10: You'll find a side-profile Mickey on a huge popcorn box that's on display across from the *Toy Story Midway Mania!* attraction. Look behind the "Hey Howdy Hey!" sign.

Hint 11: On the left lower side of a large "Prospector" plate, which stands on the left side of a shelf on the rear wall of the "Hey Howdy Hey" snack area, a horseshoe and two circles resemble a classic Mickey.

– Rock 'n' Roller Coaster Starring Aerosmith

Hint 12: Look down for a tiled floor just as you step inside the building along the Standby entrance queue. In the middle of the walkway at the end of this tiled-floor section, before you enter the carpeted room, two classic Mickeys are each formed by three tiny round tiles. The circles are all the same size, but these images are purposeful and they're sentimental favorites.

Hint 13: Along the entrance queue, when you reach the inner room past the tile floor, distorted classic Mickeys are in the carpet.

Hint 14: On the last wall before you enter the lower level of the pre-show video room, a poster labeled "Cosmic Car Show" has a tiny classic Mickey on the bottom right under the front tire of the car. The Mickey image is at the end of the signature of "J. Mouse."

Hint 15: Cables coiled into a classic Mickey lie on the rear center of the floor in the pre-show room where Aerosmith appears.

Hint 16: You'll find three Mickey Mouse stickers along the right side of a framed collage: one at the upper right and two at the middle. (One of the middle right stickers is a full-body Mickey Mouse; the other two stickers are of Mickey's face.) The poster is on the wall to your left, at the first right turn in the inside queue near the boarding area.

Hint 17: On a wall across from the front of the loading dock area, various items are hanging from a row of hooks to the left of a wall cabinet and to the right of a garage door. One of the hanging items is a pink hat with the word "Mickey" across the front. (Note: The arrangement of these items changes from time to time.)

Hint 18: On the rear license plate of each limo ride vehicle, the year sticker at the upper right is a classic Mickey.

Hint 19: Look to your far left as you exit the ride vehicle. A black classic Mickey is on the wall where the side of a gate connects to the wall.

Hint 20: Just as people exit the ride vehicle, look for "Box #15" on the right side of the room with the guest photo screens. The "o" in "Box" is a classic Mickey.

Hint 21: On the box next to box #15, "Sash Cord" is written at the left side of a piece of tape. The "o" in "Cord" is a black classic Mickey.

Hint 22: A green guitar stands upright in a merchandise display in the middle of the gift shop. Three tiny classic Mickeys are on a silver plate at the base of the guitar. They're formed of holes for the "ears" and screws for the "heads."

Hint 23: An image of Oswald the Lucky Rabbit's head and ears is made of wires. Find him behind the glass door of a cabinet on the right wall of the room that's at the left side of the gift shop (as you exit the ride).

Hint 24: On cashier's counters at the right rear of the gift shop, just before you reach the exit walkway, spot a Hidden Mickey and a Hidden Minnie made of guitar picks under laminated surfaces. Look for Mickey on the left counter top and Minnie (with her red bow) on the right.

Hint 25: Walk outside into the courtyard of *Rock 'n' Roller Coaster* and glance above the order windows of "The Rock Station" snack kiosk. Holes in the "R" form a distorted image that resembles a classic Hidden Mickey.

Hint 26: In the front courtyard, check the outside wall mural to your left for:
  - a boy wearing Mickey ears.
  - black classic Mickeys on a singer's light blue shirt.
  - a gold "bling" Mickey on the necklace of the man in the black suit.

– The Twilight Zone Tower of Terror

Hint 27: During the pre-show film in the library, the little girl on the elevator holds a plush Mickey Mouse doll.

Hint 28: Look for sheet music on a desktop and under a trumpet to the right of the television in the left library. The words "Mickey Mouse" are part of a song title: "What! No Mickey Mouse?"

Hint 29: A black, slightly distorted classic Mickey stains the wall of the boiler room at the spot where the queue branches. He's about eight feet up from the walkway, between an "Exit" sign and a red electrical box.

Hint 30: At the first stop on the ride, a small, dark classic Mickey can be seen above the ghostly images in the lower center of the ornate design on the closest archway.

Hint 31: Also at this first stop, the little girl in the ghostly images is still holding her Mickey doll.

Hint 32: On the ride itself, you'll see a bright star field just before the doors open into the elevator shaft. Look closely as the stars you're watching converge in the middle into a small classic-Mickey shape for a split second. (Tip: You see it best from the rightmost ride vehicle.)

Hint 33: On the left side of the last room as you exit the ride (and before the gift shop), three distinct floor tiles form a classic Mickey. (It's not proportioned correctly but it is clearly purposeful.)

Hint 34: In the trellis-covered smoking area across from the gift shop exit, a tiny rock classic Mickey sticks out from the last arch on the left of the upper rear rock wall. It's about four feet from the end column and close to the bottom of the arch.

– Star Tours—The Adventures Continue

Hint 35: About halfway along the outside winding queue, a white classic Mickey is high on a tree trunk, just below the walkway platform for the Ewok village above. It's on the huge central tree, directly across from the Imperial Walker.

Hint 36: Along the right side of the inside entrance queue, circles make a Mickey hat with ears on the upper part of the control panel behind C-3PO's head. It's at the lower center of the upper screen.

Hint 37: In a wall display along the entrance queue, the silhouette of R2-D2 appears several times in a continuous video loop of moving shadow figures. At one point, R2-D2 sprouts satellite ears that rotate into round "Mickey ears" for a few seconds.

Hint 38: Along the entrance queue, a robot watches a continuous scan of luggage moving along a conveyor belt. You can spot images of a plush Mickey Mouse and a plush Goofy, along with images of Buzz Lightyear, Aladdin's lamp, a Sorcerer Mickey hat, a Mr. Incredible shirt, Madame Leota's crystal ball, and some other Disney images.

Hint 39: Just after you're seated, C-3PO appears on a screen at the front right of the room. A small classic Mickey is on his right forearm near his wrist.

Hint 40: At the end of the *Star Tours* ride, there are four classic Hidden Mickeys in the Coruscant landing sequence, which is one of three different and random end destinations for the ride. After the *Star Tours* vehicle crash lands on the platform and is lowered below into the hanger, look for four recessed panels in the top half of the back wall of the hanger. A classic Mickey is in the center of each panel. To see them, focus on the background wall instead of the droid in the foreground that's flying around with the two light batons.

Hint 41: A small classic Hidden Mickey formed of blue lights is in the Tatooine Traders gift shop at the exit of *Star Tours*. As you exit the ride, turn to face the long counter to your right. The light image is at the lower right of the counter.

Hint 42: At the "Build Your Own Lightsaber" station at the other end of the long counter in the exit gift shop, a classic Mickey is on the lower right front panel. It's formed by bullet holes with surrounding black burn marks as the "ears" and a central raised circle as the "head."

Hint 43: At the left side of the exit doorway from the gift shop, a faint classic Hidden Mickey is stenciled on the wooden wall, to the left of a fire alarm box.

– *The Great Movie Ride*

Hint 44: Harry Anderson's celebrity impression is at the front left of the Chinese Theater (as you face the entrance). Look for a classic Mickey on Harry's tie.

Hint 45: Four squares to the right of Harry Anderson's impression, Carol Burnett's square has classic Mickey ears in the upper right side.

Hint 46: In the loading dock area, a shadow of Minnie Mouse's head in side profile is visible on the wall mural during loading and unloading. To find it, first spot the house in the middle of the mural. Then look above and to the right of the house to spot Minnie's shadow. She's looking to your left. Having trouble? Look at the stationary ride vehicles. The Minnie shadow is to the left of the front section of the second of the two vehicles.

Hint 47: On the right side of the loading dock mural, in the second to last house on the right, a tiny black classic Mickey peeks out of the bottom center of a top-floor window. It's on the side of the house and nearest the corner.

Hint 48: In the first part of Gangster Alley, Mickey Mouse's brown shoes and tail poke out at the lower left from under a James Cagney poster, "The Public Enemy," on the left side of the ride vehicle.

Hint 49: At the end of Gangster Alley, a silhouette of Mickey in side profile appears in the rightmost window, near the top of the "Chemical Company" building. It's to the rear left of your ride vehicle.

Hint 50: In the Western scene, look for two paper bulletins advertising "Pocahontas Remedies." One is on a wall to your right behind a barber pole. The other is to the left of your vehicle, just past John Wayne on a wood fence. (It's one of the lower bulletins on the fence and can generally be spotted toward the right of the collection of bulletins.) Note: The locations of the bulletins in this scene sometimes change.

Hint 51: In the "Raiders of the Lost Ark" room, R2-D2 and C-3PO are together in the hieroglyphics on the left wall. Look midway between the two huge statues. The two robots are etched on the second level of panes, to the right of a kneeling figure.

Hint 52: In the "Raiders of the Lost Ark" room, a small white classic Mickey is on a broken tablet (or flat rock) that leans against the foundation that the Ark container is sitting on. Two white men are painted on the side of the container, and the tablet with the Mickey image is below and between them.

Hint 53: At the end of the "Raiders of the Lost Ark" room, Mickey and Donald can be found in the far left corner on the left wall. They're facing one another and Mickey is to the right of Donald, on the third row of panes up from the floor.

Hint 54: At the end of the right wall in the "Raiders of the Lost Ark" room, a hieroglyphic classic Mickey is at the right lower part of the first full pane above the stones on the floor. It's to the right of the lower leg of a standing figure etched in the pane.

Hint 55: In the latter part of the "Tarzan" room, a basket high in a treehouse to the right contains three eggs that form a classic Mickey. (The eggs are all the same size, but this is a sentimental favorite Hidden Mickey among guests and Cast Members.)

Hint 56: In the "Wizard of Oz" room, several groups of flowers, among them three large blue flowers above a hut at the middle left of the room, form acceptable classic Mickeys.

Hint 57: A green classic Mickey is nestled in the top of the trees, midway along the mural above the exit from the "Wizard of Oz" room. This classic Mickey is tilted slightly to the right.

Hint 58: Near the top of the flames directly above the small gold statue that is standing over the entrance doors to the attraction, a red circle with swirls for ears resembles a classic Mickey.

– Voyage of The Little Mermaid

Hint 59: Opposite the entrance doors to the in-side waiting room, an ornate map of the Earth's hemispheres hangs on the left side of the wall. The brass frames encircling the hemispheres form the "head" of a sideways classic Mickey, while the decorative circular elements between them form a set of "ears." (Note: There's just one set of "ears" but two possible "heads.")

– Disney's Hollywood Studios Guidemap

Hint 60: The face of Mickey Mouse on the park map has been distorted over time, but you can still spot it. The ear on the right is formed by Echo Lake, while the buildings on the left (for The Hollywood Brown Derby and Disney Junior—Live on Stage!) form the distorted ear on the left. His round head is the central plaza, and his forehead "widow's peak" shows up behind the word "Hollywood." Two faint gray patches in the center of the plaza form his eyes.

Hint 61: On the park map, tiny pink classic Hidden Mickeys adorn the right side of the entrance plaza.

– Lights, Motors, Action! Extreme Stunt Show

Hint 62: Walk through the entrance turnstile and look through the windows of the building on your right. Classic Mickey magnets are stuck on red tool chests behind the first set of windows you encounter and behind the middle set of windows as you turn right at the first corner. These magnet Mickeys change positions on the tool chests at times.

Hint 63: In the right section of the background set, look for a window under an "Antiquities" sign and near a large "Café" sign. A full-body drawing of Mickey Mouse is near a chair in the window's lower right side.

Hint 64: A classic Mickey is behind the upper right windowpane at the rear of the set, under the sign "Motomania."

Hint 65: Near the end of the show, a fireball erupts at the front center of the stage set ("downstage center" in stage parlance). The fire forms Mickey ears for a split second.

Hint 66: As you exit, walk to the left side of the show lagoon. A dark classic Mickey formed of rocks lies in the water at the bottom.

– MuppetVision 3D

Hint 67: In a fountain outside *MuppetVision 3D,* Gonzo is balancing on a character with bulging eyes and face who resembles Mickey.

Hint 68: On the wall near the far turn of the long outside waiting queue, you'll find a classic Mickey in the center left of a blue poster that says, "5 reasons to return . . . 3D glasses."

Hint 69: Near the middle of the left wall of the waiting room for the pre-show, bicycles sit on luggage, which is, in turn, on top of a wooden chest. A round black hatbox at the side of the luggage forms a classic Hidden Mickey with two bicycle wheels above it.

Hint 70: During the first part of the pre-show on the video monitors, a test pattern appears after you see the words "Video Display Test." The black lines on a white background form a classic Hidden Mickey.

Hint 71: During the first part of the movie, as Kermit walks past the long hall and toward the lab, look for shelves with trophies on the wall before he reaches the lab entrance doors. It appears that a full-body Mickey Mouse trophy is at the middle of the top left shelf.

Hint 72: After the cannon shoots holes in the theater and Kermit rides in on a fire truck, you can see that some of the observers outside are holding Mickey Mouse balloons.

Hint 73: An image of Cinderella Castle (a Hidden Surprise) is on a license plate at the right lower corner of the fire truck Kermit is riding.

Hint 74: Across from and outside the exit doors from the *MuppetVision 3D* theater, a poster on the right wall advertises "Rowlf." At the lower left of the poster, a classic Mickey is formed by the nose and eyes of the dog's face.

– Studio Catering Co.

Hint 75: At the side of the restaurant, a red classic Mickey lies on a black tile under a fire alarm on the right wall of the High Octane Refreshments Bar.

– Walt Disney: One Man's Dream

Hint 76: On the left side of the display aisle, in the 1940 *Fantasia* exhibit, a young Walt Disney holds a painting. Three large round bushes in the painting form an upright classic Mickey.

Hint 77: On the left side of the aisle (and before you are ushered into the theater), you see Walt Disney standing with a pointer in front of a wall map. On a desk to Walt's left, a coffee mug near a telephone has Donald Duck on it.

Hint 78: In the same scene, you can spot a green classic Mickey tilted slightly to the right. He's on the wall to the left of Walt.

Hint 79: In the Tokyo DisneySea model, a classic Mickey is formed by the large round gold-domed fortress and two nearby towers. If you crouch and look up, you can spot this Mickey image in the reflection on the glass over the fortress. (The platform for the gold dome and two nearby round structures come close to a classic Mickey shape, but one "ear" is a bit too far away from the "head.")

– Disney Junior—Live on Stage!

Hint 80: Classic Mickeys appear at times in the lighting and stage effects as well as on various stage props during the live show. Look for a partial classic Mickey on the blue TV screen on the right front door after it swings open on stage.

– The Hollywood Brown Derby

Hint 81: Classic Mickeys are in the clouds on the mural on the outside wall above the restaurant. One is at the far upper right of the mural, and another is at the far mid-left of the mural, above the "Stage 5" sign.

Hint 82: On a wall to the left in the waiting area, in the second row of pictures, you'll find a caricature of Jimmy Dodd (with his Mouse ears) from the 1950s "Mickey Mouse Club" TV show.

– Sunset Boulevard

Hint 83: Midway down Sunset Boulevard toward the *Tower of Terror*, the outside scrollwork about halfway to the top of a blue building on the right side of the street has an upside-down classic Mickey in its design.

– Rosie's All-American Café

Hint 84: Mickey's smiling face is at the right lower corner of a photo collage at the right side of Rosie's leftmost food order window.

– Beauty and the Beast—Live on Stage

Hint 85: A classic Mickey is on a wind-up device on Cogsworth's back. The device has two holes for the "ears" and a larger circle for the "head." Sometimes this image is upside down.

– Hollywood & Vine

Hint 86: Outside the restaurant, a silhouette of Roger Rabbit is in a window above and to the left of the entrance.

Hint 87: On the left wall inside, the "San Fernando Valley" mural has a stick-figure Mickey on the far right, behind a pole.

Hint 88: Bushes form several classic Mickeys to the immediate left of the stick-figure Mickey and also above him.

– 50's Prime Time Café

Hint 89: In the waiting area, washers shaped like classic Mickeys secure the white tabletops.

– Mulch, Sweat & Shears

Hint 90: An orange side-profile Hidden Mickey is on the blade of a shovel that lies along the right side of the top of their vehicle.

– Backlot Express

Hint 91: Several full-body two-dimensional Mickeys are on the bulletin boards inside the Backlot Express restaurant. One bulletin board is near the exit door facing *Star Tours*. A second is close by at the side of the seating area across from the mural of the city park.

– Sci-Fi Dine-In Theater Restaurant

Hint 92: In the waiting area on the left wall (as you enter) is a poster for the movie *Attack of the 50 Ft. Woman*. A classic Mickey is behind her right knee, just off the highway.

Hint 93: Mickey Mouse in a graduation outfit is on an "Educational Reimbursement Program" notice on the lower middle of a bulletin board on a wall in the waiting area.

Hint 94: Just past the check-in counter, at the beginning of the left-side hallway, a classic Hidden Mickey is drawn on the right wall.

HINTS HINTS HINTS HINTS HINTS HINTS HINTS HINTS HINTS HINTS HINTS HINTS HINTS

Hint 95: Face the kitchen, then look to the right of it at the tall fence. You'll find two Hidden Mickeys in the mural above the right side of the tall fence. Look at the treetops. A classic Mickey, tilted slightly to the right, is above the right corner of the tall fence. A second Hidden Mickey is just to the left of the first one; this one appears to be waving with his left hand.

Hint 96: In the multicolored tiles above the kitchen door entrance (on the right as you face the kitchen) is a side profile of Mickey. He is outlined in yellow tiles and appears to be looking to his left (our right). Look first for his jaw, a curving line of yellow tiles in the middle of the mosaic square.

Hint 97: Watch the movie reel for Donald Duck, Mickey Mouse, and Tinker Bell. Donald is in a cartoon segment about a secretary who is kidnapped to another planet; Donald is one of the characters who chases her. The segment follows a clip of Walt Disney. Mickey appears in person later in the reel, in a "News of the Future" segment; he wears a spacesuit and waves to the crowd. Tinker Bell flies around above the word "Tomorrowland."

Hint 98: Stay alert for a youngster in a spacesuit during the movie reel, when the words "Calling All Boys! All Girls!" appear on the screen. A classic Mickey formed by a circle and two knobs is on the upper chest of the spacesuit, just below the helmet.

Hint 99: Watch for popcorn popping all over the movie screen. One lone morsel of popcorn, on the table between the popcorn popper and the bucket, forms an upside-down classic Hidden Mickey (actually more of a Mickey hat and ears).

Hint 100: Silver classic Mickeys are at the sides of the dining-car seats, on the running boards.

– The Writer's Stop

Hint 101: Some of the theater lights hanging from the ceiling sport yellow classic Mickeys.

Hint 102: In an outside display window, a jar contains classic Mickey-shaped chocolate chip cookies.

– Pizza Planet Arcade

Hint 103: A classic Mickey is one of the constellations of stars above the counter registers. Focus on the left side of the rear wall, between Woody and the "Disney's Toy Story" sign.

Hint 104: A small, bright classic-Mickey star cluster appears above the counter registers on the right side of the rear wall. Look near the pizza-slice constellation.

Hint 105: Above the arcade games, in the moon near the top of the mural, you can spot a three-quarter Mickey profile facing left.

– Stage 1 Company Store

Hint 106: Blue birds are stuck high on side doors of one of the tall merchandise cabinets inside the store. Classic Mickeys decorate the ends of red scarves that are draped over the birds.

Hint 107: Look for an old bureau that's loaded with hats for sale and has paint cans at the very top. You'll find a green, painted classic Mickey near the center of the desktop.

Hint 108: In the middle of the store, across from the green-paint Hidden Mickey on the bureau, circles in the middle of a cloud at the upper left of a mural with a rainbow form an approximate classic Mickey.

Hint 109: Mickey Mouse's shorts (red with white buttons) are hanging on a line near one of the exit doors.

Hint 110: Walk around the outside of the Stage 1 Company Store and admire at least five Mickey images formed by yellow and purple paint that's spilled on the ground. One yellow classic Mickey is between a Cast Member door and a big bull's-eye on the walkway between the *Muppet-Vision 3D* building and the Stage 1 Company Store.

– Mama Melrose's Ristorante Italiano

Hint 111: Just inside the entrance, to your right, the Dalmatian has a black classic Mickey spot on its right shoulder (your left).

Hint 112: A slightly distorted classic Mickey hides in the plaster of the right wall between the waiting room and the dining area. Look in the upper right corner, near the entrance door.

Hint 113: To the right of the check-in podium (as you face it), a green classic Mickey leaf is about one and a half feet above the bottom of the window, along the left edge. (Note: This Hidden Mickey moves around or disappears at times!)

Hint 114: Look for a red classic Mickey marking on the exposed brick wall behind the check-in podium and to the left of the hanging grapes and grape leaves. It's about six feet up from the floor and near the edge of the wall next to the opening with the hanging grapes.

Hint 115: The left wall between the waiting room and the dining area has a smaller classic Mickey plastered on the brick. You'll find it in the middle left part of the wall, just above the counter.

– Stars of Cars Greeting Area

Hint 116: The wing nut on Mater's engine air filter has Mickey ears.

– Streets of America

Hint 117: Some of the newspapers in a newsstand in the left lower area of a mural at the end of San Francisco Street feature articles about Steamboat Willie.

Hint 118: In the lower right and left sides of the same mural, some papers in a small newspaper dispenser feature articles about a Disney movie (at presstime, the movie was *Up*).

Hint 119: A poster entitled "The Osborne Family Spectacle of Dancing Lights" hangs on a wall across from the San Francisco mural. A faint image of the Earful Tower is in the lower middle of the poster, below a man wearing Mickey ears. Several faint sideways classic Mickeys are scattered in the background of the upper half of the poster.

Hint 120: Near the office of David L. Davies – Funeral Director, just to the left (as you face the office) of the steps up to the second floor, a small classic Mickey is etched in the cement sidewalk. Locate the face of a man that's also etched in the sidewalk near the street curb. The Hidden Mickey is above and to the right of the man's face.

Hint 121: Along San Francisco Street, you'll find a Dalmatian on an address plaque on the wall above a barber pole. Three black spots above its front leg form a slightly distorted classic Mickey.

Hint 122: A watch with Mickey on its face is in the window of Sal's Pawn Shop, near the passage to *Honey, I Shrunk the Kids Movie Set Adventure*.

Hint 123: On the upper left wall of the second window (on the left as you face Venture Travel Agency) is a picture of Walt Disney holding a Mickey Mouse doll in his right hand.

Hint 124: The same window holds four other Hidden Characters: classic Mickey holes decorate the lower edge of a lampshade; in a photo propped on the desk below the shade, Mickey and Minnie are sitting on a bench looking out to a cruise ship at sea (we see just the backs of their heads), and small white classic Mickeys are in the corners of the window.

Hint 125: A classic Mickey sand trap is in the left-most window as you face the New York backdrop at the end of the Streets of America.

– Animation Courtyard

Hint 126: Donald Duck and Goofy are etched on the ornamental arches that are adjacent to Animation Courtyard's main entrance arch.

Hint 127: On the large sign over the entrance for the *Voyage of The Little Mermaid,* a classic Mickey made of bubbles floats high above Ursula's left hand.

– The Magic of Disney Animation

Hint 128: The stage set in front of the seating area for *The Magic of Disney Animation* theater usually includes a number of Hidden Mickeys. Check the large animator's desk first. There's a blue classic Mickey on a coffee mug on the right side of the desk's middle shelf, and you can usually find a Mickey Mouse pen sticking out of a container on the desk's top shelf. At the far right side of the stage (as you face the stage), a ceramic of Mickey's face is peeking out from near the front corner of a high shelf.

Hint 129: In the video shown in the theater, a classic Hidden Mickey is formed by a large cloud of smoke when Mushu the dragon is transforming into a double-headed Mushu.

Hint 130: Later in the video, a man holds a coffee mug covered with classic Mickeys.

Hint 131: Outside *The Magic of Disney Animation* theater is an interior courtyard with cement squares in the pavement that commemorate a few Disney Legends. Mickey is traced in Ward Kimball's square.

Hint 132: The circles in the carpet design near the Animation Academy room inside the Animation building usually include classic Mickeys.

Hint 133: In the Character Greeting areas, Mickey hats, the Earful Tower, and Pluto are in the background mural of the Sorcerer Mickey set. Pluto's outline is at the lower right of the mural.

– Toward Hollywood Boulevard

Hint 134: On the plaza near *The Great Movie Ride*, a full-face Mickey Mouse formed by lights can often be spotted in the afternoon and evening.

Hint 135: Maneuver around the plaza near *The Great Movie Ride* and stare toward Min and Bill's Dockside Diner. Above the food order windows, the diner's oval sign lines up with the portholes ("ears") to produce a classic Hidden Mickey.

– Intersection of Hollywood & Sunset Blvds.

Hint 136: On both sides of Sunset Boulevard near its intersection with Hollywood Boulevard, you'll find small impressions in the cement sidewalks, near the curb. They read, "Mortimer & Co, 1928, Contractors." "Mortimer Mouse" was Mickey Mouse's first (and soon discarded) name; 1928 was the year he was "born." (Two more of these stamps are at the other end of Sunset Boulevard. One is near the curb just before the walkway to *Rock 'n' Roller Coaster*. The other is across the street close to the entrance walkway to the *Fantasmic!* show.)

– Keystone Clothiers

Hint 137: At Peevy's Polar Pipeline drink service, behind Keystone Clothiers, gauges or regulators form a classic Mickey, especially when viewed from behind.

– Mickey's of Hollywood

Hint 138: Classic Mickey holes are drilled in some of the store's metal support poles.

Hint 139: The round merchandise bins have classic Mickeys in the band around the top and classic Mickey-shaped feet.

Hint 140: "MICKEYS" is spelled out on four vertical dividers (two on each side of the store) that separate the sections of the store.

– Cover Story

Hint 141: You'll find a design containing classic Mickeys on the outside of the store, next to The Darkroom. Look on the horizontal frieze below the second-floor windows.

– Sid Cahuenga's Antiques and Curios

Hint 142: Just inside the park entrance, a statue of a Dalmatian stands on the porch to the left of the shop's entrance doors. A black classic Mickey spot hides on the dog's left rear thigh.

– Near the charter bus area

Hint 143: Outside the park, near the charter bus area, a classic Mickey is stamped in cement. It's about nine or so benches (and three light poles) away from the main entrance promenade as you head toward the walkway to the BoardWalk Resort. Look across from the Bus Stop 25 cement marker and sign.

– Fantasmic!

Hint 144: When animated characters float up in large bubbles on the water screen, watch for Pinocchio. His bubble forms the head of a classic Hidden Mickey. Two bubbles beside it form the ears. (Other bubbles on the screen may come together at times to form classic Mickeys.)

CHAPTER 5

Disney's Animal Kingdom Scavenger Hunt

Before You Start

• *Many great Hidden Mickeys are in Standby queues. You'll miss them if you take the FastPass queue, so I recommend reserving FastPass+ for the following rides: Kilimanjaro Safaris, Festival of the Lion King, and Finding Nemo—The Musical. Be sure to keep track of your three FastPass+ windows and return to those attractions at the appropriate times. In the Scavenger Hunt below, if you come to your FastPass+ attraction and it's not time for it yet, skip to the next stop in the Hunt and return to the FastPass+ attraction during your time window.*

• *Some of the Hidden Mickeys in this park are in restaurants and shops. Be considerate of fellow guests and Cast Members as you search. Tell them what you're looking for, so they can share in the fun. Avoid searching restaurants at busy meal times unless you are one of the diners.*

★ Your first stop is **Expedition Everest** in Asia. Walk through the Oasis, turn right in Discovery Island, and follow the path to Asia. One of the queue Hidden Mickeys (number 20) is only visible from the Single Rider and FastPass+ queues. The rest are in the regular line, which Disney calls the Standby queue because you just walk into it and stand by for the attraction. Join the Standby queue to search for the Mickeys in Clues 1 through 13. After you exit the ride, you can look for Hidden Mickeys in and just outside the gift shop and then step into the Single Rider queue to look for Clue 20.

Clue 1: In the Standby queue, search for a classic Mickey in the first sunken courtyard. 3 points

155

Clue 2: Locate Mickey depressions on a red wall.
4 points

Clue 3: Look around for cloud Hidden Mickeys in a mural.
4 points for spotting two

Clue 4: Keep alert for pipes on a shelf that form a classic Mickey.
3 points

Clue 5: Find small Mickey ears in this room.
4 points

Clue 6: Look for a Hidden Mickey made of light-switch devices in a display.
3 points

Clue 7: Stay alert for Mickey on a book.
4 points

Clue 8: Search for Mickey on a handrail.
5 points

Clue 9: Spot a Hidden Mickey in a kettle.
4 points

Clue 10: Squint for a Hidden Mickey in an animal track.
5 points

Clue 11: Search for an animal with Mickey's ears!
3 points

Clue 12: In the last room before boarding for both the Standby and FastPass+ lines, glance around for Sorcerer Mickey near something blue.
5 points

Clue 13: In the loading area outside the Standby and FastPass+ lines, look for a classic Mickey.
3 points

Clue 14: After the ride starts, stay alert for a classic-Mickey melted spot in the snow.
5 points

discovery island

1 The Tree of Life

2 It's Tough to be a Bug!

3 Rivers of Light (opening 2016)

africa

4 Festival of the Lion King

5 Kilimanjaro Safaris

6 Pangani Forest Exploration Trail

7 Wildlife Express Train

rafiki's planet watch

8 Conservation Station

9 Affection Section

10 Habitat Habit!

asia

11 Flights of Wonder

12 Maharajah Jungle Trek

13 Kali River Rapids

14 Rivers of Light (opening 2016)

15 Expedition Everest

dinoland u.s.a.

16 Finding Nemo – The Musical

17 The Boneyard

18 TriceraTop Spin

19 Primeval Whirl

20 Cretaceous Trail

21 DINOSAUR

22 Dino-Sue T Rex

★ After disembarking, study the photo monitors.

Clue 15: Earn bonus points if you find a Hidden Mickey in the ride photos.
4 bonus points

Clue 16: Find a small classic Mickey made of gold balls in the gift shop at the ride exit.
3 points

Clue 17: Look around the gift shop for classic Mickey circles on a brown chest.
3 points for one or more

Clue 18: Admire a Hidden Mickey on a yellow flower near the ceiling.
4 points

Clue 19: Search outside, near the Serka Zong Bazaar shop, for a classic Mickey.
3 points

Clue 20: In either the Single Rider or the FastPass+ queue, find a Hidden Mickey on a lantern.
4 points

Clue 21: Locate a cloud Hidden Mickey outside on a truck.
4 points

Clue 22: Now walk around to spot a classic Mickey in camp supplies near a post.
3 points

★ Stroll to Africa at your FastPass+ time to enjoy riding **Kilimanjaro Safaris**.

Clue 23: Along the queue, watch a video monitor for spots on a leopard.
5 points

Clue 24: Observe the island in the flamingo pond.
4 points

Clue 25: Near the lions, watch for Donald in the rocks.
4 points

Clue 26: Locate a Hidden Mickey on a drink cart as you exit from Kilimanjaro Safaris.
4 points

★ Go to **Kali River Rapids** in Asia and find a classic Mickey formed by plates on the wall of one of the rooms you pass through on your way to the ride. (You can exit when you get to the loading dock if you don't want to ride. Ask a Cast Member to point the way out.)

Clue 27: You're getting close when you see stone statues in the grass.
2 points

★ Visit **DINOSAUR** next. Go back through Discovery Island and then follow the walkway into DinoLand U.S.A. Find Hidden Mickeys on paintings just inside the *DINOSAUR* building.

Clue 28: Mickey is on a tree trunk.
4 points

Clue 29: Look for Mickey ears above a dinosaur.
3 points

Clue 30: After the ride begins, be alert for a Hidden Mickey on a greaseboard. (Note: This Mickey image changes locations and even disappears at times.)
4 bonus points

Clue 31: Find a classic Mickey on the red dinosaur in the mural behind the counter in the ride's photo-purchase area.
4 points

★ Walk into the queue for **It's Tough to be a Bug!** on Discovery Island.

Clue 32: When you get inside *The Tree of Life*, look for Mickey above the handicapped entrance doors.
4 points

★ Stroll over to the **Maharajah Jungle Trek**. At the tiger exhibit area, find seven classic Hidden Mickeys in the building with arches.

Clue 33: Check in the water in the painting to the right of the first arch.
2 points

Clue 34: Look for the earring Mickey on the left mural inside the first arch.
2 points

Clue 35: Find a leaf Mickey on the left mural inside the first arch.
2 points

Clue 36: Search the right mural inside the first arch for a Hidden Mickey on a man.
2 points

Clue 37: Inside the building with arches, on the right wall, check the flowers on two square panels to find classic Mickeys.
2 points for one or more

Clue 38: Look for a classic Mickey in the mountains inside the second arch.
2 points

Clue 39: Now find a classic Mickey in the cloud formation inside the same arch.
2 points

Clue 40: After you exit the temple ruins, search for two Hidden Mickeys in the leaves to your left.
8 points for spotting both

Clue 41: Scan the huge mural on the left outdoor wall at the Elds Deer Exhibit for a classic Hidden Mickey in orange flowers.
5 points

Clue 42: Further along the trail, before you get to the aviary entrance, try to spot a classic Mickey in a man's necklace in a carving on the wall.
2 points

Clue 43: On another carving, locate a Hidden Mickey on an ear.
2 points

★ Eat an early lunch to avoid the crowds. The Rainforest Cafe at the park entrance is a good place to eat and has an interesting ambiance.

★ Before or after lunch, wander over to the **Pangani Forest Exploration Trail** in

Africa. Look for two Hidden Mickeys in the building with the Naked Mole Rat exhibit.

Clue 44: Find Mickey on a small box. (Note: At times, this box is moved around and may even disappear.)
4 bonus points

Clue 45: Spot a backpack with a Mickey emblem.
3 points

Clue 46: Past the gorilla viewing area, search for a Hidden Jafar.
5 points

★ Be aware of your FastPass+ times for *Finding Nemo –The Musical* and *Festival of the Lion King*.

★ See **Finding Nemo–The Musical** at Theater in the Wild in DinoLand.

Clue 47: Look around for a Hidden Mickey near the stage.
3 points

Clue 48: Find two Hidden Mickeys in the show-time signs outside.
4 points for spotting both

★ Go to Africa and see **Festival of the Lion King**.

Clue 49: Be alert for an upright classic Mickey on Timon the meerkat's float.
4 points

Clue 50: Now search for an upside-down classic Mickey on Timon's float.
4 points

Clue 51: Study the center stage for a classic Mickey.
4 points

Tip: If Timon's float and the props are still there after the show has ended, you can look for the Hidden Mickeys in Clues 49 to 51 as you exit. If you need help, ask a Cast Member.

★ Take the *Wildlife Express Train* to Rafiki's Planet Watch to search **Conservation Station** for a Hidden Mickey bonanza.

Clue 52: Look at the mosaic in the pavement outside the main entrance to *Conservation Station* for a tiny classic Mickey.
4 points

Clue 53: Find the Hidden Mickey profile in the changing, repeating panels inside the entrance.
4 points

Clue 54: On the wall mural just to the right, spot a Mickey Mouse profile on an opossum.
4 points

Clue 55: Look for a butterfly wearing classic Mickeys.
3 points

Clue 56: Gaze closely at a spider nearby with a classic Mickey marking.
3 points

Clue 57: Spot a classic Mickey on an ostrich.
3 points

Clue 58: Look for a classic Mickey on a green snake.
3 points

Clue 59: Search for another classic Mickey on a lizard's ear.
4 points

Clue 60: Locate a side-profile Mickey on a hippo.
4 points

Clue 61: Glance at a llama for a classic Mickey.
3 points

Clue 62: A squirrel nearby sports a classic Mickey.
3 points

Clue 63: Look for a classic Mickey on an alligator.
3 points

Clue 64: Find a frog bearing a tiny image of Mickey's face.
5 points

Clue 65: Scan a walrus for a Hidden Mickey.
4 points

Clue 66: Find the Hidden Mickey on an owl.
3 points

Clue 67: Search for the amazing Mickey image on a second butterfly!
5 points

Clue 68: Look up for a classic Mickey on a frog behind a monkey.
5 points

Clue 69: Scan the mural for a fish with a partially hidden classic Mickey.
5 points

Clue 70: Locate a butterfly with two Hidden Mickeys.
4 points for both

Clue 71: Look around carefully for a frog with a side-profile Mickey.
5 points

Clue 72: Find a yellow butterfly with a classic Mickey.
3 points

Clue 73: Look lower for a chameleon with Mickey spots.
3 points

Clue 74: Admire this chameleon a bit longer so you don't overlook another Hidden Mickey!
4 points

Clue 75: Scan overhead for a Mickey in tree leaves.
3 points

Clue 76: Next to the "Song of the Rainforest" area, spot a fly with a tiny classic Mickey on its back.
5 points

Clue 77: Search for a tiny flower Hidden Mickey at the first entrance to the "Song of the Rainforest" area.
4 points

Clue 78: Look for a classic Mickey indentation on a tree toward the front of the Rainforest area.
3 points

Clue 79: Don't stray far for a Mickey hole in a leaf.
4 points

Clue 80: Check the trees inside the Rainforest area for a side-profile Mickey shadow.
4 points

Clue 81: Look for the classic Mickey shadow on the ceiling near door number eight in the "Song of the Rainforest" area.
4 points

Clue 82: Now find a Hidden Mickey on a tree near door number six.
3 points

Clue 83: Search for a green moss side-profile Mickey in the Rainforest area.
4 points

Clue 84: Walk out to the front of the Rainforest area and search for a side-profile Mickey.
4 points

Clue 85: Spot a classic Mickey made of short plant stalks on the Grandmother Willow tree.
3 points

Clue 86: Also in the Rainforest area, spot a classic Mickey on a cockroach.
4 points

Clue 87: Now find a classic Mickey on a lizard on the same tree.
3 points

Clue 88: Stay with this tree and admire a berry Hidden Mickey.
4 points

Clue 89: Look for a butterfly wearing a tiny Hidden Mickey on this tree.
5 points

Clue 90: Examine the grates around the bottoms of the trees in the main lobby.
2 points

Clue 91: Locate a Hidden Mickey on a plate in a window display at the rear of the lobby.
3 points

Clue 92: Spot a reptile classic Mickey on a ledge in the rear area displays and laboratories.
3 points

★ Walk outside to **Affection Section** to spot another classic Hidden Mickey.

Clue 93: Study the animals in the petting zoo. (Note: These Hidden Mickeys come and go.)
4 bonus points

★ Wander on over to the **Wildlife Express Train station** and look for classic Mickeys.

Clue 94: Examine the rafters inside the station.
2 points

★ Ride the train to Africa, then explore the area around **Harambe Fruit Market** to spot a large Mickey Mouse head in the cement.

Clue 95: Check the beginning of the cement and flagstone path at the side of the Fruit Market.
4 points

Clue 96: Turn left at the opposite end of the path and follow the cement walkway a few feet to find a large, faint classic Mickey in the cement.
5 points

★ Outside the **Mombasa Marketplace** store, look for a classic Mickey formed by a small utility cover and the pebbles adjacent to it.

Clue 97: It's near an entrance door to the store.
5 points

★ Stroll inside **Tusker House Restaurant**.

Clue 98: Locate a classic Mickey on an Assignment Board on a wall.
4 points

★ Go to the far side of **Tamu Tamu Refreshments**.

Clue 99: Find another classic Mickey formed by a small utility cover and adjacent pebbles.
5 points

Clue 100: Marvel at a Hidden Baloo the bear inside the small seating area behind Tamu Tamu Refreshments.
5 points

Clue 101: Search for another Hidden Character here.
4 points

★ Walk a short way down the **path to Asia**.

Clue 102: Look over to *The Tree of Life* and spot the Hidden Mickey on it. (Psst! It's near the hippo.)
4 points

★ Cross the bridge from Africa to Discovery Island and amble on into **Pizzafari** restaurant to find six Hidden Mickeys.

Clue 103: Spot Mickey in the room across from the food order counters.
3 points

Clue 104: In the first dining room to the left as you walk down the hall, search for a tiny orange classic Mickey.
5 points

Clue 105: In the Nocturnal Room (the dining room directly to the left of the food counters as you face the counters), study the firefly wings.
3 points

Clue 106: In the Nocturnal Room, look around for a classic Mickey in the trees.
4 points

Clue 107: In the large room past the Nocturnal Room, find some spots on the wall in the tree branches.
3 points

Clue 108: Study an animal near these tree branches for a classic Mickey.
2 points

★ Return to DinoLand U.S.A. Enter **The Boneyard** and find two classic Mickeys.

Clue 109: Walk upstairs. Go to the rear and observe the small classic Mickey in an archeology display.
2 points

Clue 110 Look around the children's dig area for Hidden Mickey hard hats.
2 points

★ Walk to the **Cretaceous Trail** in the middle of DinoLand and go dino hunting.

Clue 111: Find a dark Mickey on a dinosaur's back.
3 points

★ Go to **TriceraTop Spin**.

Clue 112: Search in front of the attraction for a classic Mickey on a dinosaur with a ball.
3 points

Clue 113: Spot a classic Mickey in one of the parking spaces near the attraction.
3 points

Clue 114: Study the nearby horned dinosaur studded with gems and find a Mickey pin.
4 points

★ Check inside **Chester & Hester's Dinosaur Treasures** shop.

Clue 115: Find a marionette Mickey in the shop.
2 points

Clue 116: Study the pavement outside the store entrance that faces *Primeval Whirl* for a classic Mickey.
5 points

★ Cross back to **Primeval Whirl** and look for classic Mickeys on the outside of the attraction.

Clue 117: Check the meteors.
5 points for two or more

★ Walk along the outer walkway **behind the Fossil Fun Games area**.

Clue 118: Check out the fence signs for a classic Hidden Mickey.
3 points

★ Walk to the **Creature Comforts** shop on Discovery Island between Pizzafari restaurant and the bridge to Africa.

Clue 119: Search inside Creature Comforts for black classic Mickeys on creatures.
5 points for finding two or more Hidden Mickeys on two creatures.

★ Enter the **Island Mercantile** shop.

Clue 120: Look for three classic Mickeys made of spots.
5 points for all three

★ Back outside on **Discovery Island**, find a classic Mickey made of green moss.

Clue 121: Study the front of *The Tree of Life*.
5 points

★ Step inside the **Disney Outfitters** shop.

Clue 122: Locate a Hidden Mickey in a constellation high on a wall.
5 points

★ Stroll to the **Flame Tree Barbecue Restaurant** to find two classic Mickeys.

Clue 123: Search the ground in the food order area for a rock classic Mickey.
4 points

Clue 124: Now find a classic Mickey in the seating area outside.
2 points

★ Go to the **Rainforest Cafe entrance sign** inside the park.

Clue 125: Look for a Hidden Mickey on the sign.
3 points

★ Keep your eyes open **as you leave the park**.

Clue 126: Search the outside walls of the ticket booths for Hidden Mickeys.
4 points for two

Clue 127: Outside the entrance turnstiles, check the metal grates around some of the trees near the tram loading area.
2 points

Now turn the page and tally your score.

Total Points for
Disney's Animal Kingdom =

How'd you do?

Up to 179 points – Bronze
180 to 357 points – Silver
358 points and over – Gold
448 points – Perfect Score

You may have done even better if you earned bonus points in *Expedition Everest, DINOSAUR, Pangani Forest Exploration Trail*, and/or *Affection Section*.

**Caution:
Don't peek at this
section unless you
really want help!**

Asia

– Expedition Everest

Note: Hints 1 through 13 apply to Hidden Mickeys you'll find in the Standby queue. The Hidden Mickey in Hint 20 can only be spotted from the Single Rider and FastPass+ queues.

Hint 1: A classic Mickey made of a central circle with swirls for ears hides in the base of a Yeti statue. You'll find it in a sunken outdoor courtyard past the first room (an office).

Hint 2: Just past the first room, a classic Mickey is formed by shallow depressions in the left wall of a small red building. The upright image is at the far left lower corner of the wall, below and to the left of a small curved drainpipe.

Hint 3: On the rear wall of the same red building just past the first room, classic Mickeys lie in the clouds on the left and right sides of a Yeti mural.

Hint 4: As you enter the second building (Tashi's Trek and Tongba Shop), an upside-down classic Mickey is formed by the highest pipes on the top shelf in the right corner.

Hint 5: Along the far wall of Tashi's Trek and Tongba Shop, a small white Yeti doll on the top right shelf inside a cupboard wears black Mickey ears.

Hint 6: In Tashi's Trek and Tongba Shop, light-switch devices in a glass case on the left side of the queue form a classic Mickey.

Hint 7: Inside the Yeti Museum, on the right side of the queue after the first left turn, look for a Yeti book at the far left of the book display. A partial image of Mickey's head and ears is imprinted in the snow on the book's front cover.

Hint 8: Just past the snow Mickey of Hint 7, a classic Mickey is etched into the top of a wooden handrail.

Hint 9: Dents in a kettle in the Yeti Museum's second display form a classic Mickey.

Hint 10: Also in the museum a classic Mickey is hiding in an "animal track." It's at the lower left of a tall glass cabinet in a display labeled "Documenting Bio-Diversity." Look near the top of the third paper from the left, above the label "Small Mammal Tracks."

Hint 11: The next-to-last display cabinet in the museum has a photo of a bear with ears that look like Mickey's ears. The bear is on the right side of the cabinet, under the words "The Yeti, Interpreting the Findings."

Hint 12: In the last room before boarding, look for a photo of a woman in blue listening to a hand-held radio. Mickey in his Sorcerer's Hat is etched on a wall to the woman's left.

Hint 13: Outside in the loading area, look for a classic Mickey in the blue scrollwork above the first window. (You can see this Hidden Mickey from both the FastPass+ and Standby queues.)

Hint 14: In the first part of the ride, as your train is climbing the mountain, a dark, melted classic Mickey-shaped spot appears in the snow to your left. The "ear" farthest away from the train is contiguous with a larger dark spot above it.

Hint 15: The ride photos from various WDW attractions often include Hidden Mickeys. Check the photos on the monitors at the unloading area. A small white classic Hidden Mickey may be present on the ground to the left of the ride vehicle.

Hint 16: Small gold balls form classic Mickeys at the bottom of both sides of a merchandise display in the middle of the gift shop at the ride exit. The display is across from the photo pickup area.

Hint 17: Brown chests sit on an upper shelf of a merchandise cabinet at the right side of the gift shop's right exit door (as you exit the ride). Circles along the front and sides of the lower chest form several classic Mickeys. One is at the middle bottom of the left front. It's tilted to the left.

Hint 18: Find a yellow flower at the top center of this same merchandise cabinet (at the right side of the right exit door). A petal at the seven o'clock position on the flower forms a classic Mickey.

Hint 19: Outside and across from the Serka Zong Bazaar shop, an upside-down classic Mickey is etched near the top of the second stone tablet from the edge closest to the shop.

Hint 20: In the Yeti Museum as seen from both the FastPass+ and Single Rider queues, a sideways classic Mickey is formed by three dents in a lantern in the second glassed-in display. (Note: You cannot spot this lantern image from the Standby queue.)

Hint 21: At the front of the left side of the Anandapur Ice Cream Truck, look for a painting with two towers. A classic Hidden Mickey, tilted to the left, hides in the clouds at the upper right of the painting. (Note: the images on this truck change from time to time.)

Hint 22: Outside the attraction, base camp supplies hang in the Gupta's Gear area. A three-circle image hangs among these supplies, near the second post from the end nearest the restrooms.

Africa

– Kilimanjaro Safaris

Hint 23: Near the end of the entrance queue, just before you reach the final loading dock, a monitor above you shows a continuous video loop. Look for the resting orange-and-white leopard with black spots. Three spots on white fur form a classic Mickey on the left side (your right) of the leopard's neck.

Hint 24: In elephant country, and about halfway through the ride, the island in the flamingo pond is shaped like a classic Hidden Mickey. It's to the left of your ride vehicle.

Hint 25: The rocks in the lion area are arranged to resemble Donald Duck. Spot his cap first, then his face, eyes, and beak. (Note: These rocks have shifted positions slightly over time.)

Hint 26: Walk to a cashier's cart at the end of the exit path from *Kilimanjaro Safaris* and not far from the entrance to the *Pangani Forest Exploration Trail*. A Hidden Mickey is on a tile on the top (not the side or front) of the counter of the drink and merchandise cart. Small ceramic circles (a white and blue "head" and two black "ears") stuck in the surface of the cart form a classic Hidden Mickey.

Asia

– Kali River Rapids

Hint 27: Along the entrance queue, keep your eyes peeled for stone statues in the grass. As you enter the next room, look at the lower left corner of the wall. Three of the plates on the wall above the bicycle form

a classic Mickey, tilted down to the right. (Note: These images change from time to time.)

DinoLand U.S.A.

– DINOSAUR

Hint 28: Just inside the building entrance, on the right side of the queue, look at the tree at the far left of the painting. There is a classic Mickey on the tree trunk; it's across from a lower right branch.

Hint 29: In a painting on the wall that you face before you take the first right turn in the entrance queue, you can spot classic Mickey ears along the left side of the reddish explosion cloud above the middle dinosaur.

Hint 30: Just as the ride starts and before you travel back in time, a classic Mickey at the lower left corner of a white greaseboard appears to the left of your vehicle. (This Mickey image changes locations and even disappears at times.)

Hint 31: On the mural behind the counter in the ride's photo-purchase area, a large red dinosaur has a small classic Mickey on its lower neck.

Discovery Island

– It's Tough to be a Bug!

Hint 32: Inside *The Tree of Life*, look for the handi-capped entrance doors to *It's Tough to be a Bug!* (You reach them before you get to the main en-trance doors to the theater.) Look at the upper left area near the doors—and just to the right of the "Cast Members Only" door—to find a small dark classic Mickey.

Asia

– Maharajah Jungle Trek

Hint 33: To the right of the first arch, swirls in the water under a tiger form a classic Mickey.

175

Hint 34: Inside the first arch, on the left mural, the king's gold earring forms an upside-down classic Mickey.

Hint 35: Inside the first arch, on the left mural, three leaves under the wrist of the king's extended arm form a classic Mickey.

Hint 36: Inside the first arch, on the right mural, a man is wearing an upside-down classic Mickey gold earring.

Hint 37: On the right wall inside the building with arches, two square panels are decorated with flowers. Some of the outer flowers have circles at the bases of their petals that form classic Mickeys.

Hint 38: Inside the second arch, on the left mural, there's a small classic Mickey in a brown rock formation on the left side of the mountains.

Hint 39: Inside the second arch, on the right mural, a classic Mickey appears in the upper part of the left cloud formation.

Hint 40: As you exit the temple ruins, turn to your immediate left to a large wall mural. Among the leaves is a dark green classic Mickey. It's about nine feet above the ground and one foot from the bricks at the left side of the mural. Another even darker green classic Mickey is further to the right on this mural. It's above the tiger running toward the left, and between two large, light green fan-shaped leaves.

Hint 41: In the Elds Deer Exhibit, look left to the huge outdoor mural. Mickey is hiding in the right center of the mural, below the third (from the left) of four vertical brick cracks, in some orange flowers and green leaves.

Hint 42: On a wall to the right, just before you reach the aviary entrance, you can spot an upside-down down classic Mickey in the necklace of a man in the middle carving.

Hint 43: On the wall carving to the left of the above Hidden Mickey, an earring on a crouching man (his right ear—on the left as you face the man) forms a classic Hidden Mickey.

Africa

– Pangani Forest Exploration Trail

Hint 44: To the left of the entrance to the building with the Naked Mole Rat Exhibit, a small box of Asepso soap on a desk near a lamp has a classic Mickey as the "o" in "Asepso." (Note: At times this box is moved around and may even disappear.)

Hint 45: In the far left corner of the room with the Naked Mole Rat Exhibit, the left side of a back-pack sports a small classic Mickey emblem.

Hint 46: A three-dimensional head of Jafar is carved out of a 25- to 30-foot rock. You'll find it past the gorilla viewing area, to the right of the first section of the first suspension bridge.

DinoLand U.S.A.

– Finding Nemo–The Musical

Hint 47: Three bubbles touch to form a classic Mickey at the lower left of the stage.

Hint 48: Two sideways classic Mickeys formed by bubbles hide in each of the two outdoor signs announcing the show times for the day. One is in the bottom right corner of the signs and the other is under the 1:00 time disk. These signs are posted on both the walkway from Asia and the walkway from the rest of DinoLand U.S.A.

Africa

– Festival of the Lion King

Hint 49: A white classic Mickey is painted on the lower middle front of Timon's (and the giraffe's) float. You can see it as the float enters the arena.

Hint 50: An upside-down white classic Mickey is on the lower right side of Timon's float, under the giraffe's front leg.

Hint 51: A classic Mickey in relief is on the lower side of the movable center stage, to the right of some steps. It is usually facing the Elephant section of the audience.

Rafiki's Planet Watch

– Conservation Station

Hint 52: A classic Mickey made of circles (two dark and one light) hides in the circular mosaic in the pavement right outside the main entrance to *Conservation Station*. Mickey is above the second "T" in "Station" and below the elephant's trunk.

Hint 53: The front wall facing you as you enter the building has a section of changing, repeating panels. A small side profile of Mickey Mouse is in the center of the orange starfish.

Hint 54: Find an opossum on the right side of the mural just inside the entrance. There is a side profile of Mickey Mouse in its eye.

Hint 55: Above the opossum, at the upper right, a butterfly has classic Mickeys on its wings.

Hint 56: About six feet up from the floor, not far from the opossum, a spider has a light pink classic Mickey marking on its thorax.

Hint 57: On the wall to the left of the restrooms, near the entrance, the pupil of an ostrich's eye is a classic Mickey.

Hint 58: Toward the middle of the mural at the front, near the entrance, a green snake sports a black classic Mickey on its upper back.

Hint 59: Near the upper right border of the changing screen, a dark classic Mickey marking is at the top of a green lizard's ear, above a deer.

Hint 60: A hippopotamus is the fifth animal from the left at the bottom of the entrance mural on the left wall. A side-profile Mickey is on its lower jaw, under the middle tooth.

Hint 61: To the immediate left of the hippopotamus, a llama sports a dark brown classic Mickey on its neck.

Hint 62: Under the hippopotamus, a squirrel's eye has a black classic Mickey pupil.

Hint 63: On the hippo's right side, an alligator has a small dark classic Mickey to the left of its green eye.

Hint 64: To the right of the alligator, Mickey Mouse's smiling face is under a frog's right eye.

Hint 65: Directly above the frog with the smiling Mickey is a walrus with a dark classic Mickey on the left side (your right) of his neck.

Hint 66: A bit farther along on this left wall mural, the pupils of an owl's eyes are classic Mickeys.

Hint 67: The entrance murals curve toward the inside of the building. On the right curving mural, look closely for the butterfly with an image of Mickey's face on its body (not on its wings!).

Hint 68: Midway along the right curving mural, high up near the ceiling, a classic Mickey-shaped marking is on the white skin of the chin under the middle of a frog's face. The frog is behind a red-faced monkey.

Hint 69: Toward the top and near the end of the left side of the entrance mural, a dark classic Mickey, partially hidden by an octopus nearby, is on the side of a fish, to the left of the fish's fin.

Hint 70: Along the bottom of the right mural as you near Rafiki's Theater, two black classic Mickeys are near the bottom of the wings of an orange butterfly under a monkey.

Hint 71: Near the bottom of the same mural, just before the theater, a side-profile Mickey is in a silver frog's left pupil.

Hint 72: Before the first entrance to the "Song of the Rainforest" area, about halfway up the wall and above a bat, a yellow butterfly has a black classic Mickey on its left wing.

Hint 73: In the same area, a tan and green chameleon has a group of spots directly behind the eye that form an upside-down classic Mickey.

Hint 74: This same chameleon sports a small dark classic Mickey behind the neck and just above the front leg. It's at about the same level as the upside-down Hidden Mickey described above.

Hint 75: A hole in the tree leaves overhead resembles a classic Mickey. It's directly above the first entrance.

Hint 76: The fly with a tiny classic Mickey on its back is on the left panel of the first entrance to the "Song of the Rainforest" area.

Hint 77: On the same panel, a tiny yellow-flower classic Mickey blooms on a green plant near the floor.

Hint 78: Turn to the right panel at the same entrance to the Rainforest area to see a classic Mickey indentation on a tree. It's about four feet up from the floor.

Hint 79: Look for a classic Mickey hole in a green leaf near the Mickey indentation in Hint 78.

Hint 80: Now go inside to see a side-profile Mickey shadow about seven feet up from the floor on the front of a tree inside the Rainforest area.

Hint 81: Above and in front of door number eight in the Rainforest area, you can spot a dark classic Mickey shadow on the ceiling to the right.

Hint 82: A white classic Mickey is outlined on a tree by door number six, to the left of the words "The Accidental Florist."

Hint 83: Turn around and walk out toward the lobby to look at the right side of the tree with "The Song of the Rainforest" sign (the Grandmother Willow tree). A rear horizontal panel has a green moss side-profile Mickey about six feet up from the floor.

Hint 84: A side-profile Mickey indentation appears on the same tree under the sign and to the lower right (as you face her) of Grandmother Willow's face. (Tip: You have to walk farther into the lobby to spot it.)

Hint 85: Three plant stalks form a classic Mickey in the mural near the floor on the bottom left of the Grandmother Willow tree (as you face it from the lobby).

Hint 86: To the right of the Grandmother Willow tree, there is a cockroach display inside a tree in front of the "Song of the Rainforest" area. A cockroach inside and toward the back of the tree bears a dark classic Mickey on its back.

Hint 87: A lizard above the "Giant Cockroach" sign on the same tree has a classic Mickey above its front leg.

Hint 88: On the right front side of this tree, locate a long strand of red berries. The three berries at the very bottom of the strand form a classic Mickey.

Hint 89: On the left front of the tree with the cockroach display, a light brown butterfly about six and a half feet up from the floor has a tiny black classic Mickey on its back between the wings.

Hint 90: The grates around the bottoms of the trees in the lobby have classic Mickey patterns, as do those outside by *Affection Section*.

Hint 91: A classic Mickey on a "Microtiter Plate" is usually in the first display room to the right in the rear of the lobby. Look into the second window of the "Wildlife Tracking Center." The plate changes color as you watch it!

Hint 92: A classic Mickey made of three containers with reptile skins is on a ledge in the far left window of a room with reptiles.

– Affection Section

Hint 93: One of the animals usually has a classic Mickey shaved into its coat.

– Wildlife Express Train station

Hint 94: High up in the rafters inside the train station, look for classic Mickeys where the beams intersect.

Africa

– In and around Harambe

Hint 95: At one side of the Harambe Fruit Market, a short cement and flagstone path with benches leads through some trees. A large Mickey Mouse head in the cement marks the beginning of the path. It's several feet in diameter.

Hint 96: At the opposite end of this short path, turn left onto the cement walkway and walk a few feet. Nearby you'll find a faint depression in the cement that forms a very large classic Mickey (six feet or more in diameter). This Hidden Mickey is best seen after a rain when the pavement is wet. It is often partially covered with parked strollers.

Hint 97: Outside, near an entrance door to the Mombasa Marketplace store, you'll find a classic Mickey formed by a small utility cover (with the letter "D" in the middle) and the pebbles adjacent to it. The cover is on the path, on the side facing the Tusker House Restaurant.

Hint 98: In Tusker House Restaurant, walk to a small dining room on the left side of

the hallway to the restrooms. A classic Mickey is formed by one of the magnets on an Assignment Board on a wall inside the room.

Hint 99: Near Tamu Tamu Refreshments, on the walkway that connects Africa and Asia, a small utility cover and the pebbles adjacent to it form a classic Mickey. Here, the utility cover has the letter "S" in the middle.

Hint 100: Inside the small seating area behind Tamu Tamu Refreshments, a white Hidden Baloo (the bear) is on the wall nearest the path to Asia. He's often covered by a curtain.

Hint 101: Also inside the small seating area behind Tamu Tamu Refreshments, a Hidden Scar (the lion) is formed by the exposed brown brick on a corner wall and under a vase in a recessed opening.

Hint 102: On the back of *The Tree of Life*, and visible from the path between Africa and Asia, is an upside-down classic Mickey. Look above the eye of the hippopotamus to spot him.

Discovery Island

– *Pizzafari restaurant*

Hint 103: A yellow classic Mickey image is under a bat, which is on a wall in the seating area across from the food order counters. As you enter the room, turn left to face the rear wall and look for the bat on the right.

Hint 104: On the rear wall of the first dining room to the left (as you walk down the hall away from the food order area), a tiny orange classic Mickey is at the lower left of a turtle shell.

Hint 105: On the left rear wall of the Nocturnal Room (the dining room directly to the left of the food counters as you face the counters), the wings of the lower left firefly resemble Mickey Mouse ears.

Hint 106: In the same room, a classic Mickey made of tree leaves lies near a reddish raccoon. It's tilted with the "ears" to the left as you face the wall.

Hint 107: In the large room just past the Nocturnal Room, a gray spot with two white ears on the far wall forms a classic Mickey in the tree branches, to the right of the leopard.

Hint 108: On this same wall, a classic Mickey formed by black spots is directly behind the middle of the leopard's front leg.

DinoLand U.S.A.

– The Boneyard

Hint 109: Upstairs to the rear left, in a fenced off archeology display, three coins on a table form a classic Mickey.

Hint 110: On the right side of the children's dig area, in a small display, a fan and two hard hats form a classic Mickey.

– Cretaceous Trail

Hint 111: At one end of this short trail in the middle of Dinoland, you'll find a large dinosaur. Three dark spots on its middle back form a classic Mickey.

– TriceraTop Spin

Hint 112: In front of *TriceraTop Spin*, a green dinosaur balances a red and yellow striped ball on its horns. A classic Mickey is formed in the scales on the dino's right side, under the front horn.

Hint 113: In the parking spaces across from *TriceraTop Spin*, a classic Mickey can be found in the cement at the front of the second parking space from the horned dinosaur.

Hint 114: On the right side of the horned dinosaur (as you face it), a gold "Steam-

boat Willie" Cast Member pin is located on a spine on the dinosaur's upper back, near a large silver medallion.

– Chester & Hester's Dinosaur Treasures shop

Hint 115: Inside, near the middle of the shop, look up to see a Mickey Mouse marionette.

Hint 116: In front of the store, near the restrooms, a tiny orange image is embedded in the cement a few feet to the right of the leftmost post (as you face the store with your back to *Primeval Whirl*).

– Primeval Whirl

Hint 117: In the outside decorations, the sides of three meteors sport classic Mickey craters:
- One is under "Head for the Hills."
- Another is over the "Primeval Whirl" sign at the entrance to the attraction.
- The third *Primeval Whirl* classic Mickey crater is on the right side of the attraction near a dinosaur holding a sign.

– Behind Fossil Fun Games

Hint 118: Along the outer walkway behind the *Fossil Fun Games* area, look for a sign on the fence that says "Games of Chance." An upside-down classic Mickey made of gold spots lies on the upper left thigh of the blue dinosaur, on the right side of the sign.

Discovery Island

– Creature Comforts shop

Hint 119: Black classic Mickeys are on the backs of the large beetles that decorate some of the store's merchandise stands. One is on the mid left of a beetle under a zebra. Another beetle on the lower part of a stand (usually found at the rear of the store) has a classic Mickey on each of its wings.

- Island Mercantile shop

Hint 120: Three classic Mickeys made of spots hide on two orange and blue bumblebee honeycombs on posts inside the shop. These posts are along a rear wall opposite the entrance doors closest to the walkway to the Oasis. Two classic Mickeys are on the honeycomb on the right as you face the rear wall. Find the bee inside a hexagon at the upper center of the honeycomb. One Hidden Mickey is in the hexagon adjacent to the bee at the upper right, and a second Hidden Mickey is one hexagon away to the lower left of the bee. A third classic Mickey hides on the left honeycomb, three hexagons away from the central bee, counting down and to the right. Collections of spots in other hexagons on the honeycombs may also resemble the classic Mickey shape, but these three images are the best proportioned.

- The Tree of Life

Hint 121: On the front of *The Tree of Life*, facing the Oasis and about one-third the distance up the tree trunk from the bottom, is a classic Mickey made of green moss. You'll find it to the left of the buffalo. (This Hidden Mickey is becoming more distorted over time.)

- Disney Outfitters shop

Hint 122: At the far left room of the shop, look for the group of constellations above an inside doorway. One of the constellations (on the right side of the group and near the dolphin) has three stars with round gems in their centers that form a Hidden Mickey. This Hidden Mickey is more convincing when you're looking up at it than it is in photos taken straight on.

- Flame Tree Barbecue Restaurant

Hint 123: In the food order area, rocks embedded in the ground form a classic Mickey at the front edge of the rock border and next to the second post from the right wall.

Hint 124: At the outside seating area behind the food order counters, grates on the ground near trees have classic Mickey circles. Find them near the first set of tables to the right, where there is a statue of a frog holding up a pig. These grates can also be found in other areas nearby.

Oasis

– Rainforest Cafe

Hint 125: A green lizard at the Rainforest Cafe entrance sign that is inside the park has an upside-down classic Mickey in the middle of the circles on its neck.

Outside the entrance turnstiles to the park

Hint 126: When you head out of the park, turn back as you pass the ticket booths. You'll find two rock classic Mickeys, one on the right-hand lower corner of the wall of the rightmost ticket booth and the other in the wall of the leftmost ticket booth near the ground and toward the front of the booth's left side wall.

Hint 127: Outside the entrance turnstiles, near the tram loading area, the metal grates at the bases of some of the trees incorporate classic Mickeys in their design.

Resort Hotel Scavenger Hunt

• •

Walt Disney World's resort hotels are filled with Mickeys, hidden and otherwise. The majority are what I like to call décor Mickeys, imaginative decorations that vary among the hotels and change periodically over time. Hidden and décor Mickeys can be found along hotel hallways in the carpet, wallpaper, and lampshades. They appear in the guestrooms on covers for drinking glasses, bedspreads, pillows, day beds, furniture, lamps, lampshades, room curtains, shower curtains, wall pictures, wallpaper, carpets, soap, the outer wrapping of toilet paper rolls, and other items. The housekeeping staff sometimes creates Mickey images out of towels on the bed or elsewhere in your room for you to enjoy upon your return! Guest laundry rooms sometimes have Hidden Mickeys on the soap vending machines and in the bubbles on wall paintings, and resort laundry bins and carts show off classic and side-profile Mickeys.

In the restaurants, pancakes, waffles, butter pats, pasta, pizza, pepperoni on the pizza, and the arrangement of dishes and condiments, among other items, are sometimes Mickey-shaped. Sample menu displays in food order areas often have food items arranged to form classic Mickeys. Mugs, paper plates, and other items in the gift shops can sport Mickeys. Even the utilities embrace Mickey. Manhole covers and survey markers throughout Walt Disney World often have classic Mickey designs in the center.

Generally, I do not include décor Mickeys in the scavenger hunts unless they are truly unique (as many of the carpet Mickeys are) and are easily accessible to Hidden Mickey hunters at the hotels and in other WDW areas. So don't be surprised to discover dozens of Mickeys at the hotels you visit that aren't included in this scavenger hunt. They're fun to spot but you don't get points for finding them.

189

1 All-Star Resorts
2 Animal Kingdom Lodge
3 Art of Animation
4 Beach Club
5 Blizzard Beach
6 BoardWalk
7 Caribbean Beach
8 Contemporary
9 Coronado Springs
10 Disney Springs
11 Dolphin
12 ESPN Wide World of Sports Complex
13 Fantasia Gardens Mini Golf
14 Fort Wilderness
15 Golden Oak
16 Grand Floridian
17 Lake Buena Vista Golf Course
18 The Landing, in Disney Springs

19 Magnolia Golf Course
20 Oak Trail Golf Course
21 Old Key West
22 Palm Golf Course
23 Polynesian Village
24 Pop Century
25 Port Orleans – French Quarter
26 Port Orleans – Riverside
27 Saratoga Springs
28 Shades of Green
29 Swan
30 Transportation and Ticket Center
31 Typhoon Lagoon
32 Wedding Pavilion, Disney's Fairytale
33 Wilderness Lodge
34 Winter Summerland Mini Golf
35 Yacht Club
P Parking

The best way to hunt for Hidden Mickeys at the hotels is by car. However, buses to all the WDW hotels are available from Disney Springs (the major bus depot is at the far end of the Marketplace). If you choose to bus around, be prepared for leisurely hunting. You won't be able to visit as many hotels in a given time frame as you would with a car.

Of course, driving means parking, and it's not always a slam-dunk. Guard gates stand watch at most WDW hotels. When you drive up, tell the guard that you're a Hidden Mickey freak and want to look for Hidden Mickeys at the hotel. You'll generally be greeted with a smile, an opened gate, and a wave—along with a "Good luck!" or "Go freak out!" to encourage you on your quest. In the event you aren't allowed to park, drive on to another hotel on the scavenger hunt and take transportation (bus, boat or monorail) to the one you want to explore. If you're really lucky, you may have a spouse, friend, or family member who is willing to drop you off and pick you up.

Again, be considerate of other guests and Cast Members. Ask permission to look around restaurants and avoid searching for Hidden Mickeys at meal times unless you are one of the diners. Even then be careful to stay out of the way—especially of waiters with full trays. Let others share in the fun by telling them what you are up to if they notice you looking around.

Two important notes:

1. I've arranged this hunt in a logical, efficient progression that I imagine you could follow in a car. However, you may want to hunt just one hotel or group of sister hotels at a time. That's why I list the perfect score for each resort hotel (and hotel group) in parentheses after the hotel (or group) name in the Clues section. I also list the perfect score for each of WDW's four resort areas (Animal Kingdom, Disney Springs, Epcot, and Magic Kingdom) in the Scoring section on page 219.

2. This scavenger hunt includes only those WDW resorts in which I found Hidden Mickeys. If I found no convincing (to me)

Hidden Mickeys in a hotel, I didn't include it in the hunt. Keep your eyes open; you may spot one that I haven't found (yet).

★ **Bonus Points Opportunity**. During your Hidden Mickey hunt around WDW property, pay attention to the Disney buses. You may get lucky! The Disney Cruise Line bus has a Hidden Pluto on each side of the gold scrollwork on the front of the bus between the headlights. Some general Disney transport buses sometimes sport a classic Mickey on the rear of the vehicle, usually related to rear upper or lower lights. Even more subtle are faint classic Mickey images in the windows of some buses, only visible if the lighting is just right! If you spot one or more of these images, give yourself 5 bonus points for each one.

Animal Kingdom Area Resorts
(242 points)

I'll start this scavenger hunt with the seven Animal Kingdom Area resorts (Animal Kingdom Lodge, the three All-Star Resorts, Coronado Springs, Art of Animation, and Pop Century). You can start (and stop) wherever you want. Have fun!

Animal Kingdom Lodge
(108 points*)
*includes Kidani Village points

Clue 1: Look up for a classic Mickey outside near the hotel's main entrance.
2 points

Clue 2: Find a classic Mickey on a mural between the outer and inner entrance doors to the main lobby.
2 points

Clue 3: Inside the main lobby, spot a classic Mickey on a chandelier.
3 points

Clue 4: Check the logs banded to wood supports around the main lobby. Find any classic Mickeys?
2 points

193

Clue 5: Look for a classic Mickey on the rock formation next to the short bridge on the right side of the main lobby (as you face it on entering).
4 points

Clue 6: Search the Kudu Trail at the rear of the lobby for a classic Mickey on a post.
4 points

Clue 7: Try to spot a green Hidden Mickey in side profile outside the rear doors of the main lobby. He's on the vine-covered column, on your right as you exit, and he's looking into the lobby.
5 points

Clue 8: On the trail to Arusha Rock Overlook, outside the rear exit from the main lobby, explore the decorative reliefs on the rock wall for a giraffe sporting a classic Mickey.
3 points

Clue 9: Spot another classic Mickey along the walkway in Arusha Rock Overlook.
4 points

Clue 10: Search for a classic Mickey on the rock wall as you descend the stairs from the right side of the main lobby to Boma restaurant.
4 points

Clue 11: Examine the chairs inside Boma.
2 points

Clue 12: Inside Jiko restaurant, check out the ceiling above the large oven exhausts.
2 points

Clue 13: From inside Jiko, spot a classic Mickey out the window.
5 points

Clue 14: From the path alongside the walkway to the pool's water slide, find a classic Mickey impression low on a rock.
4 points

Clue 15: Farther along this walkway, around the back of the swimming pool, look for a light-colored classic Mickey cut into the rock wall.
4 points

Clue 16: From a fence at the flamingo overlook, study the rock wall for a classic Mickey.
4 points

★ Walk back to **The Mara** and then turn and walk toward the pool.

Clue 17: On your way, look down for a classic Mickey.
5 points

Clue 18: Search the wall outside in the back of The Mara eatery seating area for a classic Mickey.
4 points

★ Now find two classic Mickeys inside The Mara food area.

Clue 19: One is on the left upper wall.
3 points

Clue 20: The other is on the right upper wall.
3 points

– *Inside the Lodge* (8 points)

Clue 21: Spot a classic Mickey in the elevator to the Fitness Center.
2 points

Clue 22: Walk around to spot some classic Mickeys in the carpet below the fifth floor as well as either on or above the fifth floor.
4 points for two or more different classic Mickeys

Clue 23: Search for Mickey near the main Zebra Trail on the third floor.
2 points

Clue 24: Go to the second floor of the Zebra Trail for a Hidden Mickey near the elevators to Simba's Cubhouse.
4 points

195

– Walk to **Kidani Village**. (27 points)

Clue 25: Look for Mickey on a clock.
4 points

Clue 26: Search high for Mickey in the lobby.
5 points

Clue 27: Spot him as you approach Sanaa restaurant.
4 points

Clue 28: Locate Mickey on a wall inside Sanaa.
3 points

Clue 29: Study Sanaa's dining tables.
3 points

Clue 30: Now leave the restaurant and find Mickey on a rock outside.
4 points

Clue 31: Stroll the hallways for carpet Mickeys.
4 points for two or more

Disney's All-Star Resorts
(15 points)

★ *All-Star Sports Resort* (6 points)

Clue 32: Go to the main building gift shop and find classic Mickeys in the carpet.
2 points for all

Clue 33: Look for classic Mickeys on a wall in the food court.
2 points

Clue 34: If you know what I (the author of this book) look like, I'm a spectator at a hockey game in the food court.
5 bonus points

Clue 35: Find the classic Mickey in the cement outdoors behind and to the right of

the registration building. (Psst! It's near the Mickey Mouse statue.)
2 points

★ *All-Star Music Resort* (5 points)

Clue 36: Examine the Jazz Inn courtyard to spot classic Mickey ears.
3 points

Clue 37: Take a look at the boots in the Country Fair area.
2 points

★ *All-Star Movies Resort* (4 points)

Clue 38: Find a classic Mickey in a display window of the gift shop.
3 points

Clue 39: Check out Andy's Room in the resort's "Toy Story" section.
1 point

Coronado Springs Resort
(38 points*)
*includes Dig Site points

Clue 40: Take a good look at the large wooden doors at the front entrance to the main lobby.
3 points

Clue 41: Search in the registration area for a spotlight Mickey.
4 bonus points

Clue 42: Look around for a statue of a bird with a Hidden Mickey.
3 points

Clue 43: Now study the wooden doors at the exit labeled El Centro.
3 points

197

Clue 44: Admire the walls of Rix Lounge for a Mickey image.
2 points

Clue 45: Walk to the hallway outside the Veracruz Exhibit Hall in the Convention Center and look around for two classic Mickeys.
4 points for spotting both

Clue 46: Examine the cement near the Marina rental gazebo.
4 points

– Around the **Dig Site** (19 points)

Clue 47: Spot a classic Mickey at the Dig Site swimming pool on a wall facing the lake.
3 points

Clue 48: Now find a classic Mickey on a wall facing the Dig Site pool.
3 points

Clue 49: Look for a whitish classic Mickey on a stone block on the Mayan pyramid at the Dig Site.
4 points

Clue 50: Spot Mickey near the Dig Site restrooms.
3 points

Clue 51: Locate a classic Mickey made of rocks in the sidewalk near Ranchos Building 6A.
4 points

Clue 52: Check the bus stop signs around the periphery of the resort.
2 points for one or more

Art of Animation Resort (36 points)

Clue 53: Look around just inside the entrance doors for furniture Mickeys.
3 points for all

Clue 54: In the food court seating area, study the light covers for Lightning McQueen.
4 points

Clue 55: Search for Mickey on the bottom of another light cover in the food court seating area.
5 points

Clue 56: Walk behind The Big Blue Pool and find Mickey inside the blue coral reef kids' play area.
5 points

Clue 57: Now face Animation Hall and head to the sidewalk to your right that borders the fence around The Big Blue Pool. Spot a Hidden Mickey on a fish.
5 points

Clue 58: Explore the Boneyard outdoors in the resort's Lion King section for a Hidden Mickey.
5 points

Clue 59: In The Little Mermaid section, locate a Hidden Mickey near a clam.
4 points

Clue 60: Check the hallway carpets of the various sections.
5 points for three or more

Pop Century Resort (45 points)

Clue 61: Search for a fishbowl with a Hidden Mickey near the check-in area.
4 points

Clue 62: Find two classic Mickeys behind the registration counter.
5 points for both

Clue 63: Look low for Hidden Mickeys at the Everything Pop Food Court.
4 points for two or more

Clue 64: Now raise your eyes up for a Mickey in the lights. (Note: It's not always there!)
5 bonus points

Clue 65: Locate Hidden Mickeys on walls in the food court.
4 points for four or more

Clue 66: In the gift shop adjoining the Everything Pop Food Court, find Hidden Mickeys on the merchandise stands.
2 points

Clue 67: Also in the gift shop, search for two classic Mickeys on the wall.
4 points for both

Clue 68: Spot a classic Mickey on a wall near the Computer Pool.
4 points

Clue 69: Now look near the Computer Pool for two Hidden Mickeys that could help you type.
2 points for both

Clue 70: Marvel at a Hidden Mickey on a wall behind Mowgli on the '60s building.
5 points

Clue 71: Find Hidden Mickeys in laundry rooms near the Hippy Dippy Pool and the Bowling Pool.
4 points for four

Clue 72: Search for Mickey's name near the Bowling Pool (and, just for fun, a reference to "Disneyland" nearby).
4 points

Clue 73: Look around for a Hidden Mickey near the bus stop out front of the Pop Century lobby.
3 points

Disney Springs Area Resorts
(146 points)

The Disney Springs area resorts with Hidden Mickeys are the Caribbean Beach, Old Key West, the Port Orleans Resorts, and Saratoga Springs Resort & Spa.

Caribbean Beach Resort (24 points)

Clue 74: Examine a group of logs in the ground between Martinique Buildings 24 and 25 for a classic Hidden Mickey.
4 points

Clue 75: Spot a classic Mickey on the lighthouse behind Old Port Royale.
2 points

Clue 76: Search for a classic Mickey in the children's water play area near the main (Old Port Royale) pool.
4 points

Clue 77: Study the rockwork of the main pool for a faint classic Mickey. (Psst! Look under a cannon.)
5 points

Clue 78: Walk around just outside the main pool to marvel at this Mickey image.
5 points

Clue 79: In Shutters restaurant, find a classic Mickey in a painting.
4 points

Old Key West Resort (23 points)

Clue 80: Check the fences inside Conch Flats General Store.
2 points

Clue 81: Take a close look at the fence railings in the registration area.
2 points

Clue 82: At the pool, spot a Mickey with a big mouth.
3 points

201

Clue 83: Find a Hidden Mickey near the steps to the water slide.
4 points

Clue 84: Notice the design of certain railings on the guest buildings outside.
2 points

★ Search for classic Mickeys formed by three shell imprints in the cement on the paths leading from parking spaces to Building 36.

Clue 85: Search the pavement on the right side of the first path for imprints.
5 points

Clue 86: On the second path, explore the corner of the sidewalk after the first right turn.
5 points
(Note: More of these amazing Mickeys may be scattered around Old Key West Resort.)

Port Orleans Resort – French Quarter (5 points)

Clue 87: Find a classic Mickey in the registration area.
3 points

Clue 88: Look up for a classic Mickey in the food court area.
2 points

Port Orleans Resort – Riverside (16 points)

Clue 89: Look for classic Mickeys in the latticework of the registration area.
2 points

Clue 90: Also in the registration area, find more classic Mickeys near the giant fans.
2 points

Clue 91: Now spot Hidden Mickeys on the fans themselves.
3 points

★ Cross the river and visit Parterre Place.

Clue 92: Find some Mickeys outside the Parterre Place building.
4 points for all

Clue 93: Amble along the sidewalk next to the river and stop in front of Acadian House. Squint your eyes to locate a Hidden Mickey on the sidewalk.
5 points

Saratoga Springs Resort & Spa (78 points)

Clue 94: Locate Mickey in the registration lobby.
2 points

Clue 95: Behind The Artist's Palette shop, look around for Mickey on a door handle.
5 points

Clue 96: Notice classic Mickeys on a jacket near The Turf Club Bar and Grill.
2 points

Clue 97: Spot Mickey on a gate.
3 points

Clue 98: Find more Mickey images inside on a wall.
2 points for one or more

Clue 99: Look around inside The Turf Club for a classic Mickey on a wall.
3 points

Clue 100: Check out a statue outside the main lobby for three pairs of Hidden Mickeys. (Note: This statue also sports a décor Mickey.)
10 points for finding all six

Clue 101: Search for two Hidden Mickeys near stairs outside The Artist's Palette.
5 points for spotting both

Clue 102: In the children's play area of the pool, find a large classic Hidden Mickey.
5 points

Clue 103: Locate three Hidden Mickeys near the zero grade pool entrance.
5 points for all three

Clue 104: Look for Hidden Mickeys on the outside wall and the downstairs entrance door of the spa.
4 points for spotting both

Clue 105: Admire the guest buildings for small Mickeys.
2 points for one or more

Clue 106: Search for a Hidden Mickey on an outdoor wall, near the check-in point.
5 points

Clue 107: Now find a similar Hidden Mickey on a wall in the Congress Park section near the Disney Springs lagoon.
5 points

Clue 108: Check for a Hidden Mickey inside the Aquatic Play Area at The Paddock Villas pool.
4 points

Clue 109: Look around for Hidden Mickeys on outdoor wall lights.
4 points for one or more

Clue 110: Find classic Mickeys in the various Villa courtyards.
2 points for one or more

Clue 111: Smile at Hidden Mickeys on a gazebo at the Carousel Villas.
2 points

Clue 112: Locate Mickey in a gate near the Grandstand Pool.
3 points

Clue 113: Search near the Backstretch Bar for Mickey.
5 points

Epcot Area Resorts
(123 points)

You'll find Hidden Mickeys in Disney's BoardWalk, Beach Club, and Yacht Club Resorts, as well as the WDW Dolphin Hotel. To explore them, park at one and walk around Crescent Lake to the others. Smile and tell the guards that you're searching for Hidden Mickeys.

BoardWalk Resort (33 points)

Clue 114: Spot two classic Mickeys on a horse in the main lobby.
3 points for both

Clue 115: Search for a classic Mickey on a lobby wall.
4 points

Clue 116: Squint to spot some classic Mickeys above an elephant.
4 points for one or more

Clue 117: Look for Mickey near the Villa elevators.
4 points for one or more

Clue 118: Wander around the guestroom and elevator hallways in both the BoardWalk Inn and the BoardWalk Villas.
8 points for four or more different Mickey images

Clue 119: Find Mickey (and his hands!) at an outside bar.
2 points

Clue 120: Study a BoardWalk surrey bike for a Hidden Mickey.
3 points

Clue 121: Inside the Seashore Sweets shop, locate the Hidden Mickey on a lost sign that has reappeared (in a photo).
5 points

Beach Club Resort (67 points)

Clue 122: Search for Mickey Mouse along the inside walkway in front of the Cape May Cafe.
3 points

Clue 123: Look around just inside the entrance to Cape May Cafe for Mickey on a plate.
4 points

Clue 124: Walk along the hallway behind Cape May Cafe and find Mickey in a painting.
4 points

Clue 125: Search for Mickey in the tile floor in the hallway to the left as you enter the main lobby. (Psst! Look near the luggage room door.)
4 points

★ Walk to the **Beach Club Solarium** to find more Hidden Mickeys. (Psst! Check the walls.)

Clue 126: Spot some car tires with Mickey's full face.
3 points

Clue 127: Now look for classic Mickeys in the same general area.
2 points

Clue 128: Gaze at Mickey's face in the sky.
3 points

Clue 129: Search for Mickey on the sand.
4 points

Clue 130: Now find classic Mickeys in the water.
2 points

Clue 131: Do you see other classic Mickeys floating in the air?
2 points

Clue 132: Squint for a Hidden Mickey atop a building.
5 points

Clue 133: Walk to a guestroom hallway to find classic Mickeys under your feet.
2 points for one or more

Clue 134: Now stare at the hallway walls for more.
3 points

Clue 135: Find Mickey in the Marketplace shop.
2 points

Clue 136: Look for Mickey in an elevator near the Beach Pool (aka the Quiet Pool).
3 points

Clue 137: Study the area near the entrance to the Beach Club Villas for a classic Mickey.
4 points

Clue 138: Enter the Breezeway in the Beach Club Villas and locate three different Hidden Mickey images.
5 points for all three

Clue 139: Walk toward the nearby restrooms inside and find Mickey in a painting.
5 points

Clue 140: Wander into the Beaches & Cream Soda Shop to spot a tasty Hidden Mickey on the wall.
4 points

Clue 141: Now watch hamburger preparation on the Beaches & Cream grill for a classic Mickey.
3 points

Yacht Club Resort (20 points)

Clue 142: Study the globe in the main lobby.
5 points

Clue 143: Look for a cabinet in the main lobby with character names on the drawers.
4 points

Clue 144: Check out the lobby carpet.
2 points

Clue 145: Search other resort carpets for Mickeys.
4 points for two or more

Clue 146: In the Yachtsman Steakhouse, look for the photograph of (now deceased) Minnie Moo, a cow born with a black classic Mickey on her side. (You may have to ask a Cast Member where the photo is located. It's sometimes not on public display.)
5 points

WDW Dolphin Hotel (3 points)

Clue 147: Walk into the main lobby and look for classic Mickeys.
3 points

Magic Kingdom Area Resorts (318 points)

This area is home to seven resorts as well as Disney's Fairytale Wedding Pavilion. The resorts include Disney's Fort Wilderness, Wilderness Lodge and Villas, Shades of Green, and the three monorail resorts (Polynesian Village, Grand Floridian, and Contemporary), so-called because they are all connected to one another and the Magic Kingdom by monorail.

Tip: To explore Fort Wilderness and Wilderness Lodge, take a boat from the Magic Kingdom or from the Contemporary Resort to their respective marinas, or hop on a Disney bus or into your car for transportation to their front entrances.

Fort Wilderness Resort (15 points)

If you drive to Fort Wilderness, swing by the entrance to the **Golden Oak** commmunity at the intersection of Vista Boulevard and Bonnet Creek Parkway (not far from Port Orleans Resort – Riverside) to spot another Hidden Mickey.

Clue 148: Look for a Hidden Mickey on a sign.
3 bonus points

At Fort Wilderness, you'll need to ride an internal bus between the Hidden Mickeys at the rear near the lake (where your hunt begins) and the Hidden Mickeys near the front parking area.

Clue 149: Visit the Blacksmith (near the Horse Barn) and find a Hidden Mickey.
3 points

Clue 150: Check out Trail's End Restaurant inside for a classic Mickey.
3 points

Clue 151: Go to the Trail Ride Check-In building near the front parking area to find two Hidden Mickeys.
3 points for both

Clue 152: Stroll over to the Fort Wilderness registration building ("Reception Outpost") at the far side of the front parking area and look for Mickey.
3 points

Clue 153: Admire a trash can for a Hidden Mickey!
3 points

Wilderness Lodge
(139 points*)
*includes Cub's Den and Wilderness Lodge Villas points

Clue 154: Check out the signs on the right side of the entrance drive.
2 points

Clue 155: Search out a classic Mickey on the guard gate kiosk.
3 points

Clue 156: Near the car unloading area, look up for a classic Mickey etched in a support pole above a black metal band.
4 points

Clue 157: Now search for a classic Mickey etched in another support pole and partially hidden under a black metal band.
4 points

209

Clue 158: Glance down for a tiny classic Mickey traced in the cement on a black stripe.
5 points

Clue 159: Look up again for a classic Mickey etched on a side support pole.
4 points

Clue 160: Find a classic Mickey on a large key in the registration area.
1 point

Clue 161: Look overhead for Mickey driving a bus.
2 points

Clue 162: Find a classic Mickey on the rock of the main lobby fireplace.
5 points

Clue 163: Peek at a fireplace inside the Whispering Canyon Cafe for a classic Mickey. (Ask a Cast Member to let you into the rear of the cafe.)
4 points

Clue 164: Search around the bubbling spring in the lobby for a classic Mickey.
4 points

Clue 165: Look for a classic Mickey on a wall map at the entrance stairs to the Territory Lounge.
3 points

Clue 166: Now go inside and spot a classic Mickey on a ceiling mural above the bar.
4 points

Clue 167: Inside the Artist Point restaurant, spot a classic Mickey in a large mural above the entrance to the rear left dining area.
4 points

Clue 168: Now scan another mural for a classic Mickey near the restaurant's ceiling. (Psst! Turn back toward the entrance.)

5 points

Clue 169: Next scan the walls of the restaurant for Winnie the Pooh.
3 points

Clue 170: Search inside the Roaring Fork snack bar for a Hidden Mickey in a display case.
3 points

Clue 171: Find a classic Mickey in one or more lights near the elevators close to the snack bar.
3 points

Clue 172: Glance at the hallway walls for small Hidden Mickeys.
3 points

Clue 173: Look down in the hallways for more.
2 points

Clue 174: Locate a classic Mickey near Room 6100.
3 points

Clue 175: Explore one floor down for a classic Mickey near Room 5066.
3 points

Clue 176: Find another classic near Room 4035.
3 points

Clue 177: Search for a classic Mickey in the rock outside at Fire Rock Geyser.
4 points

Clue 178: Find stairs outside an exit door from the main building (on the side toward the Boat and Bike Rental) and look up for a classic Mickey.
4 points

Clue 179: Admire a Hidden Mickey at the Boat and Bike Rental cabin.
3 points

Clue 180: Locate a rope Hidden Mickey near the Boat and Bike Rental cabin.
4 points

– In the Cub's Den (8 points)

(Tip: Visit in the afternoon if possible. It's less crowded then and the Cast Members are more likely to let you in. Tell them you're searching for Hidden Mickeys.)

Clue 181: Spot a plush Mickey doll in a mural.
2 points

Clue 182: Look higher for a side-profile Mickey.
3 points

Clue 183: Find a classic Mickey in the same mural.
3 points

– Wilderness Lodge Villas (39 points)

Clue 184: Just inside the main entrance to the Villas, stop before you get to the elevators on your left. Check out the rock pillar to your right for a Hidden Mickey.
5 points

Clue 185: Search for four classic Mickeys near the elevators. (Psst! Look behind some fabric for one of the four.)
5 points for all finding all four

Clue 186: Look around the rock pillars near the Villas lobby for a classic Mickey in the rock.
5 points

Clue 187: Smile back at Mickey hiding in a hole in a beam in the lobby.
5 points

Clue 188: Locate a side profile of Mickey on a wall near the lobby.
4 points

Clue 189: Spot Mickeys around a painting in a room near the lobby.
3 points

Clue 190: Find Mickey in the rock in the Carolwood Pacific Railroad Room near the lobby.
5 points

Clue 191: Look up to spot Mickey in the hallways of the Wilderness Lodge Villas.
2 points

Clue 192: Search for Mickey on a hallway wall near Room 1507.
5 points

Magic Kingdom Monorail Resorts (155 points*)
*includes Disney's Fairytale Wedding Pavilion points

To find the Hidden Mickeys in these resorts and the nearby Fairytale Wedding Pavilion, park at the Polynesian Village or the Grand Floridian and ride the monorail to the other two resorts and past the Wedding Pavilion. Or if you prefer, walk or drive to the Wedding Pavilion. (Note: Polynesian Village has the bigger parking lot.)

★ *Polynesian Village Resort* (45 points)

Clue 193: On the lower level, look for a classic Mickey on the floor near the waterfall.
4 points

Clue 194: Find Mickey overhead in the lobby.
4 points

Clue 195: Study a painting on a wall in the lobby for Mickey ears.
5 points

Clue 196: Search another painting nearby for two classic Mickeys.
5 points for both

Clue 197: Spot three Hidden Mickeys in the Tiki Boutique store.
4 points for finding all three

Clue 198: Study the bamboo-ring wall decorations by the corner staircase.
3 points

★ Find a Hidden Mickey in the Moana Mercantile shop.

Clue 199: Look along a wall.
3 points

Clue 200: Walk by the Kona Cafe and find a classic Mickey.
2 points

Clue 201: At the Kona Island coffee bar, search for a small classic Mickey.
5 points

Clue 202: Look down for Hidden Mickeys in hallways and elevators.
3 points for spotting them in both places

Clue 203: Wander to the marina area and admire a Sea Raycer for a Hidden Mickey.
2 points

Clue 204: Stroll along the lagoon walkway toward Disney's Wedding Pavilion and spot small, white Hidden Mickeys near your feet.
5 points for one or more

★ *Disney's Fairytale Wedding Pavilion*
(3 points)

Clue 205: As your monorail car passes by the pavilion buildings, observe the weather vane.
3 points

(Note: A Hidden Mickey may be lurking inside, but the Wedding Pavilion isn't open to the general public.)

★ *Grand Floridian Resort & Spa* (57 points)

Clue 206: Take a good look at the weather vanes on the roofs.
3 points for one or more

Clue 207: Check the large trolley carts outside the hotel.
1 point

Clue 208: Study the lobby carpet.
2 points

Clue 209: Look at the floor tile for a classic Mickey.
2 points

Clue 210: While you're at it, check the tile for the Fab Five.
5 points for five characters

Clue 211: Look near 1900 Park Fare restaurant for a Mickey hat.
3 points

Clue 212: Also near 1900 Park Fare, find Mickey and Minnie below your feet.
2 points for both

Clue 213: Now look for other Disney movie characters, as well as Mickey and Minnie, in the floor encircling the main lobby and in front of the Grand Floridian Café.
5 points for five or more characters

Clue 214: Search a wall map for a Hidden Mickey.
4 points

Clue 215: Spot Mickey on the outside of the ornate lobby elevator by the stairs.
4 points

Clue 216: Look up high for Mickey on the ceiling above the main lobby.
4 points

Clue 217: Check out the classic Mickey in front of the M. Mouse Mercantile shop.
1 point

Clue 218: Find Hidden Mickeys in the hallway walls.
2 points for one or more

Clue 219: Now look down for others in the hallways.
2 points

Clue 220: Locate a Hidden Mickey while walking outside toward the Grand Floridian Villas.
3 points

Clue 221: Study the area around the main pool near the Villas for a Hidden Mickey in rock.
5 points

Clue 222: Find Mickey and other characters in the lobbies of the outer buildings.
4 points for four or more

Clue 223: Stroll into Gasparilla Island Grill and search for Mickey.
3 points

Clue 224: Walk into the Grand Floridian Convention Center's main entrance and look around for Mickey.
2 points

★ *Contemporary Resort* (50 points*)
*includes Bay Lake Tower points

Clue 225: From the window of the California Grill restaurant, on the top floor, spot a stretched out Mickey watchband on the ground in front of the hotel.
4 points

Clue 226: Go to the sixth floor and walk in the direction of the Transportation and Ticket Center to an outside balcony to spot this amazing Hidden Mickey.
5 points
Caution: Be sure to prop the hallway door open, as it may lock upon closing.

Tip: This Mickey can also be seen from the resort and express monorails.

Clue 227: Look for Mickey's profile inside Chef Mickey's restaurant. (You'll also encounter many décor—not Hidden—Mickey images inside the restaurant.)
1 point

Clue 228: Don't miss Mickey's ears at the rear of Chef Mickey's!
3 points

Clue 229: Find Mickey low on a wall near the Contempo Café.
3 points

Clue 230: Now study this mural higher up for a classic Mickey in a basket.
4 points

Clue 231: Look high for a classic Mickey on an animal in the next mural to the right.
4 points

Clue 232: Search around for a stick-figure Mickey near the shops.
3 points

Clue 233: Look for classic Mickeys in The Game Station Arcade.
3 points for all

Clue 234: Ride up the monorail escalator to spot a classic Mickey on the wall. (Enjoy the five-legged goat while you're up there!)
4 points

Clue 235: Find a classic Mickey silhouette in the bricks behind the main hotel. (Psst! It's near Mickey Mouse himself.)
2 points

Clue 236: Locate a Hidden Mickey in The Sand Bar.
3 points

Clue 237: Spot Mickey in the tile at the exit from the Garden Building to the parking lot.
5 points

Clue 238: Look up for Mickey at the hotel entrance.
2 points

– Bay Lake Tower (4 points)

Clue 239: Walk to Bay Lake Tower and locate Mickey from the outside. (Psst! Look high!)
4 points

Shades of Green Resort
(9 points)

(Only folks with military connections are allowed into this resort.)

Clue 240: Search for four classic Mickeys in the lobby.
5 points for finding all four

Clue 241: Find a large classic Mickey outside (or on a map of the resort).
4 points

It's time to tally your score.

A perfect score for this scavenger hunt is 829. You may have done even better if you earned bonus points at Coronado Springs registration desk, in the All-Star Sports and/or Pop Century food court(s), by finding the Hidden Mickey in the entrance sign to the Golden Oak community, and/or by spotting Hidden Characters on the WDW buses.

Total Points for Hotel Hunt =

How'd you do?

Give yourself Gold if you scored at least 80% of the points available for the places you've searched, Bronze if you scored at least 40%.

Here is a point breakdown by area and resort or resort group, so that you can compare your score with the perfect score for the areas you've covered. You'll find the total points for each section in parentheses.

Animal Kingdom Area (242)
    Animal Kingdom Lodge (108)
        - Kidani Village (27)
    Disney's All-Star Resorts (15)
        All-Star Sports Resort (6)
        All-Star Music Resort (5)
        All-Star Movies Resort (4)
    Coronado Springs Resort (38)
        - Dig Site (19)
    Art of Animation Resort (36)
    Pop Century Resort (45)

Disney Springs Area (146)
    Caribbean Beach Resort (24)
    Old Key West Resort (23)
    Port Orleans Resort – French Quarter (5)
    Port Orleans Resort – Riverside (16)
    Saratoga Springs Resort & Spa (78)

Epcot Area (123)
    BoardWalk Resort (33)
    Beach Club Resort (67)
    Yacht Club Resort (20)
    WDW Dolphin Hotel (3)

Magic Kingdom Area (318)
    Fort Wilderness Resort (15)
    Wilderness Lodge (139)
        - Cub's Den (8)
        - Wilderness Lodge Villas (39)
    Monorail Resorts Area (155)
        Polynesian Village Resort (45)
        Disney's Fairytale Wedding Pavilion (3)
        Grand Floridian Resort & Spa (57)
        Contemporary Resort (50)
        - Bay Lake Tower (4)
    Shades of Green Resort (9)

**Caution:
Don't peek at this
section unless you
really want help!**

Animal Kingdom Area Resorts
Animal Kingdom Lodge

Hint 1: Outside, above the lower roof, the second tall figure to the left of the car baggage drop-off area has a classic Mickey in its mouth.

Hint 2: On the right wall mural between the outer and inner entrance doors to the main lobby, an orange and brown creature sports a classic Mickey in a circle on its mid back.

Hint 3: Inside the main lobby, you can find a classic Mickey near the bottom of the second chandelier on the right (as you face in from the front entrance). The Hidden Mickey is near the bottom of one of the shields.

Hint 4: Around the main lobby, classic Mickeys are formed by logs banded to wood supports. One of the best is the second support on the right (as you enter the lobby from the front doors). It's on the second level, on the side away from the main lobby entrance.

Hint 5: On the right side of the main lobby (as you face in from the front entrance), a short bridge crosses a rockbound pool of water. A classic Mickey is visible on the rock from the side of the bridge nearest the lobby. It's toward the rear on the right side. To spot it, look for the first recess in the rock from the right edge of the pool. Mickey is at the back of this recess, above the water line.

Hint 6: Go down the staircase at the rear of the lobby. Turn left and walk down the Kudu Trail hallway. In the first small lobby, near the elevator, a classic Mickey is on the top end of a piece of wood that's roped to two giant "log" supports. Mickey is above the second rope binding, near the ceiling.

Hint 7: Outside the rear doors of the main lobby, a green Mickey in side profile hides in the decorative vines to the right as you exit. He is about two-thirds of the way up the side of the vine-covered column, above the middle horizontal brace, at the top of an open space in the vines. He's looking into the lobby.

Hint 8: Outside the rear exit from the main lobby, on the left side of the trail to Arusha Rock Overlook, check the rock wall for a decorative relief of a group of giraffes. You'll find a classic Mickey among the spots on the middle of the large giraffe in the center, above its inner front leg.

Hint 9: Along the walkway in Arusha Rock Overlook, a rock sports a classic Mickey. Look for it where the trail first turns left between rock walls. It's on the right side in the first small alcove, about six feet up from the path and under a large overhanging rock.

Hint 10: Toward the bottom of the staircase that winds from the right side of the main lobby to Boma restaurant, there's a classic Mickey on the rock wall.

Hint 11: Inside Boma, you'll see classic Mickeys on some of the chairs with tall metal backs.

Hint 12: Inside Jiko restaurant, a classic Mickey is formed on the ceiling above the two large orange oven exhausts and the white column behind them.

Hint 13: From the entrance to Jiko, walk to the third table on your left, next to the glass windows. Outside in the shallow pool area, a classic Mickey is sculpted on the first rock island from the left that has a pillar jutting out of it.

Hint 14: Outside the exit from the restaurants, a large rock on the left side of the path behind the water slide has a classic Mickey impressed on its lower half near the ground. The rock is about three-quarters of the way along the walkway to the water slide. A small light pole juts out of the top of this rock.

Hint 15: A light-colored classic Mickey is cut into a rock wall behind the swimming pool. The wall forms the back of the pool's water slide. The Mickey is several feet above the walkway, below a gazebo that marks the starting point for the water slide.

Hint 16: Walk behind the pool to the bird and fla-mingo overlook. From the rightmost "Bird Spotter Guide" on the fence along the main trail, look to your right to the opposite fence. About two-thirds of the distance along this fence from the main trail, a pinkish classic Mickey with a white right ear is about one foot down from the top of the rock.

Hint 17: A Mickey image is etched in the ce-ment outside of The Mara restaurant. Go to the walkway leading to the pool, which is directly opposite the rear exit door from the restaurant. Near the end of this short walkway, and on the left side as you stroll toward the pool, you'll find the Hidden Mickey.

Hint 18: A classic stone Mickey is on the rear of the short wall behind The Mara seating area. It's about three feet up from the ground, behind an emergency phone and a tall brown pole.

Hint 19: In the food area of The Mara, a classic Mickey is on the upper left wall in the third leaf from the left tree (in the mural of falling leaves).

Hint 20: Also in the food area, a classic Mickey hides in a leaf in the middle of the upper right mural of falling leaves.

Hint 21: As you enter the elevator to the Fitness Center, you can spot a classic Mickey on the lower left panel (as you face the rear of the elevator).

Hint 22: Many small classic Mickeys can be found in the carpet in the hallways in front of guestrooms. Classic Mickey images in the carpets below the fifth floor differ from those on and above the fifth floor.

Hint 23: On the third floor, at the end of the first short hall to the right of the main Zebra Trail hallway, an upside-down classic Mickey is formed by three plates on a wall.

Hint 24: On the second floor of the Zebra Trail, near a hat display and the elevators to Simba's Cubhouse, a classic Mickey is etched at the bottom end of a piece of wood that's roped to two giant "log" supports. Mickey is below the upper rope binding. (Note: these images change or disappear from time to time.)

– Kidani Village

Hint 25: A classic Mickey is at the 6:30 position on a large gold clock on a table just inside the entrance.

Hint 26: A white classic Mickey is on a ladybug on the middle level of the closest chandelier to the front lobby entrance.

Hint 27: At the entrance to Sanaa restaurant downstairs, a classic Mickey made of baskets is on the wall behind the check-in desk.

Hint 28: Inside Sanaa, a classic Mickey is above a booth on a white wall. It is to the left as you enter.

Hint 29: Classic Mickeys hide in the woodwork in the middle of Sanaa's dining tables.

Hint 30: Outside Sanaa, a classic Mickey is etched on the rockwork at the bottom rear of the lobby stairs.

Hint 31: A variety of small classic Mickeys can be found in the carpet in the hallways in front of guestrooms.

(Other Hidden Mickeys are in the Spa and Health Club area, but generally only Kidani Village guests are allowed to enter there.)

Disney's All-Star Resorts

★ *All-Star Sports Resort*

Hint 32: In the main building gift shop, classic Mickeys are part of the carpet. Each is composed of a baseball with two circles for ears.

Hint 33: Midway along the left wall of the food court seating area, one painting shows Mickey after he's hit in the head with a basketball. Some of the "stars" he sees are yellow classic Mickeys.

Hint 34: In the food court, an image of me (Hidden Mickey Guy, Steve Barrett) is on the last design pane near the rear exit from the food court seating area. I'm sitting in the stands behind hockey player Minnie Mouse, and you can find me on both sides of the pane. I'm holding a yellow *Hidden Mickeys* book with a magnifying glass on the cover, and a tiny classic Mickey is on my shirt! Needless to say, I'm incredibly honored by this!

Hint 35: Outside, behind and to the right of the registration building, and past the buildings with surfboards, a large Mickey statue stands directly over a classic Mickey (white head and black ears) in the cement.

★ *All-Star Music Resort*

Hint 36: In the Jazz Inn courtyard, classic Mickey ears top the cymbal stands. Each is a winged nut that holds a cymbal in place. (These nuts come and go.)

Hint 37: In the Country Fair area, you'll find classic Mickeys on the front and back of the huge boots.

★ *All-Star Movies Resort*

Hint 38: On a mural in an outside display window in front of the gift shop next to the lobby, a small black classic Mickey hides at the lower right of the mural. It's on the front of an orange book with the title "Future Plans."

Hint 39: The large checkers in Andy's Room in the "Toy Story" section sport classic Mickeys.

Coronado Springs Resort

Hint 40: At the front entrance to the main lobby, a medallion in the upper left rectangle of the left large, open wooden door is a three-dimensional relief of Mickey's face.

Hint 41: On the far wall opposite the main entrance to the registration area, three spotlights sometimes create a classic Mickey image. The light circles change size from time to time.

Hint 42: At the far end of the registration lobby, a statue of an eagle stands on the left side. Circles on an emblem on its chest form a classic Hidden Mickey.

Hint 43: A three-dimensional Mickey face is on the large right wooden door (as you face the doors) at the exit labeled El Centro.

Hint 44: Subtle circles form classic Mickeys in the ornate design of the outside black glass walls of Rix Lounge. They're on the walls that face the Pepper Market.

Hint 45: In the hallway outside the Veracruz Exhibit Hall in the Convention Center, a black classic Mickey pattern repeats along the sides of some of the ceiling chandeliers. Nearby, a similar Mickey pattern can be spotted on rectangular light covers that are flush with the ceiling.

Hint 46: A classic Mickey is chipped into the cement next to the lamppost nearest the Marina rental gazebo.

Hint 47: At the Dig Site swimming pool's main entrance (closest to the lake), a classic Mickey hides on a wall to your right. To spot it, check out the upper middle part of the wall facing the lake before you enter the Dig Site.

Hint 48: After you enter the Dig Site, examine the wall to your left (as you enter) that faces the pool. A classic Mickey is on the upper left side.

Hint 49: Also at the Dig Site, you'll find a whitish, somewhat distorted classic Mickey near the very top of the Mayan pyramid, on the side facing the pool. It's on the second stone block from the left, fourth row from the top.

Hint 50: To the left of the restrooms at the Dig Site, a circular stone tablet with relief images is hanging on the wall. A somewhat distorted sideways classic Mickey hides at the lower right.

Hint 51: A section of the walkway in front of Ranchos Building 6A is made of circular flat gray rocks. Some of these rocks form classic Mickeys. You'll find one of them near the far end of the rock section. It's on the right side as you approach the Ranchos buildings.

Hint 52: Mickey Mouse (side profile) is sitting in a bus on some of the bus stop signs located around the periphery of the resort (such as at Bus Stops No. 2, No. 3, and No. 4).

Art of Animation Resort

Hint 53: In the registration lobby of Animation Hall, classic Mickeys are woven in the upholstery of benches located along the wall opposite the check-in area.

Hint 54: In the Landscape of Flavors food court seating area, an image of Lightning McQueen is in the clouds on the side of a large circular light fixture hanging from the ceiling.

227

Hint 55: In the same seating area, the painting on the bottom of another large circular light fixture includes a faint full-body image of Mickey Mouse. Look for Mickey near the bright light at the center of the overhead fixture. The image is in what appears to be a framed photo that is sitting on a shelf above some books.

Hint 56: Behind The Big Blue Pool is a play area for kids formed by a blue coral reef rising from the ground. Walk to the left of the slide exit and duck your head as you enter a small passageway through the coral. Halfway along the passageway, about three-quarters of the way up on the right wall, depressions in the rock form a classic Mickey.

Hint 57: Face Animation Hall and walk on the sidewalk next to Finding Nemo Building #5. This sidewalk is to your right and follows the fence encircling the Big Blue Pool. As you walk, look for a green fish perched in the grass near the fence. You'll find the fish after you pass the end of the Finding Nemo Guest Room Building on your right. A decent sideways classic Hidden Mickey is on each side of the fish, below each eye and near both corners of the mouth.

Hint 58: Outdoors in the resort's Lion King section, there is a cave in the Boneyard play area. Walk under the elephant ribs to enter the cave on the right side and then keep your eyes peeled. About halfway through the cave, depressions in the rock form a classic Mickey on the right wall.

Hint 59: In The Little Mermaid section, three orange spots on green seaweed under a clam design form a classic Hidden Mickey. You can find this image repeated in several of the clam designs along the inner perimeter of the guest room buildings facing the pool.

Hint 60: A variety of classic Mickeys hide in the hallway carpets of the resort's various sections. Each carpet design is consistent with the décor of the specific section, so these carpet Hidden Mickeys vary, too.

228

Pop Century Resort

Hint 61: In a small TV room near the check-in area, classic Mickey bubbles rise under a fish in a fishbowl painted on the wall.

Hint 62: In a photograph on the wall behind the middle of the long registration counter, two Hidden Mickeys formed of craters and shadows lie on the moon. Look at the lower right of the television screen and below the word "moon" for a small sideways classic Mickey and above the same word for a large upright classic Mickey.

Hint 63: Several classic Mickeys are hiding on the tile floor of the food court order area. One is in the center of the order and pay area. Another is in front of the middle cash register.

Hint 64: A tiny black classic Mickey is inside one or more round lights suspended from the ceiling in the food court order area. (Note: These images change or even disappear at times.)

Hint 65: Inside the food court seating area, classic Mickeys made of circles can be found on the undulating purple, brown, blue, and green divider walls.

Hint 66: In the shop near the food court, classic Mickey holes are in the poles that hold merchandise racks.

Hint 67: Inside the gift shop, near the exit to the bus stop, check the wall behind the cash registers to spot round gift boxes that form a classic Mickey. The image appears twice in faux package-locker windows. One image is in the second window from the top of the second column of windows from the right side. The other is in the third window from the left along the top row.

Hint 68: Behind Roger Rabbit, in a mural on one of the '80s buildings near the Computer Pool, a classic Mickey hides at the top of a bush beside a building. The bush's topmost leaf is just above Mickey's head and ears, and one hand of a traffic signal points to Mickey!

Hint 69: Two black classic Mickeys are on the keyboard of the huge computer near the Computer Pool. Both are on the lower row of keys. One is on the second key from the left and the other is on the second key from the right. (More obvious decorative classic Mickeys are in the computer monitor's screensaver.)

Hint 70: Look sharp for a faint classic Mickey in green paint on an outside wall of the '60s building, behind the Mowgli figure and just past the Hippy Dippy Pool. It's on the left side of the wall with green plants, above a vertical leaf, and almost touching the yellow beam of the walkway ceiling to your left.

Hint 71: In the guest laundry rooms near both the Hippy Dippy Pool and the Bowling Pool, bubbles form two sideways classic Mickeys. You'll find them in the same places in both laundry rooms. One is on the lower right front of the soap vending machine and the other is at the upper right.

Hint 72: "Mickey Mouse Club March" is choice "C2" on the giant jukebox near the Bowling Pool. ("I've Got a Date at Disneyland" is choice "F10.")

Hint 73: Outside the main lobby, classic Mickeys are at the ends of the guardrails near the bus stops.

Disney Springs Area Resorts
Caribbean Beach Resort

Hint 74: A group of three logs stuck in the ground forms a classic Mickey. Find the image in a border of logs along the lakeside walkway between Martinique

Buildings 24 and 25. The Hidden Mickey is next to a recessed drain that faces and is adjacent to the lakeside walkway.

Hint 75: Behind Old Port Royale, a classic Mickey appears in the "Barefoot Bay Boat Yard" sign on the side of the lighthouse near the bike racks.

Hint 76: In the child's water play area near the main pool, a classic Mickey is on the helm near the wheel of the pirate ship.

Hint 77: At the main swimming pool, a tan classic Mickey is on the rockwork of the small slide's wall. To spot it, stand at the back of the pool and look under the left cannon. Mickey is on a long rock in the second row of rocks from the bottom. This great Mickey image has almost faded away.

Hint 78: Where the sidewalk from Trinidad North meets the sidewalk outside the main (Old Port Royale) pool, they are joined by a short sidewalk that takes you to the right toward the main resort parking area. As you face the parking area from this intersection, look down at the lower right corner of the first white cement section of the short sidewalk. A small classic Mickey is etched in the pavement not far from a green lamppost.

Hint 79: In Shutters restaurant, a cloud classic Mickey hides in a painting on the left wall of the room close to the rear exit door.

Old Key West Resort

Hint 80: Throughout Conch Flats General Store, the design in the fence woodwork includes classic Mickeys.

Hint 81: Classic Mickeys are worked into the design of the fence railings behind the check-in counter in the registration area.

Hint 82: At the main pool (behind the registration building), the water slide (hidden in the rock) opens into the pool through the head of a classic Mickey.

Hint 83: At the upper right of the entrance to the steps to the water slide, a classic Mickey is impressed in the white rock, above a space in the wall.

Hint 84: You'll see classic Mickeys in the outdoor railings around the guest buildings.

Hints 85 and 86: Classic Mickeys formed by three shell imprints in the cement can be found on the two paths leading from parking spaces to Building 36. On the first path, you'll find the Hidden Mickey just after the first right turn on the right side. On the second path, the three shell imprints are in the corner of the sidewalk, after the first right turn and just before the next left turn.

Port Orleans Resort – French Quarter

Hint 87: On the third painting from the left behind the registration counter, an upside-down classic Mickey is on a man's crown.

Hint 88: Upside-down classic Mickeys made of blue and white gemstones adorn the top of a crown hanging from the ceiling on the right side of the food court seating area.

Port Orleans Resort – Riverside

Hint 89: Above the registration area, classic Mickeys are repeated in the wooden latticework circling the central lobby.

Hint 90: In the registration area, classic Mickeys decorate the sides of the brackets that hold the giant fans hanging from the ceiling above the center of the lobby.

Hint 91: Classic Mickeys are at the base of the strapping on the big ceiling fans.

Hint 92: Small classic Mickeys are in the upper level side rails at Parterre Place.

Hint 93: A subtle classic Hidden Mickey is in the sidewalk in front of the Acadian House Building. Walk across Ol' Man Island

and around the right side of the pool, then cross the first bridge on the right over the waterway and turn left onto the sidewalk. Just before you reach the white benches in front of Acadian House (Rooms 8001-8432), spot a lighter coloration in the stone walkway that forms a Hidden Mickey. The image is difficult to spot, and it may fade over time.

Saratoga Springs Resort & Spa

Hint 94: In the main registration lobby, red swirls in the center carpet form a series of classic Hidden Mickeys.

Hint 95: Halfway down the hallway behind The Artist's Palette shop (turn right as you enter the shop from the main lobby), a full-body impression of Mickey Mouse swinging a golf club is on a handle on the left door.

Hint 96: In the hallway leading to The Turf Club Bar and Grill, the jacket in a display on the left wall sports black classic Mickeys.

Hint 97: Just before entering the lounge area in front of The Turf Club, notice the small, ornate gate to your right, near The Turf Club menu posted on the brick wall. Examine the right half of the gate. Three small blue circles in the left middle area form a classic Mickey image tilted sideways to the left. (This image is not proportioned perfectly, but many guests and Cast Members consider it a Hidden Mickey.) Other circles on the gate also resemble classic Mickeys.

Hint 98: On a wall inside the lounge in front of The Turf Club, Mickey and other Disney characters decorate billiard balls. They are in the first display to the left as you enter from the hallway.

Hint 99: Just inside the dining area of The Turf Club, three circles on equestrian equipment in the upper right section of a wall display form an upside-down classic Mickey. The display is on the left wall (as you enter).

Hint 100: On a statue of a horse and rider outside the main lobby, the rings attaching the bridle to the reins and bit on both sides of the horse's mouth form classic Mickeys. Tiny classic Mickeys are also hidden in the roses on both sides of the horse's winner's blanket. You'll find them in the middle of the blanket in about the third or fourth row down. Finally, large blue classic Mickeys decorate the back and front of the jockey's jersey. (In addition, a blanket on the horse includes a yellow décor Mickey.)

Hint 101: As you walk away from The Artist's Palette, look for depressions in the left rock wall at the top of the stairs to the High Rock Spring Pool. One classic Mickey is in the middle of the top horizontal rock of the wall, and a second classic Mickey is on the lower horizontal rock near the handrail post.

Hint 102: Behind Donald Duck in the children's water play area at High Rock Spring Pool, a classic Mickey about six feet tall and tilted to the left, is made of three depressions in the rock wall behind the waterfall. As you face the rock wall, the Hidden Mickey is at the left side. It's easier to see when the waterfall is off.

Hint 103: At the left side of the High Rock Spring Pool (as you face it from the main building), impressions in the rock wall that borders the zero grade entrance to the pool form three classic Mickeys. Three large circles on the middle of the rock face form an upright classic Mickey, while three smaller circles at the right middle tilt to make a sideways classic Mickey. Behind the layered stone wall, three more circles on the end of the gray rock form another upright classic Mickey.

Hint 104: Small classic Mickeys adorn the spa signs on the wall outside and on the glass door at the downstairs spa entrance.

Hint 105: Some balcony railings on the guest buildings have classic Mickey holes.

Hint 106: In the resort's Springs section (Villas 4101 to 4436), across from the check-in parking lot, a large faint classic Mickey is on an outdoor red wall.

Hint 107: In the resort's Congress Park section (Villas 1501 to 1836), near the lagoon over which you can see Disney Springs, another large faint classic Mickey is on an outdoor red wall. I stood near this red wall and could spot the Rainforest Cafe across the lagoon.

Hint 108: A classic Mickey is inside the Aquatic Play Area at The Paddock pool. This Hidden Mickey is formed by three stones in the middle front of a pillar that is on your right after you pass through the entrance gate.

Hint 109: Classic Mickeys can be found in the upper corners of some of the outside lights on the guest buildings, such as on the exterior of the enclosed stairways.

Hint 110: Classic Mickeys are at the bottom of obelisks in the various Villa courtyards.

Hint 111: Classic Hidden Mickey holes are in the corners of the decorative design work along the ceiling perimeter of the carousel-themed gazebo at the Carousel Villas.

Hint 112: Partial classic Mickeys hide in the left side of the gate to the Grandstand Pool and on the back gate next to the restrooms.

Hint 113: At the Grandstand Pool's Backstretch Pool Bar, a classic Mickey hides at the top of the green trees painted on the lower front wall below the bar counter.

Epcot Area Resorts
BoardWalk Resort

Hint 114: In the main lobby, a horse on the outer ring of the small carousel has brown spots that form two classic Mickeys, one on the neck and one on the thigh.

235

Hint 115: In the middle painting on the wall above the middle registration counter in the main lobby, a classic Mickey is formed by the second small group of trees from the right.

Hint 116: Along a side wall inside the lobby, tiny classic Mickey holes are at the very tops of the red lattice-work designs on all sides of the canopied seat (called a "howdah") atop the elephant.

Hint 117: On the first to the fifth floors of the Board-Walk Villas, a classic Mickey sits atop light fixtures alongside the elevators.

Hint 118: Classic Mickeys hide in the carpet in front of some elevators and also appear in the lobby carpets and the guestroom hallway carpets in both the Board-Walk Inn and BoardWalk Villas. (Note: The images in these areas change or disappear from time to time.)

Hint 119: Walk outside behind the BoardWalk Villas to the Leaping Horse Libations pool bar to spot a classic Mickey at the top of the wall clock behind the bar counter. Mickey's hands tell you the time.

Hint 120: Three circles make a classic Hidden Mickey in each of the small round headlights on the Board-Walk surrey bikes.

Hint 121: A lost BoardWalk sign has reappeared in a photograph on a wall inside the Seashore Sweets shop. In the photo, find the sign and then spot a fluffy white cloud classic Mickey floating in the sky between two ladies and next to the head of the lady at the left.

Beach Club Resort

Hint 122: Along the inside walkway in front of the Cape May Cafe, a full length Mickey Mouse is standing in a sandcastle. It's the sculpture farthest to the left, on the wall facing the pool. (This image disappears at times.)

Hint 123: A classic Mickey is on a blue plate inside Cape May Cafe. The plate is perched on a small shelf on the right wall

just past the check-in podium at the restaurant's entrance. Mickey is on the inside of the plate and has a red circle for a "head" and two black circles for his "ears."

Hint 124: A gold upside-down classic Mickey hides in an old painting of Florida and its landmarks that hangs in a hallway near the back entrance to Cape May Cafe. Look to the lower left of the painting at the gazebo below the words "Cape May Point." The Hidden Mickey is above the steps to the right in the gazebo's facade.

Hint 125: In the Beach Club lobby, on the left as you walk toward the Marketplace shop, a white classic Mickey surrounded by a white circle is inlaid in a floor tile. Look for it under a light fixture and in front of the luggage room door.

Hint 126: Enter the Solarium from the Beach Club main lobby. The first painting on the wall to your left has Mickey's face on spare tires on the backs of the yellow car (left side) and the blue car (right side).

Hint 127: Classic Mickey hood ornaments adorn the blue and red cars on the right of this painting.

Hint 128: In the second painting on the left wall, you can see Mickey's face looking out at you from the clouds at the upper right.

Hint 129: In this second painting, a lady on the beach is sitting on a Mickey Mouse towel.

Hint 130: The cruise ship smokestacks in this second painting have classic Mickey decals.

Hint 131: Mickey balloons are on the right side of the third painting to your left.

Hint 132: Also on the right side of this third painting is a tiny white classic Mickey atop the front post of a small building with a brown roof.

Hint 133: The guestroom hallways have carpet segments with classic Mickeys.

Hint 134: Classic Mickeys are in the wallpaper along the guestroom hallways.

Hint 135: Sand dollars form classic Mickeys in the carpet of the Marketplace shop.

Hint 136: Check the elevator that's near both the Beach Pool (aka the Quiet Pool) and Room 1571 for an ad for the Beaches & Cream Soda Shop. Onion rings in the ad form a classic Mickey.

Hint 137: Under the Ariel statue in front of the entrance to the Beach Club Villas, seashells are embedded in the ground. One group of three shells forms a classic Mickey.

Hint 138: In The Breezeway at the Beach Club Villas, three different Mickey images hide in a painting on the left wall (as you enter The Breezeway from the front doors):
- Classic Mickeys are on a fence in the lower part of the painting.
- A full-body shadow of Mickey Mouse is in a bottom-floor hotel window in the middle of the painting.
- A subtle dark smiling Mickey face drawn in the sand lies to the right of the two people standing closest to the water.

Hint 139: Near the restrooms off the lobby inside the entrance doors to the Beach Club Villas, a colorful picture entitled "Cape May" is on the left wall in the short hallway to the left of the Breezeway. Look at the top border and you'll spot a train just to the left of center. A classic Mickey is formed by the coal in the car behind the engine.

Hint 140: Onion rings form a classic Mickey in one of the food images decorating the Beaches & Cream Soda Shop. The image is on the left wall as you enter, on the second panel back from the rear wall.

Hint 141: You can spot classic Mickey holes in the hamburger press used at the Beaches & Cream Soda Shop to hold the burgers on the hot griddle.

Yacht Club Resort

Hint 142: On the globe in the main lobby, a blue classic Mickey is at the bottom right-hand corner of the sea monster, under the sea monster's head and below the island of Madagascar.

Hint 143: In a seating area in the main lobby, the names of Mickey, Minnie, Donald, Daisy, Goofy, and Huey are on small labels on the drawers of a corner cabinet. (This cabinet is moved around at times to different parts of the lobby.)

Hint 144: Near the main lobby seating area, dark classic Mickeys are in the rug.

Hint 145: Various other classic Mickey images can be found in other carpets around the resort, especially near elevators and in the guest hallways.

Hint 146: A photo of (now deceased) Minnie Moo, a cow born with a black classic Mickey on her side, often hangs in the Yachtsman Steakhouse. Examine the left wall just past the entrance podium. Minnie Moo once resided at Fort Wilderness.

WDW Dolphin Hotel

Hint 147: Walk toward the piano in the main lobby and observe the backs of the brown chairs nearby. Several classic Mickeys are formed by wooden circles on the chair backs.

Magic Kingdom Area Resorts

Fort Wilderness Resort

Hint 148: On the sign at the entrance to the **Golden Oak** commmunity on Vista Boulevard near the Fort Wilderness Resort, a classic Mickey is hidden in the tree of Golden Oak's logo.

Hint 149: A classic Mickey brand is on the left side of the Blacksmith sign near the Horse Barn.

Hint 150: Inside Trail's End Restaurant, a classic Mickey is formed by frying pans hanging from hooks on the wall behind the food serving station.

Hint 151: At the front parking lot, two Hidden Mickeys are on the Tri-Circle-D Ranch sign on the small Trail Ride Check-In building. They are in the middle of the scrollwork at both sides of the sign.

Hint 152: Inside the Fort Wilderness registration building ("Reception Outpost") at the far side of the main parking lot, a plush Mickey Mouse stands in a metal jug at the far left of a shelf directly over the registration counter.

Hint 153: A small classic Hidden Mickey, tilted to the right, is at the lower middle of the logo on the trash cans. It's under the "C" in "Campground."

Wilderness Lodge

Hint 154: On the right side of the entrance drive to the hotel, a full length Mickey Mouse is walking on top of the "Bear Crossing" sign.

Hint 155: A classic Mickey is on the slanted end of the first horizontal log beam of the guard gate kiosk as your car approaches the entrance gate.

Hint 156: As you approach the center steps from the parking lot, you'll see that the roof of the covered unloading area in front of the entrance is supported by huge wooden logs, banded together (four to a set) by black metal strips. The right rear pole of the first set to the right (as you face the entrance) has a classic Mickey etched in the wood above the upper black metal band. This Mickey faces the parking lot.

Hint 157: In the set of support poles on the left after you walk up the center steps from the parking lot, the pole in the corner closest to you and the hotel entrance has a classic Mickey etched in the wood. This Mickey is partially covered by the upper black metal band; only his head and part of his right ear are visible. This Mickey faces the steps.

Hint 158: In the cement of the car entrance drive-through, the black stripe nearest the center steps from the parking lot hides a tiny classic Mickey. From the red rectangle in the cement, follow the right (as you face the hotel entrance) diagonal crack to the black stripe. The tiny classic Mickey is traced in the cement about six inches to the right of the intersection of the crack and the stripe.

Hint 159: As you face the hotel entrance, the left rear support pole of the far left set of poles closest to the parking lot has a classic Mickey etched in the wood. It's above the lateral crossbeam on the lower part of the pole.

Hint 160: A classic Mickey hides on the left side of a large key in a wall display behind the registration counter. Look near the entrance to the Mercantile shop.

Hint 161: A sign that says "Walt Disney World Transportation" hangs from the ceiling near the Mercantile shop. Mickey (in side profile) is driving the bus at the top of the sign.

Hint 162: In the lobby, you'll find a classic Mickey on the rock in the corner at the upper right of the fireplace. Search at the level of and near the lower round wooden horizontal beam that juts toward the lobby.

Hint 163: The outer grillwork of a fireplace in the rear room of the Whispering Canyon Cafe is adorned with decorative cutouts. Bend down low and look for a classic Mickey on the bottom row. It is the third cutout from the left corner.

Hint 164: A small classic Mickey lies on the floor at the left front corner (as you face the rear of the lobby) of the rectangle of dark hardwood slats that surround the bubbling source of the water spring. The "head" is formed by a circle in the wood with small indentations in the wood for "ears."

Hint 165: At the entrance stairs to the Territory Lounge, a classic Mickey decorates a pot in the right lower section of a wall map.

Hint 166: Inside the Territory Lounge, a classic Mickey rests on the rear of a beige mule in a ceiling mural. Look above the center of the bar.

Hint 167: Inside the Artist Point restaurant, examine the large mural above the entrance to the rear left dining area. You can spot a classic Mickey in the upper part of the lowest tree on the right if you look between the third and fourth lights (counting from the left) illuminating the mural.

Hint 168: Turn left toward the Artist Point entrance and study the large mural near the ceiling and between the two front sections of the restaurant. On the clothing at the lower back of the leftmost of four horsemen is a light brown classic Mickey, tilted slightly to the right.

Hint 169: Inside the rear left dining area, the top middle part of a dark cloud in a painting on the left wall is shaped like a side profile of Winnie the Pooh. He's looking to the right.

Hint 170: A display case on an inside wall facing the entrance to the Roaring Fork snack bar contains three chestnuts arranged to form a classic Mickey.

Hint 171: You'll find classic Mickey images on a few of the wall-light covers, most often as a sideways image at the lower center of the light cover. Some of these covers are near the elevators just past Roaring Fork snack area. One or more can be found elsewhere around the hotel.

Hint 172: The wallpaper in the guest hallways on most floors (for example, near the elevators) includes classic Mickeys in the design.

Hint 173: Segments of the guest hallway carpets contain blue classic Mickeys.

Hint 174: A classic Mickey is etched near the bottom of a flat vertical wooden post around the corner from Room 6100 and near a green EXIT sign.

Hint 175: Near Room 5066, a classic Mickey is etched on a flat vertical wooden post about five and a half feet from the floor. It's across from an ice machine.

Hint 176: A classic Mickey is etched on a vertical wooden post about six feet up from the floor across from Room 4035.

Hint 177: Outside, from the walkway next to Fire Rock Geyser, scan the shallow stream running down from the small pool by the geyser. You'll find a slightly distorted classic Mickey with white rocks for ears in the rock of the streambed about a third of the way up to the geyser.

Hint 178: Walk toward the Teton Boat and Bike Rental cabin and locate stairs to an exit door in the corner of the main building. A classic Mickey is impressed in a vertical wooden beam at the left side of the exit door (as you face the door) across from the fourth-floor balcony. Mickey is on the right side of the beam, just below the log that juts out to the right.

Hint 179: On an upper shelf behind the counter of the Boat and Bike Rental cabin, the Cast Members maintain a classic Hidden Mickey made of towels.

Hint 180: At the marina, to the left of the Boat and Bike Rental cabin, the Cast Members usually maintain a classic Hidden Mickey made of coiled rope. Look for it on the front of a display boat that sits on the marina pier.

– In the Cub's Den

Hint 181: A plush Mickey doll sits in the rightmost tee-pee in the mural on the right wall.

Hint 182: In this same mural, a side-profile shadow of Mickey (standing and looking right) falls on the side of a mountain to the right of the center of the mural and above the tree line.

Hint 183: On the far left of this mural, about midway up and left of the mountains, you can spot a classic Mickey.

– Wilderness Lodge Villas

Hint 184: Turn left toward the elevators after you enter the Villas' main entrance. On the rock pillar to your right as you walk toward the elevators, an almost upside-down classic Hidden Mickey is etched in a square, dark gray rock. Find it on the second rock from the floor, about two and one-half feet up.

Hint 185: Near the lobby elevators to the left of the entrance to the Villas, four classic Mickeys hide on the wall. One is to the right of the elevators near the lower left corner of a picture frame. Two more are part of the wall decoration between the elevators, and a fourth can be found to the left of the leftmost elevator. This last Mickey is hiding behind the red tapestry.

Hint 186: A classic Mickey made of depressions in the rock is tilted to the right on the last stone pillar to your left as you enter the Villas. You can spot this image just before you step into the lobby. It is about three feet from the floor, on the corner (facing the entrance) of the second horizontal rock from the floor.

Hint 187: Mickey Mouse is peeking out of a hole on the outer side of the first overhead beam to your right as you enter the lobby of the Wilderness Lodge Villas. The beam is jutting out into the lobby and has a rattlesnake on top.

Hint 188: A side profile of Mickey Mouse is on the upper part of a wall, between two moons, near the lobby of the Wilderness Lodge Villas (and to the right as you face the lobby).

Hint 189: Examine the art hanging in the first room to the right after you pass through the Villas' lobby entrance doors. A painting that's hanging on the room's right wall has a frame with classic Mickeys in the corners.

Hint 190: Walk to your right (as you face the Villas lobby) to the Carolwood Pacific Railroad Room. On the left side of the fireplace, a classic Mickey is embedded in the stonework at about the height of the fireplace mantel.

Hint 191: High along the hallways of the Villas, you'll find classic Mickey corner brackets.

Hint 192: To the left of the entrance doors to the Villas, in a hallway on the left past the elevators, a dark classic Mickey appears on the baseboard near the hall carpet. It's down the hallway on your right, about eight to ten feet before you reach Room 1507.

Magic Kingdom Monorail Resorts

★ *Polynesian Village Resort*

Hint 193: On the lower level, just inside the main lobby, there's a classic Mickey design in the flagstone tiles a few feet in front of the waterfall.

Hint 194: Overhead in the lobby, some rope knots securing the round lights resemble Hidden Mickeys.

Two paintings with Hidden Mickeys hang on the lobby wall to the left of the registration counter:

Hint 195: In the painting on the right, a person with Mickey ears stands at the back (aft) of the sailboat on the left.

Hint 196: In the painting on the left, two classic Mickeys are formed in the water, one on the front of a brown rock at the left middle of the painting and another in the breaking surf in the middle of the second wave from the beach.

Hint 197: Inside the Tiki Boutique store on the first floor and near the various entrances, three wooden statues holding merchandise are adorned with classic Mickeys. Two of the Mickeys are blue and white while the third is red.

Hint 198: Along the right rear corner staircase from the lobby, bamboo wall decorations are composed of rings. Seen end on, some of the lower rings in the decoration on the right side form classic Mickeys.

Hint 199: Inside Moana Mercantile Shop upstairs, a classic Mickey is formed of blue and green balls hanging in knotted ropes high along the middle of the rear wall, above the merchandise shelves.

Hint 200: The carpeting on the floor of the Kona Cafe includes many flowers. Some of the flowers contain classic Mickeys of different colors. You can see these carpet images from the railing outside the cafe.

Hint 201: At the Kona Island coffee bar, in front of the Kona Cafe, small purple tiles on top of the mosaic tile counter form a classic Mickey. You'll spot it to the left of the glass case.

Hint 202: The carpet in some of the hallways and elevators sports classic Mickeys.

Hint 203: On the display Sea Raycer boat outside by the marina, three dials at the left side of the dashboard form a classic Mickey. (You can see other Sea Raycers with this dashboard classic Hidden Mickey on display at other Walt Disney World Resorts.)

Hint 204: Four sets of tiny, white classic Mickeys in pairs lie along the lagoon walkway, about halfway between the Polynesian Village Resort and Disney's Fairytale Wedding Pavilion. Look for them in the area where you see a wooden wall a few feet to the side of the walkway and opposite the lagoon. The Hidden Mickey pairs appear every few feet along the length of the wall. One is on the walkway itself and the other on the curb just above it. I hope they last!

★ Disney's Fairytale Wedding Pavilion

Hint 205: The weather vane on top of the building closest to the monorail has a full-length side profile of Mickey Mouse.

★ Grand Floridian Resort & Spa

Hint 206: Weather vanes on various roofs at the front of the resort sport classic Mickeys.

Hint 207: The large trolley carts outside the hotel have classic Mickeys in the woodwork around the luggage storage areas at the back of the carts.

Hint 208: In the main lobby, gold classic Mickeys are in the carpet.

Hint 209: Green classic Mickeys are in the corners of the marble tile designs on the floors of the first and second levels of the main building.

Hint 210: You'll find the Fab Five Disney characters (Mickey, Minnie, Pluto, Donald, and Goofy) in the tile floor near the main lobby's front entrance—and directly above in the tile on the second floor entrance from the monorail.

Hint 211: Along the entrance hall to 1900 Park Fare restaurant, a Mickey-hat image is at the left lower corner of the left lower picture in a group of carousel pictures on the wall.

Hint 212: Minnie is here with Mickey (green full-body images) on the tile floor of the foyer in front of the dining area of the 1900 Park Fare restaurant.

Hint 213: Other Disney movie characters are in the tile floor encircling the main lobby and in front of the Grand Floridian Cafe. They include Tinker Bell, Cinderella and Prince Charming, Peter Pan and friends, Mrs. Potts and Chip, and of course Mickey and Minnie.

Hint 214: Wall maps of the Grand Floridian Resort are on the first and second floors, toward the front of the building. A small sideways classic Mickey is formed by bushes at the upper right of the Sago Cay building, located at the left middle of the map.

Hint 215: Ornate ironwork encloses the elevator out in the lobby, and the decorative sections between the floors host multiple classic Mickeys. You'll find four classic Mickeys in each ironwork panel at the intersection of the diagonal spokes and the large circle. The ears are oriented toward the center. (Tip: Stand inside the main lobby elevator for the best view of these classic Mickeys.)

Hint 216: A classic Mickey design is at the bottom of each of the four tall blue flowers in the stained-glass dome above the main lobby of the Grand Floridian.

Hint 217: On the second floor, a classic Mickey hides on the top of a pole on the M. Mouse Mercantile sign in front of the shop.

Hint 218: Most guestroom hallways have classic Hidden Mickeys in the wallpaper.

Hint 219: Classic Mickeys are also in the guest hallway carpets.

Hint 220: Along the covered walkways outside the Grand Floridian Villas, look up for classic Hidden Mickeys in the latticework design. They occur only at certain points along the walkways.

Hint 221: A classic Mickey is two-thirds of the way up the huge rock wall at the side of the main pool near the Grand Floridian Villas. The Hidden Mickey, made of circular depressions in the rock, is behind the waterfall and is sometimes difficult to make out if the water flow is heavy and obscures the image.

Hint 222: In the lobbies of the outer guest buildings, the carpets have Hidden Mickeys as well as a Hidden Minnie Mouse, Donald Duck, Goofy, and Pluto.

Hint 223: Inside Gasparilla Island Grill, classic Mickeys are in the metalwork above the individual lights on the ceiling light fixtures.

Hint 224: Step into the main entrance area of the Grand Floridian Convention Center and look up for a hot air Mickey balloon painted on the ceiling.

★ *Contemporary Resort*

Hint 225: From the window of the California Grill restaurant on the hotel's top floor, you can see a stretched out Mickey watchband on the ground in front of the building. It's among the conical-shaped trees. (You can see part of this watchband from the monorail.)

Hint 226: *(Caution: Prop the hallway door open before you step out onto the balcony to look for Mickey.)*

From the sixth floor outdoor balcony closest to the front of the hotel, look left to see Mickey sitting on the edge of a roof below! This Mickey can also be spotted from either monorail just outside the hotel (the opening nearest the Transportation and Ticket Center). If you're on the resort monorail, you have to bend down to view Mickey through the lower part of the window (to the left of forward motion) and below the express monorail track next to you. On the express monorail, look to the right of forward motion.

Hint 227: Inside Chef Mickey's restaurant, a large side-profile Mickey decorates both sides of the large black, white, and red tile divider.

Hint 228: Mickey ears are atop posts at the rear of Chef Mickey's restaurant.

Hint 229: On the lower part of the wall mural facing Contempo Café, the fourth girl from the right corner of the wall has a classic Mickey on her dress.

Hint 230: At the upper middle of this wall mural facing Contempo Café, a girl in a blue and white dress is carrying orange and light purple round fruits in a basket on her head. In the right side of the basket, a light purple "head" and two smaller orange "ears" form a classic Mickey tilted to the left.

Hint 231: High on the wall mural facing Bay Lake, a black classic Mickey is on an owl perched on a girl's head. It's on the red right wing (as you face the mural).

Hint 232: On the fourth floor, a stick-figure Mickey is in an artwork display on the side of the Bayview Gifts store facing the monorail.

Hint 233: On the fourth floor, classic Mickeys are in the carpet inside The Game Station Arcade.

Hint 234: On the wall mural facing the monorail, an upside-down classic Mickey has a blue circle for a "head" and yellow circles for "ears." It's at the top of a tree that is positioned to the lower left of the five-legged goat.

Hint 235: Behind the main hotel, a classic Mickey silhouette can be found in the bricks under the metal Mickey Mouse sculpture. (The sculpture itself is a decorative Mickey, not a Hidden Mickey.)

Hint 236: In The Sand Bar by the pool, near the middle of the upper left wall border, one of the semaphore figures is wearing Mickey ears.

Hint 237: At the exit from the Garden Building to the parking lot (facing the monorail), a huge classic Mickey is traced in the tile under the exit canopy between the benchs.

Hint 238: Large white classic Mickeys are frosted into glass partitions that support the curved roof that covers the vehicle drive-though entrance area to the hotel.

– Bay Lake Tower

Hint 239: Classic Mickeys are at the top of both elevator towers at the sides of the hotel. (Ceiling lights hang from these Mickey-shaped metal plates.) You can spot one of them from the monorail and either or both from the ground.

Shades of Green Resort

Hint 240: In the lobby, a Mickey statue stands in front of a framed picture of a blue sky with puffy clouds. Three classic Mickeys are in the clouds and another, made of fireworks, decorates the statue Mickey's right ear.

Hint 241: The Millpond pool is shaped as a classic Mickey. You can visit this pool outside or spot it on a resort map posted on hallway walls.

CHAPTER 7

Hither, Thither & Yon Scavenger Hunt

A car is the most efficient method for hunting the following areas. I've planned the hunt taking time of day and location into consideration. However, some backtracking will help keep you ahead of the crowds. Don't forget to be courteous to the shoppers, diners, golfers, swimmers, other guests and Cast Members you encounter during your hunt. (Note: Because you may want to hunt only one area at a time, I've listed the perfect score for each area in parentheses after its name in the Clues section.)

★ **Bonus Points Opportunity.** As I advised in Chapter Six, pay attention to the Disney buses during your Hidden Mickey hunt around WDW property. You may get lucky! The Disney Cruise Line bus has a Hidden Pluto on each side of the gold scrollwork on the front of the bus between the headlights. Some general Disney transport buses sometimes sport a classic Mickey on the rear of the vehicle, usually related to rear upper or lower lights. Even more subtle are the faint classic Mickey images in the windows of some buses, only visible when the lighting is just right! If you spot one or more of these images, give yourself 5 bonus points for each one you find.

Magnolia Golf Course (5 points)

Clue 1: If you're a golfer, look around you for a classic Mickey sand trap.
5 points

Vista Boulevard (5 points)

Clue 2: Drive east along Vista Boulevard away from Fort Wilderness and stay alert for a classic Mickey on a sign to your left.
5 points

1 All-Star Resorts
2 Animal Kingdom Lodge
3 Art of Animation
4 Beach Club
5 Blizzard Beach
6 BoardWalk
7 Caribbean Beach
8 Contemporary
9 Coronado Springs
10 Disney Springs
11 Dolphin
12 ESPN Wide World of Sports Complex
13 Fantasia Gardens Mini Golf
14 Fort Wilderness
15 Golden Oak
16 Grand Floridian
17 Lake Buena Vista Golf Course
18 The Landing, in Disney Springs

19 Magnolia Golf Course
20 Oak Trail Golf Course
21 Old Key West
22 Palm Golf Course
23 Polynesian Village
24 Pop Century
25 Port Orleans – French Quarter
26 Port Orleans – Riverside
27 Saratoga Springs
28 Shades of Green
29 Swan
30 Transportation and Ticket Center
31 Typhoon Lagoon
32 Wedding Pavilion, Disney's Fairytale
33 Wilderness Lodge
34 Winter Summerland Mini Golf
35 Yacht Club
P Parking

255

Disney Vacation Club Way (5 points)

Clue 3: Head south down Bonnet Creek Parkway, turn left onto Disney Vacation Club Way, and scan the area to your left for a Hidden Mickey.
5 points

ESPN Wide World of Sports (15 points)

Clue 4: Search hard for a three-dimensional Mickey Mouse head near the high central ceiling of The Milk House (the Field House). He's on an upper rafter opposite the main entrance.
5 points

Clue 5: Don't miss Mickey in the outfield if you go to a game in the stadium! (Tip: You can only see this Hidden Mickey from Champion Stadium.)
5 points

Clue 6: Now head for the softball fields and check out the pitcher's mounds for possible bonus points.
5 bonus points for one or more

Clue 7: Stroll around the Sports Fields to locate a Hidden Mickey on the discus field.
5 points

WDW Water Parks (48 points)

★ *Blizzard Beach* (15 points)

Clue 8: Take a close look at the Beach Haus store's right rear wall near the dressing rooms.
3 points

Clue 9: Inside the Beach Haus, spot Hidden Mickeys near the merchandise.
2 points

Clue 10: Hop on the *Chairlift* to spot a classic Mickey formed by three round rocks on the ground near one of the support poles for the ride.
256
5 points

Tip: The Singles line for the *Chairlift* is usually shorter than the Standby line.

Clue 11: Go to the rear of the park (by tube or on foot) to find a classic Mickey with a sorcerer's hat that's formed by three stones topped by a small triangular rock. (Psst! He's near the center of the side of a stone bridge that crosses over *Cross Country Creek*.)
5 points

★ *En Route to Typhoon Lagoon* (4 points)

Clue 12: On your way to Typhoon Lagoon from Blizzard Beach, spot Mickey on the Disney Vacation Club white tower, which will appear on your left at the intersection of Buena Vista Drive and Bonnet Creek Parkway.
4 points

★ *Typhoon Lagoon* (29 points)

Clue 13: Check out a Tip Board for a Hidden Mickey. (Note: These images come and go.)
3 bonus points

Clue 14: Look around the *Crush 'n' Gusher* elevator for a Hidden Mickey.
4 points

Clue 15: Search for Mickey on a bridge over *Castaway Creek*, near *Shark Reef*.
4 points

Clue 16: Marvel at Mickey if you snorkel with the sharks in *Shark Reef*.
5 points

Clue 17: Don't pass by Mickey on the steps up to the *Storm Slides*.
4 points

Clue 18: Climb the trail up to *Humunga Kowabunga* and locate a classic Mickey along the way.
4 points

Clue 19: Spot the Main Mouse hiding under a cannon along *Castaway Creek* at the rear of the park.
4 points

Clue 20: Squint for Mickey in the wall of a cave at *Ketchakiddee Creek.*
4 points

Disney Springs West Side
(79 points)

★ *Cirque du Soleil* (8 points)

Clue 21: Look down for a Hidden Mickey in the sidewalk near Parking Lot Q.
5 points

Clue 22: Head for the outside restrooms (they're under the main entrance staircase to the theater) and examine the floor in either one (men's or women's). See a small classic Mickey?
3 points for either (or both)

★ *House of Blues* (3 points)

Clue 23: Search for a classic Mickey on the ceiling.
3 points

★ *DisneyQuest* (31 points)

Clue 24: On the third floor inside, look above you in Ventureport for a Hidden Mickey.
2 points

Clue 25: Check the carpet on Ventureport's third floor.
3 points

Clue 26: Look for track lighting shaped like a classic Mickey on the second through fifth floors. (Psst! It's not on the same side on all four floors.)
5 points for spotting all four

Clue 27: Find similar lighting near *"Invasion! An Extra-TERRORestrial Alien Encounter."*
3 points

Clue 28: Check out the air hockey tables for Hidden Mickeys!
2 points for one or more

Clue 29: Be aware of Hidden Mickeys on the front of some games on various floors.
2 points

Clue 30: Don't tread on Hidden Mickeys near the *Living Easels*!
2 points for one or more

Clue 31: To play games, children can elevate themselves on these Hidden Mickeys.
2 points

Clue 32: Spot classic Mickey markings on the back of one of the creatures you encounter during *"Aladdin's Magic Carpet Ride."* (You don't have to take the ride; you can watch the overhead video screens as others ride.)
4 points

★ Find two classic Hidden Mickeys at the *"Virtual Jungle Cruise."* (Again, you needn't take the ride; you can stand behind one of the ride pods and watch.)

Clue 33: Before the ride starts, watch the left side of the screen.
4 points

Clue 34: Keep watching the screen during the first part of the ride to see if the raft exits a glacier area. (The riders have optional routes, so they may not enter the glacier area.) If it does, watch carefully as it exits. (The ears on this Hidden Mickey aren't perfectly formed, but you'll recognize them.)
3 bonus points

Clue 35: Along the queue for *"Pirates of the Caribbean,"* examine the walls for a Hidden Mickey.
2 points

★ *Splitsville Luxury Lanes* (12 points)

Clue 36: Admire the mural inside on the lower level for Hidden Mickeys.
5 points for three different kinds of Mickey images

Clue 37: Find Mickey on a huge orange on the upper level.
3 points

Clue 38: Search the orange trees on the upper level.
4 points

★ *Wolfgang Puck Cafe* (5 points)

Clue 39: Study the mosaic tile pyramid behind the reception counter to find a classic Hidden Mickey.
5 points

★ *Disney's Candy Cauldron* (4 points)

Clue 40: Go inside to find a classic Mickey marking on a stone.
4 points

★ *D Street* (10 points)

Clue 41: Spot Mickey on the ceiling.
2 points

Clue 42: Now search for a small classic Mickey wall impression.
3 points

Clue 43: Observe Mickey in the bricks.
2 points

Clue 44: Find a Hidden Mickey on Mickey!
3 points

★ *Starbucks* (4 points)

Clue 45: Locate a Hidden Mickey on a wall in the seating area. (Tip: You may need to wait a few minutes for it to appear!)
4 points

★ *Bus stop in The Landing* (2 points)

Clue 46: Look down near one of the bus stops.
2 points

Disney Springs Marketplace (193 points)

★ *Entrance to the Marketplace* (8 points)

Clue 47: Find Hidden Mickeys at the bus stop area near the main entrance.
5 points for five or more

Clue 48: Check out the signs over the entrances.
1 point for one or more

Clue 49: Study the green benches for Hidden Mickeys at the entrance and elsewhere around Disney Springs Marketplace.
2 points

★ *Disney's Wonderful World of Memories* (3 points)

Clue 50: Search for Mickey outside the store.
3 points

★ *Disney's Days of Christmas* (15 points)

Clue 51: Step inside and search for a Mickey made of rocks.
3 points

Clue 52: Find at least one classic Mickey on each of three large trees.
4 points total for one or more on each tree

Clue 53: Study the walls and carpet for classic Hidden Mickeys.
3 points for two or more

Clue 54: Take a good look at the ceiling in the rear room of the shop.
2 points

Clue 55: Admire an outside window of the store for subtle Hidden Mickeys.
3 points

★ *Goofy's Candy Company* (10 points)

Clue 56: Search for a Goofy shadow in the store.
4 points

Clue 57: Find Goofy and other characters on the wall.
4 points for three or more characters

Clue 58: Find Mickey in a store window.
2 points

★ *Rainforest Cafe* (4 points)

Clue 59: Look for Hidden Mickeys on the outdoor signs.
4 points for both

★ *Sassagoula River Cruise ferry* (5 points)

Clue 60: If you have time, take the *Sassagoula River Cruise* ferryboat to Port Orleans – French Quarter, disembark, and then ride the next boat back to Disney Springs Marketplace. During both your crossings, study the Treehouse Villas for Hidden Mickeys.
5 points for one or more

★ *Marketplace Carousel* (5 points)

Clue 61: Study the decorative inner and outer panels on the Carousel for four classic Mickeys.
5 points for spotting all four

★ *Once Upon a Toy* (38 points)

Note: This store sports numerous Mickeys and other Disney characters in the décor in addition to the Hidden Mickeys below.

Clue 62: Examine the interactive fountain near the store. (Note: Two Hidden Mickeys are there all the time, a third appears only when the water is on.)
4 points for two, 5 points for spotting all three

Clue 63: Find a faint classic Mickey in the cement outside.
5 points

Clue 64: Outside the main entrance, look for classic Mickeys with tires for ears.
2 points for one or more

★ Now enter the store and keep your eyes open.

Clue 65: Gaze up for classic Mickeys.
2 points for one or more

Clue 66: Check out the tops of merchandise stands. (Only some sport Hidden Mickeys.)
1 point for one or more

Clue 67: Now examine the bottoms of these stands.
1 point for one or more

Clue 68: Search for a classic Mickey on large and small sandals in the middle of the first room.
3 points for both

Clue 69: In the first room, find a tiny Mickey near Mrs. Potato Head. (Note: Three other more obvious décor Mickey images are on or near her body.)
4 points

Clue 70: Examine the mural behind the service desk in the same room.
2 points for two or more images

Clue 71: Look at the upper beams of the wooden merchandise displays.
1 point for one or more

Clue 72: Now observe the bolts on those displays.
1 point for one or more

Clue 73: Study the floor for a Mickey.
3 points

Clue 74: Find a classic Hidden Mickey cloud in a central room.
3 points

Clue 75: Look for a Mickey shadow in a central room.
3 points

Clue 76: Look for Hidden Mickey lollipops.
2 points for one or more

★ *Disney's Pin Traders* (8 points)

Clue 77: Spot a Hidden Mickey on a Mickey statue inside the store.
3 points

Clue 78: Find three Hidden Mickeys on Donald's statue.
5 points for all three

★ *Tren-D* (27 points)

Clue 79: Look around for classic Mickeys on the tops and sides of various merchandise tables in the store.
3 points for two or more

Clue 80: Check out Mickey in wallpaper.
2 points

Clue 81: Find Mickey on a mannequin.
4 points

Clue 82: Look for a Mickey ring on Minnie Mouse, a Mickey watch on another Minnie, and a gold Hidden Mickey on a third Minnie.
5 points for all three

Clue 83: Spot a blue Hidden Mickey on the wall inside the store.
264 5 points

Clue 84: Smile at the initials of two Disney characters on a countertop!
5 points

Clue 85: Locate Mickey circles on a countertop.
3 points

★ *Marketplace Co-Op* (7 points)

Clue 86: Find a classic Mickey in the Disney Vacation Club (DVC) display near Marketplace Co-Op.
2 points

Clue 87: Check out the signs inside Marketplace Co-Op for a red Hidden Mickey.
2 points

Clue 88: Find classic Mickeys in the Caricature Booth nearby.
3 points for one or more

★ *Ghirardelli Ice Cream & Chocolate Shop* (4 points)

Clue 89: Locate Mickey on a wall inside.
4 points

★ *Near the lake* (3 points)

Clue 90: Do you see any chairs with Hidden Mickeys outside the Ghirardelli Shop?
2 points

Clue 91: Spot Mickeys in the fence around the lake.
1 point

★ *World of Disney* (46 points)

Clue 92: Look up for Mickeys on the store sign.
1 point

Clue 93: Find light brown Mickeys outside the store.
2 points

Clue 94: Look for classic Mickeys in some of the clothing racks.
2 points

265

Clue 95: Find a classic Mickey emblem on the Chinese Theater in a mural in the high-ceilinged central room.
4 points

Clue 96: In the same room, find an upside-down classic Mickey on the Pocahontas airship.
4 points

★ Now find the two classic Mickeys below on the Tweedle Dee and Tweedle Dum mural in the same room.

Clue 97: Look for a flag.
2 points

Clue 98: Check out an apron.
2 points

Clue 99: Study the mannequins in this room.
4 points

Clue 100: Find Mickey near Cinderella Castle.
4 points

Clue 101: Stare up high for classic Mickeys.
2 points for four

Clue 102: Spot classic Mickeys on paintings in the central Genie Room.
2 points

Clue 103: In the same room, take a close look at the "antique" maps decorating the walls. (Psst! Think character profiles.)
5 points for three or more

Clue 104: Next door in the Villain Room, spot Cruella De Vil's Hidden Mickey.
3 points

Clue 105: Look for Mickey on top of and underneath merchandise bins.
3 points for both

Clue 106: Now find him on a wall near the restrooms.
3 points

Clue 107: Outside the store, in an entrance area to the Marketplace, look around for a classic Mickey. (Psst! Examine the pots.)
3 points

★ **T-REX** (10 points)

Clue 108: Admire a classic Mickey in the bar area.
5 points

Clue 109: Find a Hidden Mickey just outside the main entrance.
5 points

The Landing in Disney Springs (3 points)

★ **Raglan Road Irish Pub and Restaurant** (3 points)

Clue 110: Locate a Hidden Mickey near the stage.
3 points

WDW Casting Center (3 points)

Clue 111: Drive to the Casting Center building, across Buena Vista Drive from Disney Springs Marketplace, to locate more classic Mickeys. (These Hidden Mickeys can also be spotted from Interstate 4.)
3 points

Miniature Golf Courses (22 points)

You can find these Hidden Mickeys while you play the courses. Or you may be able to walk the courses without playing if it's not crowded, due to rain or luck. (Tell the attendants that you're hunting Hidden Mickeys and ask if you can take a look around.)

★ **Fantasia Gardens** (4 points)

Clue 112: Check the tee-off areas.
1 point

Clue 113: Take a good look at the 12th hole on the Gardens Course.
3 points

★ *Winter Summerland* (18 points)

Clue 114: Find Mickey on the third hole.
3 points

★ Now head straight for the 16th holes.

Clue 115: Spot Goofy on the 16th hole of the Winter Course.
3 points

Clue 116: Now check around the same hole for a Mickey Mouse gingerbread cookie.
2 points

Clue 117: Find Mickey and Minnie on the 16th hole of the Summer Course. (Psst! This Hidden Mickey is also visible from the 16th and 17th holes of the Winter Course.)
3 points for both

Clue 118: Wait for Mickey on the 17th hole of the Winter Course.
1 point

Clue 119: Study the Christmas tree on the 17th hole of the Summer Course for Hidden Mickeys.
3 points for three Hidden Mickeys

Clue 120: Look around for Mickey near the 18th tee for the Summer Course.
3 points

Near Celebration, Florida (4 points)

Okay, I admit it, this Mickey isn't hidden. Just the opposite, in fact. But it is unique. So I decided to include it anyway. You'll find a huge classic Mickey near Celebration, Florida, on the west side of Interstate 4.

Clue 121: Look for it as you get close to Exit 62.
4 points

Near the Magic Kingdom (5 points)

Clue 122: You can only see this classic Mickey made of tree groves from the air or on an image from a Google Earth search. It's a few miles northwest of the Magic Kingdom. Good luck!
5 points

**Total Points for
Hither, Thither & Yon Hunt =**

How'd you do?

A perfect score for this hunt is 387. You may have done even better if you earned bonus points in ESPN Wide World of Sports, Typhoon Lagoon, Disney-Quest, and/or by spotting Hidden Characters on the Disney buses.

You'll find a breakdown by area below, so that you can tally your score for only those places you've covered. Give yourself Gold if you scored at least 80% of available points, Bronze if you scored at least 40%.

Magnolia Golf Course (5)

Vista Boulevard (5)

Disney Vacation Club Way (5)

WDW Water Parks (48)
   Blizzard Beach (15)
   En route to Typhoon Lagoon (4)
   Typhoon Lagoon (29)

ESPN Wide World of Sports (15)

Disney Springs West Side (79)
   Cirque du Soleil (8)
   House of Blues (3)
   DisneyQuest (31)

Disney Springs West Side, cont'd.
Splitsville Luxury Lanes (12)
Wolfgang Puck Cafe (5)
Disney's Candy Cauldron (4)
D Street (10)
Starbucks (4)
Bus stop in The Landing (2)

Disney Springs Marketplace (193)
Entrance to the Marketplace (8)
Disney's Wonderful World of Memories (3)
Disney's Days of Christmas (15)
Goofy's Candy Co. (10)
Rainforest Cafe (4)
Sassagoula River Cruise ferry (5)
Marketplace Carousel (5)
Once Upon a Toy (38)
Disney's Pin Traders (8)
Tren-D (27)
Marketplace Co-Op (7)
Ghirardelli Ice Cream & Chocolate Shop (4)
Near the lake (3)
World of Disney (46)
T-REX (10)

The Landing in Disney Springs (3)
Raglan Road Irish Pub and Restaurant (3)

WDW Casting Center (3)

Miniature Golf Courses (22)
Fantasia Gardens (4)
Winter Summerland (18)

Near Celebration, Florida (4)

Near Magic Kingdom (5)

270

**Caution:
Don't peek at this
section unless you
really want help!**

Magnolia Golf Course

Hint 1: A sand trap at the sixth green is shaped like a classic Mickey.

Vista Boulevard

Hint 2: If you drive east from Fort Wilderness along Vista Boulevard, you can spot a sign for the Golden Oak community on your left. A classic Mickey is hidden in the tree of Golden Oak's logo.

Disney Vacation Club Way

Hint 3: Along Disney Vacation Club Way, when you reach the entrance drive to Saratoga Springs' Treehouse Villas, look to the opposite side of the road at the golf course and spot three bushes that form a classic Mickey at the side of the golf cart path.

ESPN Wide World of Sports

Hint 4: A three-dimensional Mickey Mouse looks out over the court from near the high central ceiling in The Milk House (the Field House). He's on an upper rafter above the sign, "The Milk House," in front of a yellow triangular wall partition that is opposite the main entrance. I spotted him to the upper left of the lower seats of section 104.

Hint 5: A large, pale green classic Mickey image lies in the outfield grass in the Wide World of Sports Champion Baseball Stadium.

Hint 6: On some days, you may spot classic Mickey circles around the pitcher's mounds on the nearby softball fields.

Hint 7: Walk past Champion Baseball Stadium, the Field House, and several multipurpose sports fields to the Track and Field Complex way in the back. A clever classic Mickey forms the base of the discus-throwing launch pad. (Tip: You can get a better vantage point for viewing this Mickey image by climbing up into the nearby bleachers.)

WDW Water Parks

– Blizzard Beach

Hint 8: Find a lighting fixture on the wall at the right rear of the Beach Haus store near the dressing rooms. There's a painting on the cover in which a small classic Mickey is formed by rocks at the lower center of an outdoor mountain scene.

Hint 9: As in many WDW shops, one or more of the merchandise stands has classic Mickey-shaped holes on its center pole.

Hint 10: From the *Chairlift* ride that takes you to the Mount Gushmore water slides, look to the ground on the second level of the mountain just past support pole

#4 (counting from the beginning of the lift) and below the right side of your chairlift to spot a classic Mickey made of three round

rocks. (Depending on the foliage, sometimes you can spot part of this rock Hidden Mickey from the left edge of the Observation Deck at the top of Mount Gushmore.)

Hint 11: At the rear of the park, a classic Mickey is formed by three stones jutting out from near the top edge of a stone bridge crossing *Cross Country Creek*. It is on the side of the bridge, near the center. A small triangular rock over this Hidden Mickey gives it the appearance of wearing a sorcerer's hat.

Tip: You can see this Mickey from the water or dry land. It is visible from the floating tubes as you approach the bridge by water. On land, you can see it through the trees (past the "Runoff Rapids Tube Pickup" area) either from just past the *Runoff Rapids* "Red Slope" entrance sign or from several points on the walkway on the other side of the bridge.

– En Route to Typhoon Lagoon

Hint 12: Classic Mickey holes are in the railing around the Disney Vacation Club (DVC) white tower that stands to the left of Buena Vista Drive at its intersection with Bonnet Creek Parkway.

– Typhoon Lagoon

Hint 13: Tip Boards with wait times written in chalk are situated around Typhoon Lagoon. If there is zero wait time for an attraction, the zero is drawn in the shape of a classic Mickey. (These images come and go.)

Hint 14: At *Crush 'n' Gusher*, on the upper floor near the elevator, paint circles on the cement form a classic Mickey.

Hint 15: Mickey ears are at the bottom of a vertical strut in the railing of a bridge. You can see the ears if you enter *Castaway Creek* at Shark Landing (near *Shark Reef*) and look behind you as you float under the first bridge. The ears are toward the right side of the bridge. You can also usually see the ears if you walk downstream on either side of the creek and look back at the bridge.

Hint 16: As you snorkel along in *Shark Reef,* you can often see a classic Mickey resting on the bottom of the swim route. Recently, the Mickey was located on the right side, about halfway along the route after the island.

Hint 17: About halfway up the wooden steps to the *Storm Slides,* and past the stranded motorboat on the right side of the path, Mickey ears are on the left side of a walkway slat.

Hint 18: Near the end of the long trail up to *Humunga Kowabunga,* three of the last short logs in the ground under the rope fence to the left of the walkway form an upside-down classic Mickey when viewed from above. (Note: You may spot other groups of short logs in the ground along walkways that resemble classic Mickeys.)

Hint 19: You'll find a classic Mickey formed by cannonballs along *Castaway Creek.* He's on your left by the second cannon past the waterfall if you're drifting in the creek. If you're walking on the nearby trail, you'll see him just past *Forgotten Grotto* in the rear of the park as you walk alongside the drifters. (Sometimes this cannonball image is moved around in this area.)

Hint 20: In the walk-through cave at the rear of *Ketchakiddee Creek,* there is a classic Mickey impression in the rock. It's on the back wall of the cave, about one and a half feet up from the ground, and near the drain at the right side of the cave as you enter the cave from the water.

Disney Springs West Side

– *Cirque du Soleil*

Hint 21: A classic Mickey is etched in the sidewalk near *Cirque du Soleil,* on the

second slab back from Parking Lot Q, just past a manhole cover and near the grass.

Hint 22: Under the main entrance staircase to the show are restrooms for men and women. You will find tiles laid to approximate a small classic Mickey on the floor of each restroom, in a corner just inside the entrance doors. These circles don't touch, but the design is convincing to my eyes.

– House of Blues

Hint 23: Walk through the front door and down the right side aisle. A classic Mickey is on the ceiling past the first server's station.

– DisneyQuest

Hint 24: At the bottom of the large three-dimensional ray gun poised over the lobby of Ventureport, three spheres form a classic Mickey from certain perspectives.

Hint 25: Symbols and figures that include classic Mickey designs are woven into the carpet on the third floor in Ventureport.

Hint 26: Track lighting shaped like a classic Mickey hangs above the elevator doors on floors two, three, four, and five. You'll find it near the *"Mighty Ducks Pinball Slam"* (on the third floor) and near *"Ride the Comix"* (on the fourth and fifth floors). On the second floor, near *"CyberSpace Mountain,"* the lighting is above an elevator door on the opposite side of the elevator bank.

Hint 27: Similar track lighting can be found in front of pod 4 of *"Invasion! An ExtraTERRORestrial Alien Encounter."*

Hint 28: On the fourth floor, the classic Mickey-shaped DisneyQuest logo is on the playing surface and on the sides of the air hockey tables.

Hint 29: Small yellow classic Mickey-shaped information stickers are on the fronts of some games on various floors.

Hint 30: Classic Hidden Mickeys are formed by some of the circles in the brown carpet near the Living Easels on the second floor.

Hint 31: Classic Mickey-shaped holes are in the sides of some of the wooden stools on the floor that children can stand on to play games. Find them on the second floor and other floors.

Hint 32: During *"Aladdin's Magic Carpet Ride,"* the golden beetle you encounter bears classic Mickey markings on its back.

Hint 33: At the "Virtual Jungle Cruise," classic Mickey-shaped balloons periodically float up from the left side of the screen, in front of the castle, before the ride starts.

Hint 34: On the screen in the first part of the *"Virtual Jungle Cruise"* ride, the raft may exit a glacier area under a distorted classic Mickey-shaped ice bridge over the river.

Hint 35: In the wall murals along the queue for *"Pirates of the Caribbean,"* the rightmost bunch of palm tree coconuts near the stairs is shaped like a classic Mickey.

– Splitsville Luxury Lanes

Hint 36: In the right wall mural inside the main entrance on the lower level, you can see the Mickey Earful Tower, balloons with Mickey ears, and classic Mickey holes in a red bowling ball.

Hint 37: On the upper level near the escalator, holes form a classic Mickey in a huge "orange" in the left wall mural.

Hint 38: A few classic Mickeys are formed by groups of oranges in the trees in the upper level left mural.

– Wolfgang Puck Cafe

Hint 39: Behind the reception counter, about two thirds of the way up the mosaic pyramid, a white tile and two smaller black tiles form a classic Mickey.

– Disney's Candy Cauldron

Hint 40: Inside the store, on the upper wall above the candy display, a dark marking on a stone near the ceiling forms a classic Hidden Mickey.

– D Street

Hint 41: Above you, various Mickey images float as clouds on the ceiling just inside the store entrance.

Hint 42: A somewhat distorted image on the wall to your immediate left as you enter the store resembles a classic Mickey.

Hint 43: A large classic Mickey image is formed by exposed bricks on the wall behind the main counter and across from the store entrance.

Hint 44: On the wall to the right of the exposed-brick classic Mickey, a full-body menacing Mickey has a black classic Mickey on his belt buckle.

– Starbucks

Hint 45: On a wall inside the seating area, an interactive electronic screen periodically allows you to draw inside white picture frames. Classic Mickeys are in the corners of a frame at the top middle of the screen.

– Bus stop in The Landing

Hint 46: A large classic Mickey hides in the cement between Bus Stops 5 and 6, across from the Planet Hollywood restaurant.

Disney Springs Marketplace

– Entrance to the Marketplace

Hint 47: Coca-Cola vending machines stand near Bus Stops 2, 3, and 4 in the Disney Springs Marketplace bus stop area. In colorful paintings on these machines, one full-body Mickey is pouring water and several classic Mickeys can be found on signs, a tower, and an awning.

Hint 48: Signs over the entrances to the Marketplace sport classic Mickeys at their sides.

Hint 49: Green benches with classic Mickey emblems on the top and sides are scattered around the Marketplace and the interactive fountain.

– Disney's Wonderful World of Memories

Hint 50: The sign on the store contains a full-figure Hidden Mickey on the page of a book.

– Disney's Days of Christmas

Hint 51: A large dark brown circular rock and two smaller rocks for "ears" form a classic Mickey on the middle side of the "chimney" inside the store. You'll see Dalmatians on the mantelpiece around this chimney.

Hint 52: Inside the shop, three large trees surrounded by merchandise have classic Mickeys carved in their bark near the tops of their trunks. The trees are not Christmas trees, and each of the three has one or two Mickey carvings.

Hint 53: Various sections of wallpaper and carpet often hide classic Mickeys.

Hint 54: In the rear room of the shop, classic Mickeys hide in the scrollwork on the ceiling.

Hint 55: At the corners of the store's far right outside windows that look toward the Marketplace Carousel, subtle classic Hidden Mickeys are in snowflakes.

278

– Goofy's Candy Co.

Hint 56: A shadow of Goofy is on the upper back wall of the store, behind the large Krispy Treat display.

Hint 57: Goofy, Mickey Mouse, Pluto, and other characters hide in the light brown mural on the upper wall around the store.

Hint 58: Classic Mickey circles are part of the design in the middle of the side window that faces the lagoon.

– Rainforest Cafe

Hint 59: A green lizard on the large sign outside Rainforest Cafe has an upside-down classic Mickey in the middle of the circles on its neck. On the smaller sign at the left of the cafe entrance, the lizard's mid-neck classic Mickey is tilted sideways to the left.

– Sassagoula River Cruise ferry

Hint 60: From the Marketplace boat dock, take the ferryboat to Port Orleans – French Quarter and then back to Disney Springs Marketplace. Both ways, spot small white classic Mickeys in some of the Treehouse Villas' windows.

– Marketplace Carousel

Hint 61: At least four classic Mickeys are hiding on the inner and outer decorative panels on the Carousel near Disney's Days of Christmas store. (You may find more than four Mickey images, but these are the ones I like best.)
   - A blue classic Mickey is on the sign under Minnie Mouse.
   - Two light green classic Mickeys hide on the dragon's nose. (For the best view of the dragon, check out an inner panel.)
   - Two tiny classic Mickeys hide on the pink window awnings on the right side of the panel that shows part of a store from a

distance. You'll see blue umbrellas on the left side of this panel.

- Pink classic Mickeys formed of roses hide in the upper part of the panels in the center of the Carousel.

– *Once Upon a Toy*

Hint 62: In the interactive flat fountain near the Once Upon a Toy store, water-tube heads are shaped like classic Mickeys, recessed lights in the cement are arranged in a classic Mickey shape, and the fountain water collects into a huge classic Mickey on the cement!

Hint 63: Outside the store, you'll find several faint classic Mickey hats in the cement near the side entrance.

Hint 64: Outside the store's main entrance, classic Mickeys are formed by truck tires (the "ears") atop Lincoln Logs.

Hint 65: Classic Mickey pincers or clamps (holding toys) circulate on a track that hangs from the ceiling in the room with Mr. Potato Head.

Hint 66: Tinker Toys on top of merchandise stands around the store form classic Mickeys.

Hint 67: At the bottom of these merchandise stands, you'll find classic Mickey supports.

Hint 68: Two black classic Mickeys are on blue sandals on one of the Mr. Potato Heads in the first room just inside the store's main entrance. Also notice black classic Mickeys at the sides of the small sandal accessories in the bins.

Hint 69: In the center of this Mr. Potato Head display in the first room, a tiny white classic Mickey adorns the clasp of Mrs. Potato Head's handbag. (Note: She's holding decorative Mickey balloons, wearing Mickey sunglasses, and has a Mickey sticker on her shoe.)

Hint 70: In this same room, the mural behind a service desk includes a classic Mickey balloon, several pairs of Mickey ears, and a Mickey ice cream bar.

Hint 71: The centers of the upper beams on wooden merchandise displays sport classic Mickey shapes.

Hint 72: On the same merchandise displays, large wing nuts on some of the bolts form Mickey ears.

Hint 73: Across the first and second rooms (as you enter from the front main entrance), large letters in Scrabble tiles on the floor spell "MICKEY."

Hint 74: In a central room of the store, a classic Mickey cloud appears in a window in a mural behind the service desk.

Hint 75: In the same room, a partial classic Mickey shadow is at the top of a wall mural. It's to the left of the classic Mickey cloud and above a checkout counter.

Hint 76: In the rear room, lollipops are arranged to form classic Mickeys on the outside of a merchandise stand.

– Disney's Pin Traders

Hint 77: On the large statue of Mickey and Minnie, Mickey wears a classic Mickey pin on his tie.

Hint 78: On Donald's statue, a red, white, and blue classic Mickey pin is on the upper right side of Donald's duffel bag. You'll find a second classic Mickey, a red one, at the front of Donald's purple suitcase, on the inside of one of the black Mickey-shaped pins spilling out of the suitcase.

– Tren-D

Hint 79: Look for Hidden (and decorative) classic Mickeys on the merchandise tables in the store. You can find decent Hidden Mickeys on the tops and sides of various tables.

Hint 80: Classic Mickeys are repeated in sections of framed wallpaper artwork inside the store.

Hint 81: A tiny black classic Mickey is on a female mannequin's cheek, under the left eye.

Hint 82: Minnie Mouse is painted on several columns inside the store in a variety of costumes and poses. In three of these paintings, she sports accessories adorned with Hidden Mickeys. In one, she wears an upside-down classic (Hidden) Mickey ring and clothing with purple decorative classic Mickeys. In another, she wears a Mickey watch and enjoys a decorative Mickey lollipop. In a third painting, Minnie's necklace has a small, gold classic Mickey pendant that stands out against her green outfit. (Other Mickey images in paintings of Minnie are decorative, not Hidden.)

Hint 83: A blue paint-splash classic Mickey is high on the wall inside the store near the entrance from the Marketplace Co-Op. If you enter the store from the main promenade, the image is on the upper wall to the right.

Hint 84: On the check-out countertop to the right as you enter from the outside promenade, smile at a reference to Mickey and Minnie. On the side closest to the main entrance, and near the angle of the countertop, "M M + M M" is carved into the counter.

Hint 85: Near the end of the left side of the check-out countertop, circle impressions form a classic Mickey. (The circles are all the same size, but this image is accepted by guests and Cast Members as a Hidden Mickey.)

– Marketplace Co-Op

Hint 86: Outside the entrance to the Marketplace Co-Op, you'll find a classic Mickey repeated in the white picket fence bordering the Disney Vacation Club display.

Hint 87: Along the main inside corridor of Marketplace Co-Op, a red classic Mickey is at the bottom of the overhead sign for "The Trophy Room."

Hint 88: Classic Mickeys hide in the clouds in the background of several paintings on the rear wall of the Caricature Booth near Guest Relations.

– Ghirardelli Ice Cream & Chocolate Shop

Hint 89: A dark side-profile image of Mickey looking to the left appears as a shadow in a painting on a rear wall of the shop (to the left as you enter). Look for a streetcar in the painting. The shadow is in the streetcar's second window from the left.

– Near the lake

Hint 90: Green chairs with classic Mickeys on top are scattered around outside in the Marketplace and near the Ghirardelli shop.

Hint 91: Several sections of the green fence around the lake have repeating classic Mickeys near the top of the railing.

– World of Disney

Hint 92: Blue classic Mickeys are on the far sides of the World of Disney entrance signs.

Hint 93: Light brown classic Mickeys can be found near the tops of the columns outside the store.

Hint 94: Classic Mickey holes are drilled in some of the metal posts that support the clothing racks.

Hint 95: In the high-ceilinged central room, behind the three little pigs floating overhead, a wall mural has a classic Mickey emblem above the doors of the Chinese Theater.

Hint 96: In the same room, the Pocahontas airship has an upside-down classic Mickey at the very bottom of the rear vertical tail fin, near where the tail fin connects to the body of the airship.

Hint 97: In the same room, you'll find a classic Mickey on a flag in the background of the Tweedle Dee and Tweedle Dum wall mural.

Hint 98: That mural also includes a classic Mickey on Tweedle Dee's apron.

Hint 99: In the same room of the store, some of the female mannequins have classic Mickey freckles under their eyes.

Hint 100: In the large central room, the clouds that encircle the model of Cinderella Castle hide a small classic Mickey.

Hint 101: In this same room, four black classic Mickeys are high on a wall under air vents near the ceiling.

Hint 102: On the walls in the central Genie Room, blue classic Mickeys can be spotted in the compass paintings.

Hint 103: Also on the Genie Room walls, antique-looking maps on wood panels painted to look like tapestries have land masses that resemble the side profiles of Mickey Mouse, Winnie the Pooh, Goofy, and possibly Donald Duck. (Donald is a bit of a stretch.)

Hint 104: On the wall in the Villain Room, next door to the Genie Room, Cruella De Vil's left wrist is wrapped with fur that has a classic Mickey dark spot on the side.

Hint 105: Display bins that hold merchandise in some of the rooms have classic Mickey-shaped feet and a band of classic Mickeys around the top. (Mickey bins like these can sometimes be found in other Disney stores as well.)

Hint 106: Near the restrooms at the far end of the store, a picture frame on the wall is lined with small classic Mickeys.

Hint 107: Near the World of Disney store, in an entrance to Disney Springs, there is a fountain surrounded by colorful flowers in clay pots. The fountain is composed of pots and bowls of varying sizes and shapes arranged so that water flows from one to another. A decorative topiary Mickey pours water into the topmost pot. Lower down, three clay pots form a classic Mickey when viewed from above.

– T-REX

Hint 108: Just inside the entrance and over the bar, a pink classic Mickey hides on the body of an octopus across from a green praying mantis.

Hint 109: A classic Mickey is formed by a clearing in the dirt (or sawdust) in the covered truck bed at the rear of the truck parked outside and to the right of the restaurant entrance.

The Landing in Disney Springs

– Raglan Road Irish Pub and Restaurant

Hint 110: A girl with Mickey ears is at a table at the left middle of a painting on the wall behind the stage.

WDW Casting Center

Hint 111: Classic Mickey holes can be seen in the upper outside walls of the Casting Center building. (These Hidden Mickeys can also be spotted from Interstate 4.)

WDW Miniature Golf Courses

– Fantasia Gardens

Hint 112: The tee-off areas on both courses are marked with classic Mickeys.

Hint 113: On the Gardens Course, the green at the 12th hole is shaped like a classic Mickey.

– *Winter Summerland*

Hint 114: On the third hole of the Winter Course, candy canes, milk, and gingerbread men pop out of "Defrosty" (the cooler). One is a gingerbread cookie featuring Mickey ears.

Hint 115: On the 16th hole of the Winter Course, you'll find a Goofy nutcracker on the left side of the mantelpiece.

Hint 116: A Mickey Mouse gingerbread cookie pokes out from a stocking hanging on the right side of the same mantelpiece.

Hint 117: On the left side of the 16th hole of the Summer Course, Mickey and Minnie are sitting in a sleigh on the mantelpiece, along with Pluto. Since the 16th holes of both courses are close together, this mantelpiece is also visible from the 16th and 17th holes of the Winter Course.

Hint 118: Mickey pops out of the present on the 17th hole of the Winter Course when you putt the ball under the gift box. This Mickey is big, but he is hiding most of the time!

Hint 119: At least three classic Mickey ornaments hang on the Christmas tree at the 17th hole of the Summer Course.

Hint 120: A red classic-Mickey Christmas ornament hangs from a rafter above your right shoulder as you face the 18th tee of the Summer Course.

Near Celebration, Florida

Hint 121: On the west side of Interstate 4, south of exit 62 near Celebration, you'll find a huge classic Mickey atop an electrical transmission line pole.

Near the Magic Kingdom

Hint 122: A few miles northwest of the Magic Kingdom, a huge green classic Mickey made of groves of trees can only be seen from the air (or on a Google Earth image). The Hidden Mickey is in a field just off Highway 27 and near the 192 merge.

Other Mickey Appearances

● ●

These Hidden Mickeys won't earn you any points, but you're bound to enjoy them if you're in the right place at the right time to see them.

★ Look for holiday Hidden Mickeys if you're at WDW during the Christmas season or any major holiday. For example, the "Osborne Family Spectacle of Dancing Lights" along the Streets of America in Disney's Hollywood Studios includes many hiding Mickeys.

★ Other "Hidden" Mickeys—décor and deliberate —appear with some regularity throughout WDW. Notice the Mickster on popcorn buckets, WDW brochures, maps and flags, Cast Member name tags, guestroom keys, pay telephones and phone books, menus, and restaurant and store receipts. The restaurants sometimes offer classic Mickey butter and margarine pats, pancakes and waffles, pizzas and pasta, as well as Mickeys on napkins and food trays. They also arrange dishes and condiments to form classic Mickeys, and some condiment containers are shaped like Mickey. You might notice classic Mickey holes in the backs of some high chairs.

The Mickey hat and ears on top of the "Earful Tower" are obvious to every visitor in the vicinity of Disney's Hollywood Studios. Many road signs on WDW Resort property sport Mickey ears and classic Mickey images, and WDW vehicles and monorails have Mickey Mouse images and insignia.

Cleaning personnel will often spray the ground, windows, furniture, and other items with three circles of cleaning solution (a classic Mickey) before the final cleansing. Or they may leave three wet Mickey Mouse circles or other Disney character images on the pavement after mopping! Mickey even decorates manhole covers, survey markers, and utility covers in the ground, as you've had a chance to find out for yourself on some of the scavenger hunts. In the evenings, you may encounter Mickey spotlight images on the pavement or on outside walls near WDW attractions.

Enjoy all these Mickeys as you explore WDW. And if you want to take some home with you, rest assured that you can always find "Hidden" Mickeys on souvenir mugs, merchandise bags and boxes, T-shirts, and Christmas tree ornaments sold in the Disney World shops. So even when you're far away from WDW, you can continue to enjoy Hidden Mickeys.

Note: There are usually some especially good Hidden Mickeys on souvenir mugs—tiny and hard to spot. The designs change every couple of years, and every time they come up with a new design, the Hidden Mickeys change.

My Favorite Hidden Mickeys

In this book, I've described over 1,250 Hidden Mickeys at Walt Disney World. I enjoy every one of them, but the following are extra special to me. They're special because of their uniqueness, their deep camouflage (which makes them especially hard to find), or the "Eureka!" response they elicit when I spot them—or any combination of the above. Here then are my Top Ten Hidden Mickeys and, not far behind, Ten Honorable Mentions. I apologize to you if your favorite Hidden Mickey is not (yet) on the lists below.

My Top Ten

1. Once-a-Year Mickey. *Under the Sea ~ Journey of The Little Mermaid*, Fantasyland, Magic Kingdom. Each year around noon on Mickey Mouse's birthday (November 18), sunlight shines through holes in the rock to form a classic Mickey on the wall of the inside entrance queue. Stay alert because Mickey might show up here at other times of the year! (Chap. 2, Clue 23)

2. Fern Mickey. The Garden Grill restaurant, The Land, Epcot. This Mickey hides behind a fern in the big mural inside the restaurant. When I outline this Mickey (a Cast Member often helps me by handing me a broom to reach it and highlighting it with a flashlight), I have witnessed folks in the restaurant smile and shout, "I see him! Look, there's Mickey!" (Chap. 3, Clue 98)

3. Minnie Mouse's Shadow. *The Great Movie Ride*, Disney's Hollywood Studios. This shadow on the mural by the loading dock is hard to spot, but once you see Minnie, you'll never forget her. (Chap. 4, Clue 46)

4. Golf Ball Mickey. *Soarin'*, The Land, Epcot. Your first reaction is to duck down to avoid the ball that's flying right at you. But stay still and don't blink, or you'll miss this great Hidden Mickey! (Chap. 3, Clue 15)

5. Jafar Rock. *Pangani Forest Exploration Trail*, Africa, Disney's Animal Kingdom. This three-dimensional head of Jafar is one of the most remarkable sculpted characters you'll see anywhere on Disney property. (Chap. 5, Clue 46)

6. Bush Rock Mickey. Japan, World Showcase, Epcot. This is one amazingly well-concealed rock Mickey! (Chap. 3, Clue 69)

7. Steamboat Willie Mickey. *Under the Sea ~ Journey of The Little Mermaid*, Fantasyland, Magic Kingdom. The Imagineers sculpted Mickey in his Steamboat Willie persona on a series of large rocks at the exit of the attraction. It's a tour de force in the world of Hidden Mickeys! (Chap. 2, Clue 31)

8. Light Cover Mickey. Art of Animation Resort. In the food court seating area, don't miss this faint image of Mickey Mouse smiling down on you. (Chap. 6, Clue 55)

9. Beam Mickey. Wilderness Lodge Villas. This Hidden Mickey peeks out of a hole in an overhead beam in the Villas lobby. Outstanding effect! Most folks don't even know he's up there, hiding! (Chap. 6, Clue 187)

10. Roof Mickey. Near the Contemporary Resort. Sitting on the edge of the roof of a backstage building next to the Contemporary Resort, this playful Mickey welcomes you to the Magic Kingdom. When you're on the monorail, show this Mickey to fellow travelers so they can join in the fun! (Chap. 6, Clue 226)

Ten Honorable Mentions

1. Grim Reaper Mickey. *Haunted Mansion*, Liberty Square, Magic Kingdom. A classic, this wonderful Mickey image has survived refurbishments and seems even better and spookier than ever! (Chap. 2, Clue 61)

2. 3-D Volcano Mickey. *Toy Story Midway Mania!*, Pixar Place, Disney's Hollywood Studios. While you're racking up points in the game, stay alert for this Hidden Mickey behind the target balloons. A convincing 3-D effect! (Chap. 4, Clue 5)

3. Sorcerer Mickey. At the rear of Blizzard Beach, Sorcerer Mickey is formed by stones jutting out from a bridge over *Cross Country Creek*. Very clever! (Chap. 7, Clue 11)

4. Purple Tile Mickey. Polynesian Village Resort. A classic Mickey in tile hides on the counter of the Kona Island coffee bar. This one's a real winner, especially when you point it out to folks who've never seen it. It's hiding in plain sight! (Chap. 6, Clue 201)

5. Tattered Fabric Mickey. Be Our Guest Restaurant, Fantasyland, Magic Kingdom. While you're marveling at the décor inside this restaurant, make a point of strolling through the West Wing room to enjoy this subtle classic Mickey hiding high above you. (Chap. 2, Clue 36)

6. Tiny Fly Mickey. "Song of the Rainforest" area, *Conservation Station*, Rafiki's Planet Watch, Disney's Animal Kingdom. Journey to spot one of the smallest classic Mickeys ever created. (Chap. 5, Clue 76)

7. Aquarium Rock Mickey. *The Seas with Nemo & Friends*, Future World, Epcot. At the bottom of the aquarium lie one or more classic Mickeys formed of rocks. Cast Members (and guest divers) do a great job of maintaining these images. (Chap. 3, Clue 105)

8. Vine Mickey. Animal Kingdom Lodge. This green classic Mickey hides on the vine-covered column outside the rear lobby doors. Well-camouflaged and hard to find, but fun to spot. (Chap. 6, Clue 7)

9. Octopus Mickey. T-REX restaurant, Disney Springs Marketplace. The octopus over the bar has many colorful spots, including one cool Hidden Mickey. (Chap. 7, Clue 108)

10. Star-Field Mickey, *Buzz Lightyear's Space Ranger Spin*, Tomorrowland, Magic Kingdom. Ride the attraction several times if you need to; this tiny Hidden Mickey is worth discovering! (Chap. 2, Clue 93)

CHAPTER 10

Don't Stop Now!

Hidden Mickey mania is contagious. The benign pastime of searching out Hidden Mickeys has escalated into a bona fide vacation mission for many Walt Disney World fans. I'm proud to include myself among them. Searching for images of the Main Mouse can enhance a solo trip to the parks or a vacation for the entire family. Little ones delight in spotting and greeting Mickey Mouse characters in the parks and restaurants. As children grow, the Hidden Mickey game is a natural evolution of their fondness for the Mouse.

Join the search! With alert eyes and mind, you can spot Hidden Mickey classics and new Hidden Mickeys just waiting to be found. Even beginners have happened upon a new, unreported Hidden Mickey or two. As new attractions open and older ones get refurbished, new Hidden Mickeys await discovery.

It may be just my imagination but I swear that every time I visit Walt Disney World, I spot a Hidden Mickey up in the clouds, watching over his domain! Do you think the Imagineers might actually have some influence on the atmosphere over Walt Disney World?

The Disney entertainment phenomenon is unique in many ways, and Hidden Mickey mania is one manifestation of Disney's universal appeal. Join in the fun! Maybe I'll see you at Walt Disney World, marveling (like me) at these Hidden Gems. They're waiting patiently for you to discover them.

Acknowledgements •••••••••••

No Hidden Mickey hunter works alone. While I've discovered many of the Hidden Mickeys in this book on my own—and personally verified every single one of them—finding Hidden Mickeys is an ongoing group effort. I am indebted to the following dedicated Hidden Mickey lovers for alerting me to a number of Hidden Mickeys I might otherwise have missed. Thanks to each and every one of you for putting me on the track of one or more of these WDW treasures and, in some cases, also helping me verify them. Extra special thanks to Sharon Dale for spotting over 235 Hidden Mickeys and to Jesse Kline for finding over 100 of these elusive gems!

Names in bold have spotted 10 or more. You can find each person's contribution(s) by visiting my website, www.HiddenMickeyGuy.com.

Candi A., Maxine A., Nancy A., Frank Abbamonte, Scott Abney, Alex Abrahamzon, Debbie Acres, Jonah Adams, Kaitlyn Rae Adams, Ron Adams, Sarah Adams, The Adornettos, Nancy Ahlsen, Michael Akers, Lindsey Albrecht, James Algatt, Katie Allen, Matt Allgaier, Anthony Almeyda, Jordan Altug, Brianna Alvarez, Eric and Danielle Ambielli, Cathy Ames, John Ames, Amy Amyot, Alex Anderson, Chelsea Anderson, Michelle Anderson, Robert Anderson, Robert Anschuetz, Sarah Anzjon, Kristin Archibald, Elena Argaluza, Jason and Tammy and Lily Armstrong, Stanley Arnold, Jennifer Ashley, Mark and Dean Ashwaite, Michelle Astuti, Tacey Atkinson, Chloe Augustine, Barb B., Dan B., Devon B., Ian B., Jason B., Jessica B., Andrew Babb, Priscilla Baer, Sarah Bagwell, Tony and Matthew and Caroline and Stephanie Banzer, Salina Barbosa, Angie Barclay and kids, Mark Barnes, Sarah Barnes and son, Daniel Barrach, Steven Madison Barrett, Vickie Barrett, Chris Barry, Diana Barry, Diane Barry, Samantha Barry, Anthony Bartiromo, Nicholas Bartoli, Johnny Bartolomeo, Fred Bastien, **James Baublitz**, Sarah Baywell, Penny and Jeff Beam, Eric Beaulieu, Mike Beckerman, Brittany and Craig Bedelyon, Jonathan Beer, The Beesinger Family, Leila Beikmohamadi, April Beisser, Heather Beland, **Annmarie and David and Josh and Rick Benavidez**, Rich Benneau,

Lauren Benson, Steve and Colleen and Michaela and Amanda Benson, The Benson Family, Richard Bent, Clark Benton, Jeffrey Berg, Patti Berg, Bryan and Stacy and Jenna and Barry Berger, Jason Berrang, Terry Berringer, David Berry, **David and Celia Berset**, Jenny Bess, Kristen Bevacqua, Tom Binder, Andy Birkett, Murray Bishop, Roberta Blackburn, Mark Blackie, **Erin Blackwell**, Trevor Blair, Louis Blanco, **Nancy Blevins**, Laurie and Rebecca Bloodworth, The Bodmann Family, Jennifer Bogdan, Tyler and Brandie Bolton, Rich Bonneau, Michael Bonnett, Jr., Kevin Booton, Storie Borgman, Katie Borland, Craig Boudreaux, Alicia Bourne, Wendy Bowen, The Bowles Family, Holly Bowling, Elizabeth Bowman, Nicole Bowman, Donna Brackin, Alan Brainard, Shane Braisdell, Brent Brandon, Tina Brannen, Leyla Brborich, Todd Breakey, David Breede, Matthew Brennan, J. Bridge, Christine Bristow, Patrick Broaddus, Colin Brooks, Larry E. and Tanya Brooks, Stuart Brooks, Daniel Brookwell, Stephen Brookwell, Chrissy Brown, Jaye Brown, Jeff Brown, Karen Brown and daughter, Peter Brown, Roberta Brown, The Brown Family, Emily Brubaker, John and Susan P. Bruederle, Paul Brune and family, Gabriella and Thierry and Matthieu Bruxelle, Erica Bryant, The Buaas Family, Cheryl Buchanan, Matt Buchanan and son, Earl Burbridge, Nancy Burke, Lisa Burleson, Todd Busby, Jon Bushee, Brett Butcher, Ruth Butler and daughter, Giovanni C., Shari C., Kimberly Cabral, Villa Cadlle, Bret Caldwell, **Peter Caldwell**, Kerri Callahan, Sarah Callanan, Abigail Campbell, Anne Campbell, David Campbell, Lisa Campbell, Rob and Annabel Campbell, Michael - Lindsay - Alex and Hailey Campe, Craig Canady, Jason Cannons, Todd Carballo, Stan Carder, Chris Carlson, Deborah Carpenter, Gary Carr, James Carraher, Kacey Cassette, Robbie Castro, Jade and Dominic Cavalco, Alexis Cavileer, Mary Anne Ceci, Christina Cella, Kelly Challand, Austin Chanu, J. Chappa, Julie Chappa, Chloe Charette, Jim Cheslin, Catherine Chiarello, Nikki Christensen, Dana Christos, Alyssa Ciaccio, Vito Ciaccio, Samantha Ciampa, Michael Ciampi, Anne-Marie L. Clanton and family, Matt Clarke, Matthew Clemons, Malcolm Cleveland, John Clover, Alexa Cohen, Serena Anne

Cohen, Rob Coile and daughter, Elizabeth Coler, John Coliton, Kent Collins, **Mary Jo Collins**, Michael Collins, William and Colleen Colmenares, Jason Colpitts, Eleanor Coltman, Greg Conlin, Joey Connors, Jeffrey Contompasis, Lindsay Contreras, Timmy Coogan, Ian Cordle, Colleen Costello, Calvin Cotanche, Bill Cote, Sherrie Cotton, Angela Coutavas, Sara Cox, Karen Crabtree, David Craig, George Crippen, Rob Croskery, Lydia and Michael Cross, Catherine Crouch, Gary Cruise, Denise and Tyler and Ashley Cruz, Kasie Culp, Erica Culver, Nancy Curl, Brian Currier, Traci Curth, Curtis D., Katie D., Nick D., Marie and Bruce Daigneault, Alicia Dakins, **Sharon and Chloe Dale**, John Anthony D'Alotto, Christina Darce and brother, Jim Darling, Christopher Dash, David Davies, Shannon DeAraujo, Anthony Dearman, Bob Decker, Keenan DeFrisco, Amy Degenstein, Dwayne Degler, Michele DeGrace, Bethany and Christine DeLaurentis, Robert Delgado, Sarah Del Grande, Dottie Del Signore, Mike Demopoulos, Michael DeRose, Stephen DeSanto, Rich DeTeresa, Wanda Deveau, **Tim Devine**, Dania Dewese, Sondra Dewey, James Dezern, The DiBenedetto Family, Cara Di Cicco, Maryt Mary DiEuliis, The Digon Family, Doug Dillard, James and Jennifer DiMaggio, Suzannah DiMarzio, Max Dinan, Sam Dinan, Mark Dingman, Mario DiPlacido, Alexander Disney, Calvin Dolsay, Gina Dorkins, Marcus Dorothy, Jim Doyle, Sarah Dozert, Kelsey Draves, Dave Drumheller, Dave Drylie, Laura Dubberly, Jim Dufek, Angelica Dufer, James Duggan, Joey Duggan, Tom Durr, Abby Dwyer, Alex Dwyer, Ian Dwyer, Robert E., Jamillia Ear, John Early, Joy and Abigail Eats, Jason Ebels, Linda Eckwerth, Susan Edgington, The Familie Edmondson, Erik Edstrom, Seth Edward, Nicholas Elardo, M. Eldred, Amber Ellis, Karen Ellis, John Emmert, Eric England, Lillie England, Ben English, David and Elizabeth Epley, Kelly and Kimberly Erickson, Michael Ethridge, Nick Exley, Eric Fabian, Alyson Fair, Nick Falco, Adam Fanjoy, Ken Fanti, Ashley Fayett, Ronald and Gianna Fazio, Joshua and Krystina Fears, Alan and Craig Fergus, Ronald Ferraco, Kathy Fetters, Dom Fiandra, Kenney Fichter, Jim Finley, John Finley, Elaine Finnigan, Ashley Rae Fischer, Dennis Flath,

Michelle Flege, Sharon Flood, Jessica Flowers, Dave Flynn, Stephanie Foley, Taylor Fong, Carlos Font, Melissa and Jacob Forbes, Mario Forcellati, Eldon J. Forcey, Chet Ford, Joseph Fortenbaugh, Mark Fowle, Joe Franceschino, Sr. and Joe and Diane Franceschino, Jessica and Brent Fraser, Debbie Frazier, Eden Frazier, Matt Freeman, Connie Freese, T.J. Frey, Eli Fried, Devon Friedman, Rachel Friedman, Ryan and Fairen Frisinger, Chip Froelich, Jake Fruci, Diane Furtado, Eric Gagnon, Jackie Gailey, Michelle Gala, **Jason Gall**, Jack Gallaher, Dave Gallant, Chrystine Gallegos, Justine Gamale, Traci Garber, Traci Gardellis, Brad Garfinkel, Marilyn Garfinkel, Scott Garland, Gunnar Garner, Tony Garon, Melissa Garrigus, Kristen Gartrell, Terry and Julia Garvey, Christy Gattis, Adam Geaneas, Anthony Gentile, Pauline Gibson, Kaela and Ryan and Jake Gilbert, Owen Gilley, **Tyler Glynn**, Chase Goeser, Mark Goldhaber, Nathan Goley, Jeremiah Good, Ty Goode, Andrew Goodwill, Jack Goodwill, June Goodwill, William Goodwill, Vanessa Gordon, Trevor Goren, James and Edward Goring, Alyssa Gormish, Ryan Goukler, Josh Graham, Jeff and Joyce Grant, Todd Grasley, Tim Grassey, Dani Gray, Jim Greenhouse, Mark Greenwald, Rick Gregg, Adam Gregorich, Bill Griffin, George Griffin, Robert Grohman, Werner Grundlingh, Louis C. Guidry, Lorri Gumanow, Amanda Gunn, Elizabeth Gutman, Ryan Gutzat, Chris and Cindy H., Christine H., Cindy H., Rick Haas, Daniel Hadden, Brandi Hall, Byron Hall, Gracie and Dana Hall, Lydia Hall, Melanie Hall, Mike Hamilton, Shannon Hamilton, Theresa Hamway, Jake Hardin, Elsa Harding, Donna Hardter, Ray Harkness, Ed Harriger, Stephen Harris, Beth Harrison, Brian Harshberger, Grant Hart and brother, David Hartzell, Bernice Hasher, Laura and Ross Haston, Bryan Hauser, Mike Hawkins, Abbi Hawthorne, Debbie Hayden, Colin Healy, Sean Heard, Ryan Hecht, Mary Heidenberg, Kurt Heinecke, Haley Heintz, Claudia and Ralph Hemsley, Carrie Henderson, Brian Henry, Liz Hernandez, Otto Hernandez, Louise Herrick, Iris and Zachary Herron, Amanda Hertel, Ricky Hett, Beth Higginbotham, Aaron Hill, Jamie Lee Hindes, Jim Hines, Joan Hinkle, Mark Hitt, Jay Hobson, Matt Hochberg,

Rick Hoefinghoff, Ed Hoffman, Paul Hoffman, Denise Hoffmann, sdmt Hogan, Chip Holland, Vivian Holland, Matt Holley, Michael Hollingsworth, Joyce Holroyd, Jamie Holz, Craig Hood, Deonna Hores, Jasmine Horning, Evelyn Horton, Noah Howard, Kim Howe, Erik Hubbard, Josh Hudson, Keith Hudson, Tony Hudson, Emily and Lynette Huey, Elton Hughes, Brennan Huizinga, Amy Hunt, William Huntley, Kaitlyn Husak, Cameron Hutt, The Huwar and Fabanich Family, **Bill and Donna Iadonisi**, Dawn and Megan Ilsley, The Ilsley Family, Alex Inman, Andy Inserra, Mike Ireland, Sarah Ireland, Amanda Iseminger, James Ivers, Ashley Izzo, Andy Jackson, Graham Jackson, Mark Jackson, Scott Jackson and niece, Andy Jasinski, Mark Jeffries, Angela Jenkins, Troy Jewell, Tammy Jimenez, Chris Johnson, Jessica Johnson, KJ Johnson, Rayanne Johnson, Trisha Johnson, Samantha and John and Brian Jonckheere, Brecken Jones, Laura Jones, The Jones Family, Tim Jones, Wendy Jones, Michael Jowett, Michelle June, Benjamin K., Julie K., Michael Kania, Gary Kaplow, Debbie Karnes, Ray Kastner, Constance Katsafanas, Kathy Katsafanas, William Katzer, Kristin Kaylor, Dan Kearns, Brent William Kee, Aaron and Evan Keller, Gayle Keller, Jennifer Keller, Robert Keller, Declan Kelly, Devin Kelly, Jim Kelly, Steven Kempa, Melanie Kemper, The Kemper Family, Deb Kendall, Jasmine Kennedy, John Kessel, Brian Keys, Heather Killough-Walden, Sam Kimport, Bonnie King, James King, Chris Kirchein, Rachel Kirk, Max Kirkpatrick, Maggie Kirkwood, Rochelle Klay, Aaron Klein, Cheryl Klein, Hilary Klein, Patty Klein, Patty and Patrick and Adam and Megan Klein, Paul and Michelle Klein, Mitchell Michini Klepac, **Jesse and Jordan Kline**, Jordan Kline, Sarah Kline, Steve Knapp, John Koerber, Deb Koma, Gloria Konsler, Rich Kordalski, Shirley Kordalski, Jack Koss, Jack and John and Christine Koss, Wendy Kraemer, Amy Krauss, Monte Kremin, Tim Kress, Chris Kretzman, Austin Kruckmeyer, Ali and Jennifer Kurtz, Matthew Kushner, Jackie Kushnier, Brenden L., Nathan L., Mikey Laing, Brian Lake, Joshua Lake, Paul Lalli, Kim Lamb, Anne Langlotz, Brian Lanier, Meris Larkins, **Bev and Scott and Dick Larson**, Tim Larson, Richard Lathrop, Allison Laudage,

Rebecca Lawler, Daniel Lawson, Lea Ann Lavy, Dr. E. Kye Layton, Melanie LeBlanc, Russell LeBlanc, Will LeBlanc, Joshua Lehrer, Becca Leipzig, Justin Lemonds, Kathryn Leonard, Lisa Leonard, Jennifer Leone, Linda Lesar, Angie Leslie, Jessica Levenson, **Justin Lewicki**, Billy Lewis, Bradley Lewis, Luke Licygiewicz, Taricia Lightfoot, Kyle Lighting, Beth Lindemann, Chuck Lionberger, Jeffrey Lipack Sara Lodgen, C. Loesch, Bryan Long, Christie Long, Kristen Long, J. Scott Lopes, **Marc and Josiah Lorenzo**, **Jeff Love**, Stephen Lovelette, John Lovett, Kent and Pam Low, Ashley Lowe, Nick Lowman, Sam Loynes, The Luckner Family, Ash Lux, Jennifer Lynch, Jim Lyon, Will Lyon, Linda Mac, Sharon Machuga (and Mei Li), Alexander Mack, Chris Macri, Michelle MacVane, Keri Madeira, Cholle Madere, Dusty Madere, Hope Madere, Karen Madere, Mason Madere, Shane Madere, Beci Mahnken, John Majcherek, Austin Malone, Michael Manall, Salvatore Manente, Katherine Manetta, Sharla Manglass, Brent Manley, Adam Manno, Kristy Mantarro, Frank Marando, Vanessa Marquez, John and Stephanie Marshall, Drake Martin, Jeffrey Martin, Breanne Martine, Brian Martsolf, Ginny Massoni, Jake Massoni, James Massoni, Brooke Matinides, Pam May, Allison and Andy Mayo, Greg Mazzella, Kelly McAdams, Isaiah McAllister, Aurora McBride, Alexander McClintick, The McCully Family, Mark McCurry, Chris McDaniel, Matthew and William McDaniel, Fawn and Holden McDonald, Mark McDonald, Chris McDonnell, Meradith McGee-Hale (and Carter), Jessica McGilvary, Sarah McGovern, Saffron McGregor, Cameron McGuire, Billy and Zoe McInerney, Andrea McKenna, Carrie McLaren, Ryan - Rachel - Samantha and Robert McMillan, **Donna McMurrey**, Allissa McNair, Michala McNair, JerriAnne and Susan McPherson, Jill Meadows, Doug Means, Mark Medley, Joseph Mehr, Matt Mellarkey, Amy Mentz, Brian Mentz, Tammy Metz, Sharon Meyer, Kim Michaux, H. Mildonian, Bill Miles, Toni-Lynn Miles, William Miles, Alexis Miller, Geoff Miller, Herb Miller, Krista and Maeve Miller, Rich Miller, Todd and Jennifer and Sean Miller, Stephen and Brianna Millevoi, Patti Minden, Sandy Modesitt, Aruna Mohan, Perry Molinoff, Kelly Monaghan, Claire Monahan, Lou Mongello, Michele

Moody, Jennifer Moon, Joy Mooney, David Moore, Rick Moore, Sharon Moore, Ron Moorhouse, Marc Moran, Denise Morelli, Mickey Morgan, The Moriarty Family, Rick Morin, Patti Lel Morris, Joseph Moschinger, Phil Motto, Scott Mueller, The Muklewicz Family, Ed Muller, Brodie Mumphrey, Baseer Muqri, Lori Murch, Christine Murphy, Marty Murray and son, Brenda N., L. Naizer, Lindsey Naizer, Kurt Nank, Michael Nemeroff, Brayson Nesbitt, Mandy Newby, Jeff Newcomb, Mary Newell, Victoria Newhuis, Benjamin and Aden Newman, Devon Newport, Debbie Newton, Darrin Nilsson, Joe Nixon, Ashley Nolf, Dennis Nordling, Annette Nuenke, Cheryl Nutter, Andrew and Matthew Nypower, Denise O., Erin O'Brien, George O'Brien, Scott O'Donnell, Eileen Knight Ogle, Steve Okeefe, Jeff Oldham, David Oliver, Mitch Oliver, Giovanni Oliveras, Beth Olliges, Kim Olsen, Bob Ondercik, Bobby Ondercik, Rita Ondercik, Sheri Ondercik, Susie Ondercik,A. O'Neill, Sarah and Jim Opaleski, Lisa O'Reilly, Nicole O'Reilly, Justin Orilio, Orlando Attractions Magazine, Rodrigo and Alejandro and Rogelio Orta, Katie Ortynsky, Greg Ostravich, Joy Ousterout, The Outra Family, Denise Owen, Annette Owens, Charles Owens, Jake Owens, Curtis P., Dom P., Kristin P., Melissa P., Glenn and Vickie Pacheco, Bill Padonisi, Doreen Pakidis, Brad and Brittany Paliswat, Jessica Paneral, Benoit Paquin, Nancy Paris, Caleb Parry, Calley Pate, Bob and Maryellen Paton, Chad and Megan Paton Evans, Sam and Lucy and Kimberly Paton Vegter, Alex Patrick, Brian Patterson, Drew Patterson, Kyla and Jen Patton, Lori Payne, Denise Peczinka, Jonathan Peczinka, Tawny L. Peedin, Glenn Peeters, Natalie Pence, **Maya Perez**, **Octavio Perez**, **Suzanne Perez**, Todd Perlmutter, Matt Perkins, Caleb Perry, Jenny Perry, John Perry III, John Perry IV, Christine Peruski, Mark Petar, Sheila Peter, Kristina Peterson, Lucy Peterson, Tony and Kara Peterson, Steve Petty, Patrick Phelan, Martin Pierce, Victoria Pike, Ray Pilgrim, Brooke Pimental, Linda Pinto, Sara Pirraglia, Tony Pirrelli, Susan Pitts, Linda Pizzuro, Amanda Plante, Cynthia Platt and family, Brian Policano, Krista Porter, Roberta Powers, Al Prete, Karen and Grace Price, Katherine Price, Kirby Price, Nathan Price, Walt Prindle, Hayden Pronto-Hussey,

Caleb Pryor, Matt Pucci, Wendy Pugh-Hummel, Todd Pushman, Erica R., Tessa R., Tim Rachuba, Deb Ragno, Richard Rando, Nicholas Ranger, Kolding Rasmussen, Chris Rathsack, Brendan Ratner, Carol Ray, Sharon Reedy, Stacy Reedy, Derrick Rees, Amber Reeves, Len Reeves, Lynne Reilly, Johnny and Jyle Reis, Michael Remy, Kathy Riccardi, Chris Ricci, Nik Ricci, Mikey Ricco, Richie Rich, Bob Richmond, D. Richmond, Richard Rick, Chuck and Sharon Ridgely, Brian Rigsby, Ron Riley, Antonio Riquelme, Jose Riquelme, Rob and Kathy Risavy, Bryan Rivera, Joy E. Robertson-Finley, Andy and Jay and Angel Robey, Joseph Robinson, Lauren Robinson, Lawrence Robinson, Lawrence Robson, S. Rodriguez, Lauren Roeser-Nordling, Geoff Rogos, Terry Rohrer, Robyn Romine, Nick Rosa, Clara Rosadas, Emily Rose, Matt Roseboom, Nancy Rosenberg, Trent Routien, Teresa Rovery, Timothy Rowe, Mitch Rozetar, Kathy Rubin, Chris Rudolph, James Rudolph, Jim Rudolph, Annmarie Rumford, Shauna Rupert-Sessions, Ed Russell, Christine Russo, Steve Russo, Callie S., Heather S., Ken S., Steve S., Tom S. and Terri, Robin Sackevich, I and Y Sakurada, Andy Salerno, Ashley Saliba, Anthony Salzano, Sheila Sanders, Tami Sanker, Christina Santoro, Hannah Savage, Rachel Savage, Andrew Savers, Dee Dee Scarborough, Jackie Scheibis, The Scheuher Family, John Schiaparelli, Josh Schickler, Matt Schimkus, Ashlea Schneider, Julie Schneider, **Sherrie Schoening**, Ashley Schultz, Hank Schultz, Steve Schultz, Spencer Schweinfurth, Bethany and Michael Scibetta, Carol Scopa, Mike Scopa, Jeri Scott, Keira Scott, Liam and Michelle Scribner-MacLean, Todd Seales, Jack Seidenberg, Steve Seifert, David and Aubree Serkoch, Debbi Sessa, Trent Sexton, Khrys Sganga, Chris Shank, Leslie Sharkey, John Sheehan, Randy Shelton, William Shelton, Yinan Shentu, Susan Shirey, Bob Shoemaker, Faith and Abby Short, Bret Shortall, Andy Shull, Bill and Kim Shultz, Stephanie Shultz, Scott Siblovin, Josh Siegel, Scott Sigouin, Deb Silhan, Tyler Silhan, Rick Simard, Stephen Simmons, Steve Simmons, James Simon, KJ Simpson, **Jimmy Sisson**, Alexander Sjursaether, Tom Skaine, Bridget Skallet, The Skazick Family from the UK, Luke Skinner, Katie Slater, Mike Sluss, Michael Smart,

Byon Smiddy, Laurie Smiley and grandsons, Bonnie Smith, Elaine Smith, Neil Smith, Rebecca Smith, John Snider, Michele Snoddy, Wesley Snyder, Jack Sorensen, Benjamin Soto, Roy Souders, Zach Souders, Douglas Southworth, Kitty Spangler, Megan Spellman, Ryan Spellman, Erica Spencer, Steve Spevak, Michele Sponagle, Kailah Spratt, Megan Stallings, Todd Standley, Rich - Diane - Andrew and James Stangle, Michael and Emily Steele, Kevin Stein, Joshua Steiner, Nicholas Steinhoff, Lindsey Stephens, Sharon Stevenson, Lori Stewart, Mark Sties, Skip and Susan and Jack Stinson, Heather Stone, **Jay Stonefield**, Ben Stowell, Branson Strawderman, Allen Stroud, The Suarez Family, Cherie Sulko, Jill Sullivan, Chris and Cathy Sutherland, David Sutton, Dan Swain, Jeff Swearingen, Jordan and Kenya Swiss, Joey Sylvester, Kathy Szczerba, Brittani T., Jen T., Jenni Tackett, Alex Taday, Sharon Tamplain, Joe Tanzillo, Kenzie Tapia, Jared Tavernari, Jordan Taylor, Karen Taylor, Leanne Taylor, Vance Taylor, Len Testa, Samantha and Mikayla Tewksbury, Alayna Theunissen, Brian Thomas, Kimmie Thomas, Roni Thomas-Patterson, Patsy Thomasson and family, Brian Thompson, Jake Thompson, Laura Thompson, Thomas M. Thompson, Pamela Thor, Emily and Kate Thorington, Albert Thweatt, Carter Thweatt, Max Thweatt, Erin Tickno, Paige Tiffany, Susie Tilley, **Martha Tischler**, Kristy and Scott and Jim and Kim Todd, Debra Tolsma and Alex, Holly Tomashek, Frank Tonra, Frank Tonra Jr., Frank Tonra III, Keith Tonra, Mallory Tonra, The Tonras, Kevin Toomey, Whitney Townsend, Lauren and Steven Tracy, Kendra Trahan, Scott Trask, Nathan Trent, Jessica Trentacosta, Marcel Troost, Beverley Tuck, Brandon Tucker, Ashley Kennedy Turner, Glenn Turner, Derek Tyler, Charles Tyner, Terry Ulrich, Melissa Uzzilia, Nicole V, Stephen Valente, Sandra Valgardson, Shivani Varma, Max-Emanuel Vingerhoets, Aninka van Staden, Frank van Wijk, Mason Vaughan, Chris Vaughn, **Wayne and Angie Vaughn**, Tairyn Velie, Tracy Vesel, Jim Vignola, The Vitrano Family, Jared Voegele, Fred Vosecky, Christpher and Alisha Vozella, Deven Wagenhoffer, Maureen Wahtera, Harry Walker, Jeanne Walker, Amanda Wallace, Michael Walsh, The Walsh Family,

Grace Walter, Christine Wang, Matthew Wang, Jonathan Ward, Rachel Ward, Sharon Ward, Kathy Warner, Sean-Paul Warnick, Matthew Watson, Mary Weaver, The Weaver Family, Dena Weber, Eric Weber, Rebecca Webster, Scott Weideman, Fred Weiner, Joshua Weiss, Cheri Weitkamp, Max Weitkamp, The Welch Family, Brett Weldon, Carrie Welf, Matt Wells, Jed Werner, Robert Wescovich, Michelle Wesolowski, James West, John Weyrich, Craig Wheeler, John Wheeler, Shona Whiddon, Jennah and Noah Whitcomb, **Alena White**, Jared White, Jeff Whitlock, Katarina Whitmarsh, Sharon Whitney, Patricia Whitson, Jack Widman, Andrew Wierzbicki and sister, Victoria A. Wieting, Jim Wiggins, Becky Williams, Carla Williams, Chris Williams, Jason Williams, Kevin Williams, Scott Williams, Shannon Williams, Susan Williams, Darrel Williamson, Ida Williamson, Garrett Willis, Deb Wills, Amory Wilson, Debbie Wilson, Jeannette Winner, Sara Witt, Darren Wittko, Chrissy Wooding, Barb Wooldridge, Harry Wootan, Marli Worden, Elizabeth Worth, Brook Wozniak, Kassidy and Cody Wright, Jeanine Yamanaka, Lynn Yaw, Trevor Yeatts, Kevin Yee, Callum Young, Heather Young, Jonathon Young, Robert and Mary Jo Young, Alexandra Z., Adam Zaner, Meghann Zanotta, Eric Zech, Christianna Ziccardi, Lea Zich, Kristine Zolciak, Julie Zanolla, Catherine Zori,

AND

Aaron, Aimee, AJ, Al, Alan, Alanna, Alex, Alexis, Alison, Allie, Allison, Alpha, Alyssa, Amanda, Amber, Amelia, Amy, Andy, Anime Hockeygrrl, Ann, Anonymous, Anubis316, Ariel, Austin, azc, Barbara, Benjamin, Beth, Bill, Blair, Bob, Brad, Brad & Courtney, Brandon, Brandy, Brian, Brianne, Brooke, Bryan, Bryan@allaboutthemouse.com, Cailin, Caitlin, Caitlyn, Captain Mike, Carlos, Caroline, Casey, Cassie, Catherine, Cathreine, Caylie, Charlene, Charles, Charlie, Charlotte, Cheryl, Chloe, Christopher, Christy, Cindy, Claire, Claudia, Cole, Colin, Colin-Kevin-Connor-Jodi-Nana and Pops, Colleen, Corey and mother-in-law, Courtney, Crispynoodle, C.T., Danielle, Darren, Dave, David, Debbie, Denise, Devon, dloncub, Donna, Donna, Ear to

There Tours, Eloy, Emily, Emma, Eric, Erik, Evan, Fernando, Foxx, Gage, Gen, Georgette, Gilbert, Giorgio, Giovanni, glaslady, Gracie, Graffix, Grant, Greg, Hanah, Hannah, Heidi, Hidden Kid, Hidden Mickster, Hoffman, Holden, Holly, Imercado, Jackie, Jake, Jake of Lake Mary, Jamie, Janelle, Jared, Jason (TrendyMagic), JB, Jean, Jeanette, JE.D, Jennah, Jennifer, Jeremy, Jessica, JG, Jim, Jodi and Nana and Pops, Joe, Jonathan, Jordan, Joseph, Josh, JP and son, Julie, Justin, Jyl, Kaela, Kasre, Katie, Kelly, Kelma, Ken, Kent, Keri, Kerri, Kimberly, Kimmie, Kira, Kitzzy, Kristin, Kristy, Kyle, Laura, Laura and Joe, Lauren, Laurie, Lea, Lea Ann, Lia, Liam, Lisa, Liz, Luis, Luke, Lyinel, Lynn, Madison, Makenzie, Marc, Maria, Marissa, Mary Ann and daughter,Mason, Matt, matt@attractionsmagazine.com, Matthew, Maureen, Max, Megan, Melanie, Melissa, Memoree, Michael, Michelle, Mike, MOEMOE55, Natalie, Nick, Nickole, Nicole, Noah, Patti, Peter, Quinten, Rachel, Rich, Rick, Rikki, rjf1423, Robert, Roman, Ronald, Rumbanana, Sam, Samantha, Sarah, Sean, Shannon, Sharon, Sharon from Auburn, She-Knows-CA, Sheri, Skiyalater, Snickers, Someone, Sonali, Stacey, Stacy, Stephanie, Taricia, Taylor, Thomas, Tim, Tony, Toontownkid4, Trevor, Tricia, Triffyboo, Trina, Tyler, Vicki, Vickie, Victoria, Wall-E, Wendy, Wendy and her Stepmom, Zach, and Zachary.

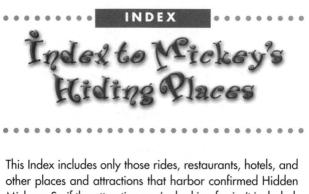
• •

This Index includes only those rides, restaurants, hotels, and other places and attractions that harbor confirmed Hidden Mickeys. So if the attraction you're looking for isn't included, Mickey isn't hiding there. Or if he is, I haven't yet spotted him.

— *Steve Barrett*

The following abbreviations appear in this Index:

AK	-	Disney's Animal Kingdom
DS	-	Disney Springs
E	-	Epcot
HS	-	Disney's Hollywood Studios
MK	-	Magic Kingdom
R	-	Resort venue
WP	-	Water Park